Shi'ism in America

Shi'ism in America

Liyakat Nathani Takim

NEW YORK UNIVERSITY PRESS

New York and London

NEW YORK UNIVERSITY PRESS
New York and London
www.nyupress.org

Library of Congress Cataloging-in-Publication Data

Takim, Liyakatali, 1957–
Shi'ism in America / Liyakat Nathani Takim.
p. cm.
Includes bibliographical references and index.
ISBN-13: 978-0-8147-8296-5 (cl : alk. paper)
ISBN-10: 0-8147-8296-5 (cl : alk. paper)
1. Shi'ah—United States. 2. Shiites—United States.
3. Muslims—United States. I. Title.
BP192.7.U6T35   2009
297.8'20973—dc22   2009013542

New York University Press books are printed on acid-free paper,
and their binding materials are chosen for strength and durability.
We strive to use environmentally responsible suppliers and materials
to the greatest extent possible in publishing our books.

Manufactured in the United States of America
10 9 8 7 6 5 4 3 2 1

To my parents, Ammijan and Abbajan

Contents

Acknowledgments

My interest in American Shi'ism was first aroused in the mid-1990s when I began to study the growing body of literature on the Muslim presence in America. I soon realized that the experience of the Shi'i Muslims, a minority group within the larger American Muslim community, had remained untold. I was determined to fill the lacuna. I began to gather data, conduct a survey, and speak to various groups and members of the Shi'i community. The present study is culmination of that endeavor.

In my research work, I have benefited from the assistance extended to me by many people and institutions. At the University of Denver, I received a Professional Research Opportunities for Faculty (PROF) grant that enabled me to visit and interview various Shi'i institutions in America. In conjunction with the Imamia Education Society, the Denver Foundation facilitated a research fund that enabled me to meet Muslim scholars, lay Shi'is, and conduct a survey. The Bayt al-Ilm Institute also provided a research stipend.

I am also indebted to various figures whose assistance was critical to this study. I would like to thank Hajja Najjah Bazzy and Eid Alwan for providing me the facilities to interview community figures in Dearborn, Michigan, in July 2007. Ron Amen of the Arab American National Museum in Detroit was exceptionally helpful, providing me with invaluable information and material regarding the early Shi'i community in Detroit and Michigan City. Many religious leaders furnished me with perspectives that helped me formulate views on the American Shi'i community. In particular, I would like to thank Shaykh Fadhil Sahlani, imam Mustafa al-Qazwini, imam Hasan Qazwini, Shaykh Jawad Ansari, imam Hisham Husainy, imam Muhammad Ilahi, and Shaykh Mukhtar Fyzee for sharing their personal insights of the American Shi'i community with me.

I have also benefited considerably from the comments and advice of scholars who read parts of my manuscript and offered many incisive comments. Professors Abdulaziz Sachedina, Vernon Schubel, John Kelsay,

Marcia Hermansen, and Hamid Mavani all made invaluable suggestions for improving this work. I would also like to mention my colleagues in the Department of Religious Studies at the University of Denver. All of them have been gracious and offered suggestions that helped me formulate ideas on this work. Ms. Jennifer Hammer, the acquisitions editor at the New York University Press, was exceptionally patient and helpful in preparing this study for publication.

Various research assistants assisted me with the mailing of the survey and making sense of the data I gathered. I am grateful to Francis Sanzaro, Danielle Dillard, Christa Kuberry, Catherine Bunge, and Patrick Bowen. Needless to say, I am entirely responsible for any mistakes or shortcomings in this study.

Many other figures within the Shi'i community also helped me with this study, too many to mention. To all of them, I would like to extend my deepest appreciation. However, I feel that I should mention the following figures who, in various capacities, shared their knowledge and personal observations of the Shi'i community: Zeinab Chami, Abbas Kanji, Madina Humkar, Julia Harajali, Nayfee Kruger, Mariam Uthman, Chuck (Khalil) Alawan, Jihad Saleh, Zahir Janmohamed, Haji Ibrahim Hakim, Haji Husein Hakim, and Hussein Abraham all devoted considerable time to respond to my various questions.

I would also like to mention John Walbridge whose wife Linda died tragically a few years ago. John volunteered to share Linda's notes with me. At the time of her death, Linda was working on a project on the role of the Shi'i *'ulama'* in America. She left behind a good deal of material that she had accumulated for this project and for her earlier work on Shi'ism in Dearborn. I benefited greatly from her observations and comments, which helped me gain a deep insight into the history and contemporary manifestation of the Dearborn Shi'i community. I am grateful to John for his generosity. Finally, I am eternally indebted to my wife Fatima and our children. They have all made great sacrifices, which have enabled me to complete this work.

Wa Ma Tawfiqi illa bi'llah.

Introduction

The twentieth century witnessed a dramatic increase in the migration of Muslims to the American shores. The increased presence and visibility of Muslims in America means that Islam can no longer be characterized as a Middle Eastern or South Asian phenomenon. Given that it is the fastest growing religion in America, Islam is now a very American phenomenon.

The composition of the American Muslim community is far from homogeneous. In fact, American Islam is a mosaic of many ethnic, racial, sectarian, and national groups. Most scholars who have studied Islam in America have limited their research to the majority, Sunni Muslims. Even in academic discourses and classes, most discussions equate Islam in America with the Sunni experience or with that of the indigenous African American Muslims. Very little has been written about the origins and experiences of minority groups within the American Muslim community.[1] Those who restrict their study to a generalized analysis of Muslims in America tend to ignore the nuances that characterize and differentiate the diverse Muslim groups in America. This monolithic view has also obscured the proper recognition and understanding of the religious experience of a significant religious minority in America. This study will examine the origins and contemporary experience of the Shi'i community in America.[2]

The Origins of Shi'ism

The term *Shi'a*[3] refers to the partisans of 'Ali b. Abi Talib (d. 661), the cousin and son-in-law of the Prophet Muhammad. For the Shi'is, 'Ali was the legitimate successor to the Prophet Muhammad having been designated by him at Ghadir Khum and at other occasions.[4] Shi'is further maintain that differences within the Muslim community regarding succession to the Prophet began even before he died, referring specifically to the Prophet's companions' refusal, at his deathbed, to give him pen and paper so that he could dictate his wishes to them.[5] Shi'is believe that the companions conspired to dispossess 'Ali of his rights as the rightful and divinely appointed successor of the Prophet.

While the majority of Muslims affirmed the leadership of the first four caliphs, Abu Bakr (d. 634), 'Umar b. al-Khattab (d. 644), 'Uthman b. 'Affan (d. 656), and 'Ali b. Abi Talib, Shi'is rejected the authority of the first three caliphs. With the coming of 'Ali to power in 656 CE, Shi'ism emerged as an effective religio-political movement. The massacre of Husayn, the son of 'Ali, and his forces at Kerbala by the Umayyad caliph Yazid (d. 684) in 680 CE was an important milestone in Shi'i history; it affirmed notions of injustices endured by the progeny of the Prophet and exacerbated a passion for martyrdom. Due to the brutal nature of his death and close connection to the Prophet, Husayn has been revered in both Shi'i and Sunni literature. He is also admired for not compromising his principles against the threats of a dictator, preferring instead to die rather than live in humiliation.

The Shi'i view that the rights of 'Ali and the family of the Prophet (also called the *ahl al-bayt*) were usurped by the companions meant that from the very beginning, Shi'ism rose as a dissenting group in opposition to the Muslim majority. This dissent manifested itself in different forms during the course of Shi'i history. Initially, Shi'i protest expressed itself by contesting Abu Bakr's succession to the Prophet, advocating instead the succession of 'Ali based on the principle of divine designation. Later conflicts between 'Ali and Mu'awiya (d. 679), Husayn and Yazid, and the various Shi'i revolts against both the Umayyad and 'Abbasid dynasties were further manifestations of these differences.[6] Subsequently, political opposition and rebellion against a central, Sunni-dominated government formed the basis of the development of a distinct sectarian movement that postulated its own concept of religious authority and leadership.

Shi'i theology and jurisprudence took definitive shape in the times of the fifth and sixth Imams, Muhammad al-Baqir (d. 733–37) and Ja'far al-Sadiq (d. 765). The latter, in particular, was largely responsible for the construction of a Shi'i legal edifice and the explication of the Shi'i doctrine of the imamate. Three principles taught by Ja'far al-Sadiq encapsulate the authority of the Imams: *nass*, *'ilm*, and *'isma*. The doctrine of divinely sanctioned authority or divine designation (*nass*) stipulates that 'Ali had been designated by the Prophet to succeed him, inheriting, in the process, his many traits. To distinguish between the divinely designated

Shi'i Imams and local prayer leaders, I will refer to the former by using a capitalized I. When referring to local scholars or prayer leaders, I will use a lower case i.

The question of *nass* is important: it links the Imams in a concatenated chain culminating in the ultimate source of authority, the Prophet. The belief in *nass* is significant in the Shi'i conceptualization of the Imam's authority because it restricts the leadership to a single candidate by negating the claims of rival contenders to the imamate. For the Shi'is, any claim to political authority without proper designation is viewed as a political innovation because it lacks divine mandate.

Besides the principle of divine appointment, the authority of the Imam came to be measured by the *'ilm* (divinely bestowed knowledge) that the Imam had reportedly inherited from the Prophet. The possession of divinely bestowed knowledge is important in the study of the Shi'i concept of religious authority because, in the absence of any political investiture, this was the only factor that could prove the claim to imamate when disputes arose regarding the identity of a true successor of an Imam. Knowledge thus becomes the source of authority and the only feasible means to legitimize any claim to authority.

The Shi'is also maintain that the *'ilm* of an Imam is transmitted in a linked chain to all subsequent Imams. Although the authority and charisma of an Imam can, theoretically, be inherited by any one of a number of his sons, it is the belief in the divinely inspired knowledge that restricts them to a particular individual. *'Ilm* acts as a mitigating factor, ensuring that only one candidate among several contenders for the imamate can inherit the Imam's charisma. The twin principles of *nass* and *'ilm* are pivotal to the Shi'i theory of leadership as they guarantee and protect the divine message from adulteration by transmitting it through a divinely protected chain of authority. Acknowledging the correct Imam becomes equivalent to accepting the original source of authoritative guidance, the Prophet.[7]

Shi'i understanding of sacred history further stipulates that this *'ilm* and the concomitant authority be fully retained in a particular line of the Prophet's family, i.e., the *ahl al-bayt*. It was therefore related from Muhammad al-Baqir, the fifth Imam, that *'ilm* should not be sought from the East or the West; rather, it was to be acquired from the *ahl al-bayt* only.[8]

To serve as exemplary models, the Imams, like the Prophet, are believed to possess *'isma*, the trait of immunity from sins. *'Isma* is important in the Shi'i concept of authority and essential to the Imams' mission to set paradigmatic precedents because the community cannot follow one whose actions are immoral or sinful. The principle of 'isma also means that as exemplary models, the pronouncements of the Imams acquire normative force. Due to the Shi'i belief in the Imams' immunity from error, the principle of 'isma can serve as a polemical weapon, for it is meant to "protect the law against the corruption which, in the Shi'i view, the use of arbitrary individual reasoning (ra'y, ijtihad) of the Sunnite lawyers and the unreliable transmission of *hadith* by the Sunnite traditionalists introduced in it."[9] It is this notion of the divinely inspired leadership of the Imams that distinguishes Shi'ism from the majority Sunnis.

Since they realized the futility of armed revolts against the political authority, the Imams, starting with Ja'far al-Sadiq, taught the doctrine of dissimulation (*taqiyya*) rather than political activism. Henceforth, Shi'is were to conceive of jihad in terms of keeping their faith intact and paying allegiance to the Imam rather than staging armed revolts against political authorities. Jihad was declared to be in abeyance until the time of the Mahdi, the promised messiah. He was expected to establish the kingdom of justice and equality and to eliminate injustice and tyranny. Belief in the Mahdi was predicated on numerous apocalyptic traditions relating to the events anticipated to unfold when the messiah reappears.

A turning point in Shi'i history came in 874 CE when the eleventh Imam, al-Hasan al-'Askari, died. Amid competing claims for succession, his infant son Muhammad was proclaimed to be the twelfth Imam and promised messiah. This group formed the backbone of the Twelver Shi'is, the largest of the Shi'i factions. It is with *this* group that the rest of this book will be concerned.

The twelfth Imam was believed to have entered a "minor" occultation from 874 to 940 CE. During this time, he reportedly communicated with agents, four of whom attained prominence. When the fourth agent died in 940 CE, the Imam was reported to have entered a "major" occultation. It was believed that he would not be accessible to his followers until his reappearance. The appearance of this eschatological messiah would coincide with the establishment of the kingdom of justice and equality.

Shi'ism during the Occultation

During the absence of the twelfth Imam, the apolitical Shi'i scholars composed many juridical and theological tracts. The most famous of these is al-Kulayni's (d. 939) monumental work, *al-Kafi fi 'Ilm al-Din*. The political milieu ameliorated for the Shi'is in the tenth century when the Buyids

(945–1055) came to power in Baghdad. Shiʻi jurists now filled the leadership vacuum that was engendered by the major occultation. Under state patronage, they used the more sophisticated intellectual tools of theology (*kalam*) to vindicate beliefs in the imamate and the occultation of the Imam.[10] Prominent scholars like Muhammad b. ʻAli b. al-Husayn al-Saduq (d. 991), Muhammad b. Muhammad b. al-Nuʻman al-Mufid (d. 1022), ʻAli b. al-Husayn Sharif al-Murtada (d. 1044), and Muhammad b. Jaʻfar al-Tusi (d. 1067) composed important theological and juridical tracts. Shiʻi works in biography, ethics, exegesis, and history were compiled by these and other scholars of the time.

The Authority of Shiʻi Scholars

After the establishment of the Safawid dynasty in Iran in 1501, Shiʻi jurists resorted to various types of hermeneutics based on rational grounds or traditions reported from the Imams in order to exercise greater control over the populace, especially after the scholars were incorporated into the state apparatus. Jurists (*fuqahaʼ*) like ʻAli b. al-Husayn al-Karaki (d. 1533) and Zayn al-Din al-ʻAmili (also called Shahid II; d. 1558) argued that in the absence of the Imam, greater religious authority was to be assumed by the *faqih* or jurist. The jurists could now occupy judicial and political offices. They could, for example, serve as judges, collect religious taxes, and enforce legal penalties on behalf of the Imam.

Under the Qajar dynasty in Iran (1794–1925), the *ʻulamaʼ* (scholars) further enhanced their authority as the sole exponents of the law. Usage of interpretive reasoning and the institutionalization and centralization of religious leadership crystallized eventually in the concept of *marjiʻ al-taqlid* (imitation of the most learned jurist). Murtada Ansari (d. 1864) was recognized as the most qualified *marjiʻ* (source of reference for juridical rulings) of his time. Later, the actions of a believer who did not adhere to a *marjiʻ*'s rulings were deemed to be invalid. In postrevolutionary Iran, based on the controversial concept of *wilaya al-faqih* (comprehensive authority of a jurist), Ayatullah Khumayni (d. 1989) established a theocratic state. Claiming the same degree of authority as the hidden Imam, Khumayni argued that the function of a jurist was equivalent to that of an Imam.[11]

Even in contemporary times, Shiʻi scholars continue to play prominent roles in the lives and religious practices of ordinary Shiʻis as they interpret the sacred sources and articulate the normative practices for the Shiʻi community all over the world (see chap. 4).

Methodology and Approach

It is important that we view Shi'ism in America within the framework of the experience of a minority religious community. With this in mind, I explore the Shi'i self-understanding and expression in America, seeking to understand individual mosques/centers in terms of their internal environment—the ethnic backgrounds of their members, attitudes, and responses of leadership and constituents—and in terms of their relationship to the surrounding culture and its ethnic, social, civil, and political institutions.

I also examine the interaction between religion and culture, how Islam has shaped Shi'i civic and political consciousness in America, the connection between religious loyalty and ethnic identity, and the role of religious texts and authorities in shaping the Shi'i religious experience. Studying the variegated roles of American Shi'is portrays an image of their being active contributors to the American social and religious milieu. Of course, not all Shi'is define themselves or engage with others in similar ways.

Tracing the origins and establishment of an immigrant community is fraught with difficulties, especially when documented sources are almost nonexistent. In many instances, I have had to rely on anecdotal narratives from senior members of the Shi'i communities in Michigan City and Dearborn. In some cases, I have had recourse to archives from the Arab American Nation Museum in Detroit. These resources are used in conjunction with material interspersed in various ethnographic works and in different genres of literature that mention the presence of Shi'is in local communities.

Given the dearth of scholarship on the topic, much of my research is based on a survey, questionnaires, and formal interviews. The statistical data included in this book reflects a 2006 survey sent to 105 Shi'i centers in America. It generated thirty-two responses. Imams or other community leaders completed the survey. Questions that were posed included (1) when the center was established, (2) the ethnic composition of the members frequenting the center, (3) the contemporary challenges that the center encounters, (4) interfaith dialogue, (5) civic and political engagement, (6) youth involvement in the center, and (7) how the center identifies itself. I also asked some open-ended questions, which included the mission statement and vision of the center.

The results of the survey are tabulated in the appendix. My observations on the Shi'i community are also based on personal engagement, insights, and knowledge of the community, all of which I have gained over a number of years. Immersion in the American Shi'i community has enabled me to comprehend the nuanced and variegated contours of various Shi'i groups. Yet, I am fully aware that many Shi'is will disagree with both my observations and conclusions. To them I say I hope we can agree to disagree, agreeably.

Studies on Shi'ism in America

To date, there has not been a comprehensive study of the American Shi'i community. Academic studies of Shi'i Muslims have often been inserted within the framework of and discourse on Sunni Islam. When scholars have discussed Shi'ism in America their approach has been ethnographic, primarily because the ethnic diversity of American Shi'ism has encouraged the study of local communities rather than the Shi'i community in its entirety. In her pioneering ethnographic study, *Without Forgetting the Imam: Lebanese Shi'ism in an American Community*, Linda Walbridge focuses on the history and contemporary challenges of the Lebanese community in Dearborn, Michigan. Vernon Schubel has discussed the ritual activities of the Khoja Shi'i community in two articles,[12] while Ron Kelley has written on the Iranian community in Los Angeles.[13] In an article, Abdulaziz Sachedina examines how the Shi'is have adapted to the challenges of living in the American milieu,[14] and I have explored the challenges confronting the American Shi'i community in two articles.[15]

None of these works has studied the American Shi'i community in depth. In particular, questions regarding identity, acculturation, and authority within the American Shi'i community have received scant attention. There is a lack of understanding regarding how different Shi'i ethnic groups have adapted their cultural and religious expressions in the American context. In the present work, I have tried to fill a crucial gap in the existing literature on this important yet neglected Muslim group.

The Present Study

To understand the history and subsequent development of Shi'ism in America, chapter 1 traces the origins and experience of the early Shi'i community. In discussing the matrix of forms through which the culture of the different Shi'i groups is expressed, I argue that scholars should abandon the essentialist, monolithic worldview of Shi'ism; nor should they see the American Shi'i community as singular. On the contrary, differences, both sociological and cultural, run deep within the community. As a matter of fact, it is possible to speak of a "rainbow" nature of Shi'i Islam in America.

The second chapter examines the establishment of early Shi'i institutions and how these have catered to the growing needs of the community. Increased migration from various parts of the world has resulted in the American Shi'i community becoming more fragmented as bonds of common faith are replaced by ties to common origins, ethnicity, and culture. This chapter also explores how members of the Shi'i community have engaged the challenges of cultural negotiations, redefinitions, and reappropriation in a new cultural context, and how they have pursued different ways to adapt to the American milieu. I focus on the Shi'is' historical, ideological, and ethnic backgrounds as these are the realms in which cultural symbols and behavioral patterns become codified in community life.

An important dimension of the Shi'i existence in America is the community's relationship with fellow Muslims. Relations between Shi'is and Sunnis in America have been contingent on political circumstances in the Middle East and South Asia. Chapter 3 discusses how political and ideological battles abroad have impacted Muslims in different spheres of their American lives. The chapter argues that polarization within the Muslim community has been exacerbated by the influx of conservative immigrants. Immigration has resulted in the spread of a conservative spirit in many institutions, accentuating sectarian divisions and disputes between the two schools of thought. Hence, there is a tendency to replicate what prevailed abroad, making America a battleground for sectarian differences.

The Shi'i experience in America is different from that of the Sunni because of the influence exerted by Shi'i scholars who are responsible for reinterpreting the relevance of Islamic norms in the modern era. Chapter 4 explores how living in America has forced contemporary Shi'i jurists to respond to the challenges of living as a minority group in America. The contemporary reformulation of Islamic law entails a meticulous examination of discrete components interspersed in different genres of both classical and modern juridical literature. To comprehend the development and interpretation of sacred texts and their implication for Muslims in America, it is essential to engage jurists who have played a significant role in the exposition as well as interpretation of those sacred texts that have shaped Shi'i religious practices and expression in the United States.

The fifth chapter explores some of the outreach and proselytization (*da'wa*) activities of the Shi'i community in America. Besides immigrants and American-born Shi'is, the Shi'i community is also composed of an increasing number of African American converts. The chapter discusses the appeal of Shi'ism for the African American community and examines the interaction between black and immigrant Shi'is. Like other immigrants, Muslims have been defined as alien. This categorization became more entrenched since the horrific events of September 11, 2001, and is directed at Muslims who, perhaps more than any other immigrant group, are more vulnerable to stereotypes and attacks. This chapter also considers the impact of the events of 9/11 on the Shi'i community and the community's attempts to reconstitute a religious and an American identity in the face of demonization and stereotypical images propagated in the media.

1

The Origins and Early History of the American Shi'i Community

The origins and experience of the early Shi'i settlers in America must be contextualized within the broader framework of the presence of the early Sunni Muslims in America. Shi'is and Sunnis arrived at about the same time, worshiped together, shared similar experiences, and encountered the same challenges. In fact, as we will see when we discuss Sunni-Shi'i relations in America in chapter three, the symbiosis between these two communities meant that many early Muslim settlers were not even aware of the sectarian differences that distinguished them.

Scholars of Islam in America have amply documented the presence of early Muslims in America. Some have argued that Muslims arrived here almost two centuries before Christopher Columbus. These Muslims are reported to have come from Spain and the northwestern coast of Africa and landed in both South and North America.[1] Other Muslims, like the Mandikos, apparently explored many parts of North America and left behind writings and engravings.[2] Some scholars have further argued that Muslim explorers from Africa intermarried with Native Americans and introduced some arts and crafts to the Americas.[3] However, a word of caution is in order. Evidence to support such claims, cited from artifacts, inscriptions, and eyewitness accounts, is circumstantial at best and, at this point, inconclusive. Further research work is necessary to corroborate them. The earliest available record of Muslims in America dates back to the sixteenth century. Estevan, a black Moroccan guide and interpreter, is said to have arrived in America with a Spanish expedition in 1527.[4]

The early American Muslim community was composed primarily of slaves who were brought here during the Atlantic slave trade in the eighteenth and nineteenth centuries. There is no evidence to indicate that there were any Shi'is among the early slaves because, until fairly recently, Shi'ism had not spread to the West African coast. Some scholars have claimed that Arab immigration to Latin America, in response to King Philip II's royal decree in 1609 ordering the expulsion of 300,000 Moriscos from Spain, started in the earliest parts of the seventeenth century.[5] Large scale migration began in the 1870s in a series of distinguishable periods or waves.[6]

The first significant wave of Muslims arrived between 1875 and 1912. They came from rural areas of what was then called Greater Syria, living under the rule of the Ottoman Empire.[7] Since most immigrants were relatively uneducated men, they worked in factories and mines or as peddlers. Many of these immigrants who came from the Middle East were Christians, but a small percentage was comprised of Sunnis, 'Alawis, and Druzes.[8] Among the early immigrants were Shi'is who accompanied other immigrants from the Middle East. Many migrated to flee conscription into the Turkish army, which, in their view, was an occupying force and not connected to their national identities. Other Muslims were emulating Christians who returned from the United States with considerable wealth. Another reason for the migration in this period was the onset of World War I, which had brought economic and political destruction to Greater Syria. Due to this factor, many chose to flee their homelands. These early immigrants settled in different parts of the States. Some went to Ross, North Dakota, in 1899.[9] In all probability, there were some Shi'is already present among the early Lebanese who settled in Ross.[10] Other Shi'is settled in Michigan City, Indiana.

The Shi'i Community of Michigan City

Most scholars of Islam in America have focused on Dearborn, Michigan, as the first city where the Shi'is settled. But the story of another area of Shi'i settlement, Michigan City, Indiana, remains largely untold. In the early twentieth century, the small communities close to the large urban areas of Detroit and Chicago were important areas of settlement for Shi'i immigrants. The nascent Shi'i community in Michigan City, made up primarily of Lebanese and Syrian merchants, built one of the first mosques in America in 1924.[11]

An early migrant to Michigan City was Hussein Hussein Ayad, who was born in Mazra'at al-Jazirat, on the banks of the Litany River in Lebanon in 1890.[12] He chose to come to Michigan City in 1902 due to the presence there of a number of Syrian immigrants. Like many others, he worked for a train company laying tracks and later worked in a steel factory. According to Ayad, the first Muslim society was formed in 1914 in Michigan City. Called "al-Badr al-Munir," it was headed by Hussein Aboudheeb. Hussein Hakim, a current resident of Michigan City, claims that this was the first Muslim organization to be registered in America.

According to Ayad, there were more than two hundred families in Michigan City in 1924, when Asser El Jadeed, another local institute, was formed and the first mosque built. The migration and settlement of Shiʻis in Michigan City at the beginning of the twentieth century is further corroborated by anecdotal accounts from their descendents. Julia Harajali was born in Michigan City in 1920. Her father had settled there in 1907. According to Julia, many of the early Shiʻi migrants settled in Michigan City, Indiana, rather than in Detroit, so that they could work in the Pullman car factory. She attests that there was a vibrant Shiʻi community in Michigan City in the 1920s and 1930s, though many left for Dearborn when better employment opportunities arose there.[13]

Ron Amen, who works at the Arab American Nation Museum in Detroit, remembers that his father was born in Michigan City in 1918. Similarly, Eddie Bedoun, a current board member of the Islamic Center of America in Dearborn, recalls that his grandfather came to Michigan City in the early 1900s. Bedoun's father, Hussein, was born in the city in 1912. Hussein Hakim's father migrated to America in the early 1900s and was drafted in the U.S. Army in 1913. Hakim recalls that virtually all of the Shiʻis in Michigan City were from Lebanon. He also remembers that a few Shiʻi families lived in Grand Rapids, Michigan.[14]

Among the migrants to Michigan City in the early 1900s was a passenger on board the *Titanic*, which sank in April 1912. The ship carried at least three Shiʻis, Fatima Masselmany and her two cousins, Mustafa Nasr and Yousif Wazli. Fatima was born in Tibnin in Lebanon; her cousins, who drowned when the ship sank, came from Bint Jbeil. All of them had planned to settle in Michigan City. An article by Henry Lange of the *News Dispatch* of April 15, 1980, shows a photograph of Fatima Masselmany, who survived the disaster. She related her story to many in Michigan City and later to the residents of Dearborn. Fatima was seventeen years old when she arrived in Michigan City a few days after the tragedy and lived with her brother, Allie Masselmany, on Wabash Street. Fatima, well known in the Michigan City community, later moved to Dearborn, where she died in 1971.

As the number of Shiʻis in Michigan City increased, there was a need for a scholar who could provide religious guidance to the community members. The famous Lebanese Shi'i religious leader, imam Muhammad Jawad Chirri (d. 1994), who had migrated to Detroit in 1949, spent two years in Michigan City in the early 1950s after a dispute arose within the Shi'i community in Detroit.

The Shi'is of Dearborn

The history of the Shi'i community in Dearborn has been amply documented by Lynda Walbridge. I will touch only on some aspects of it here. The Muslim presence in metropolitan Detroit dates to the last decade of the nineteenth century, when residents of the Lebanese Bekaa valley left an Ottoman province. Some of the inhabitants left Bekaa due to the increase in population, the decline of its silk and vineyard sectors, and instability remaining from mid-century civil wars pitting Mount Lebanon's Maronite Christians against its Druze inhabitants. Muslim peddlers and traders followed a larger number of Lebanese Christians who had already emigrated to America.

By the end of the nineteenth century, there was a small yet burgeoning Shi'i community in Detroit as more Shi'is arrived to join their relatives who had settled here. Between 1900 and 1914 several hundred settlers comprising diverse religious communities migrated from the Middle East.[15] Most of these early immigrants came from the Mount Lebanon area of what was then called the Ottoman Empire. Soon, a larger community of Shi'is started to crystallize in 1922 as other Shi'is arrived from areas like India and Iran.

The early Shi'is came primarily from the lower strata of society. Many were peddlers, laborers, and small business owners who were drawn to Detroit because of the presence of the Ford Motor Company in Highland Park, a neighborhood within the borders of Detroit.[16] Detroit became a very attractive destination for immigrants in 1913, when Henry Ford began to offer generous five-dollar daily wages for workers at his Highland Park assembly line. This was almost twice the prevailing daily wage of $2.34. Furthermore, workers had to work for eight rather than nine hours. Due to the relatively favorable economic opportunities in Detroit, some Shi'i residents of Michigan City, Indiana, relocated there.

During the second wave of Muslim immigration to America, between 1918 and 1922, immigrants from Arab countries poured into the Detroit area, as did people from different parts of the world. Not only had World War I devastated the Middle East, years of drought, various epidemics, and plagues of locusts followed on the heels of the war. The Ottoman Empire was dismantled, and the Western colonial powers, France and England, came to occupy its place. Hence, many Muslims preferred migration over the political turmoil and economic hardships in their home countries.[17] According to the *Detroit Monthly*, entire villages in Lebanon were transplanted, over time, to the Detroit area.[18]

By the 1940s, about two hundred Sunni and Shi'i families had settled in Detroit.[19] Khalil Alwan, a current member of the Dearborn Shi'i community in Michigan, was born in the United States in 1930. He recalls that his maternal grandfather came from Lebanon in 1898. His mother was born in Michigan City in 1912, further corroborating my observation that many Shi'i families had settled in Michigan City in the early 1900s. Khalil also recalls that his father migrated to South America and then went to work in Cedar Rapids, Iowa. In 1914, his father worked in Sioux Falls, South Dakota. By the time Khalil's father moved to Detroit in the 1920s, many Shi'is had settled in that area. Khalil remembers that in the 1930s, Sunnis and Shi'is would arrange joint religious and social gatherings.[20]

Marium 'Uthman, who also lives in Dearborn, was born in Michigan. She went back to Lebanon before returning to America in 1947. She recalls being told that her mother was born in Michigan at the beginning of the twentieth century and that her grandfather had migrated to the States toward the end of the nineteenth century, possibly because his brothers and cousins were already well established in Michigan.[21]

Marium 'Uthman also remembers that there was a steady influx of her Lebanese neighbors and friends after she and her family had moved to Dearborn. The steady stream of Lebanese migrants in that city led to the establishment of Shi'i institutions and places of worship. Khalil Alwan recalls that the community purchased a bank and converted it to a meeting place in 1940. The Hashemite hall, as it was then called, served as an important religious and social center for the Shi'i community until the early 1960s when a permanent mosque was built. Most of the gatherings at the hall were social rather than religious. Alwan also remembers that there were mock sword fights to raise funds for the center.

For various reasons, Detroit was an attractive place for Muslims of different schools of thought and background. For example, the charismatic Ahmadi proselyte, Mufti Muhammad Sadiq, moved the central operations of the American Ahmadiyya movement to the Detroit suburb of Highland Park soon after he arrived in 1920. This was the location of the Karoub House, one of the earliest mosques built in the United States.[22] In

1922, Muhammad Sadiq moved to Chicago where another sizable Muslim community had assembled.[23]

The early American Shi'is faced great pressure to conform to American mores and assimilate to American culture. When she came here, Marium 'Uthman remembers that neither Islam nor Muslims were widely known. She also recalls that when she arrived from Lebanon, her mother asked her to remove her *hijab* (headscarf) as it was not deemed appropriate to wear it in America. According to her, there was no *halal* meat available in Detroit until 1947, two years after she arrived. Assimilation into American culture was felt at various levels. Even at Shi'i gathering places like the Hashemite hall, many Shi'is report that mix-gendered parties were often held, in contrast to Islamic norms. Occasionally at such events, participants would even dance to celebrate marriages and other festivities.[24] According to Khalil Alwan's brother Eid, local Shi'is labeled such events as *Jahiliyya* in nature.[25] Moreover, in order to better conform to American customs, the Muslim community held religious services on Sundays instead of Fridays. Such was the sense of alienation from Islam that most of the people I spoke with in Detroit concurred that Muharram commemorations were held in Dearborn only *after* the Islamic Center of America was founded in 1963.[26]

When the early Shi'is arrived in Detroit, they tried to uphold their beliefs in an alien context, often with little institutional or religious support. The religious training available to their children and grandchildren was limited to Sunday services or religious classes. Neither schools nor businesses had facilities for daily prayers. Shi'is who wanted to fast during the month of Ramadan could expect no help or time off from their work. It was under such difficult circumstances that the Shi'is struggled to maintain their beliefs and distinct cultural and religious identities.

Practicing Islam as it had been done "back home" was proving to be difficult for these pioneer Shi'is. Imam Muhammad Jawad Chirri was one of the earliest Shi'i scholars to settle in America in 1949. Marium 'Uthman remembers that he did not force women to wear *hijab*. Instead, some women just wore hats in the mosque. She remembers that although imam Chirri did not approve of this practice, he did not enforce the *hijab* for fear that he might alienate women. He was more concerned that they remain true to their faith than insisting on their Islamic mode of dressing. As Marium states, "Today, one who does not wear *hijab* feels out of place, in the past, it was the opposite. Today, most women wear the *hijab* even outside the mosque, not just inside it."

Even after the Islamic Center of America (ICA) opened in 1963, it hosted social parties and weddings, accompanied by music and dances, while religious services were held there on Sundays.[27] A commemorative journal marking the opening of the ICA at its new location on Ford Road in Dearborn shows several photographs of women in the early days without headscarves in the old mosque. Some photos even show women with no headscarves while imam Chirri was speaking at fundraising dinners.

Chirri had to accept such acts to preserve the unity of the local community. It was the Iranian revolution and the significant wave of immigration of Lebanese and Iraqi migrants in the 1980s that led to major changes in the center. Women were now asked to wear the *hijab* in the center, and wedding dances and other celebrations were banned.[28]

Today, many Shi'i organizations are located in the suburb of Dearborn, each trying to assist in the observance of the identity of its constituent's practice. Six mosques are located in and around that city, each with its own constituency. There are about 490,000 Arabs in the Detroit metropolitan area, and Arabs make up nearly one-third of Dearborn's total population. In addition, there are about 50,000 Iraqis in the Detroit area.[29] The Arabs of Dearborn represent the largest concentration of Muslims and Arabs in the United States, making it second only to Paris for Muslim populations outside the Middle East.

Shi'i Settlement in Other American Cities

Not all early Shi'is settled in Michigan and Indiana. In the early 1900s, the first generation of Muslim immigrants came to Quincy Point in Massachusetts, attracted by the prospect of working in the New England shipbuilding industry. They were among the first wave of Muslim immigrants to enter the United States from the Middle East between 1880 and 1925. In her research of seven Muslim families who settled in Massachusetts, Mary Lahaj notes that two of the seven families were Shi'is, while the remainder were Sunnis. All of the Muslims, Shi'is and Sunnis alike, came from the areas north of Tripoli, south of Beirut, or from the east in the Bekaa Valley.[30] The first group of Shi'is settled in Quincy in the early 1880s because they were attracted by the prospect of working in the ship-building industry in New England.

The current Islamic Center of New England (ICNE) was the dream of these seven families. One of its founders, Mohamed Omar Awad, a Sunni

Muslim, offers an example of why the center grew. At the age of twenty two, Omar left his village in the mountainous area north of Tripoli. Like other immigrants from rural areas of what now constitutes Lebanon, Syria, Palestine, and Jordan, Omar came to America to flee the Ottoman army. He stated that there was no other reason for him to leave his homeland, and he did not wish to fight for the Ottomans in Yemen, having had six uncles who had gone to fight and never returned.[31] Political turmoil in the Middle East and forced conscription in the Ottoman army were important factors that led to Muslim migration to the Americas.

Some Shi'is also settled in far-flung areas like Cedar Rapids, Iowa. Husein Ali Sheronick, a distinctly Shi'i name, is said to have arrived in Cedar Rapids in 1895. Initially serving as a traveling peddler, he opened a dry goods store in 1900. By 1914 there were forty-five Muslims living in Cedar Rapids.[32] Shi'is currently residing in Detroit and other cities state there that were indeed some Shi'i families in Cedar Rapids. Khalil Alwan recalls that his father had settled there for a short period in 1913 before moving to Sioux Falls, South Dakota. In the 1930s, more Shi'is settled in Cedar Rapids. Nayfee Krugler, a Shi'i, was born in the city in 1944. Her parents married in Lebanon and then migrated to Cedar Rapids in 1938. According to Krugler, the Muslim community there was closely knit, and the Shi'is were fully integrated into the community. Both Shi'is and Sunnis worshiped in the "mother mosque" after it was constructed in 1934. Krugler states that there were a few other Shi'i families in Cedar Rapids.

Some Shi'i families settled in New York City. Nayfee Krugler's mother, Alia Kanaan, was born there in 1908. Although few in number, the Shi'is in New York interacted regularly with the local Sunni community, most of whom lived on Washington Street, now a part of Greenwich Village in the city.[33]

By the beginning of the twentieth century, Shi'is had established themselves in areas that offered attractive employment opportunities. Some settled in Fort Dodge, Iowa, in the first two decades of the twentieth century.[34] As previously mentioned, Khalil Alwan recalls that his father had worked in Cedar Rapids, Iowa, and Sioux Falls, South Dakota. Nayfee Krugler moved to Toledo, Ohio, in 1947, where she found an existing Muslim community. Muslims would rent halls or congregate in people's houses until Shi'is and Sunnis banded together to build a mosque there in 1954. For some time, the two groups worshiped in the same mosque. Abdo Elkholy confirms the presence of a sizable Shi'i community in Toledo and states that the ratio of Shi'is to Sunnis in Toledo was similar to that in Detroit.[35]

Some Shiʻi families had settled in Chicago by 1920. Edith Stein, a student at the University of Chicago in 1922, states in her master's thesis that most of the Syrians in Chicago were from Lebanon.[36] In all probability, some of them were Shiʻis. Initially, Shiʻis gathered at Sunni centers but conflicts between the two communities increased as more immigrants arrived, and the Shiʻis established their own centers.[37] It is estimated that the Shiʻi community in Chicago numbered about 15,000 in 2004.[38]

There is evidence to indicate that Lebanese Shiʻis also migrated to other parts of the Americas. Many of them went to Mexico from places such as Nabatiyeh, Damascus, Tripoli, and Aramta.[39] Some of these Mexican Shiʻis maintained strong ties with the early Shiʻi immigrants in Detroit.[40]

Other Muslims went to Canada. Some Lebanese migrants settled in Alberta, Canada, in the middle of the nineteenth century. Coming from Lala in the Bekaa Valley, ʻAli Hamilton took up the fur trade and settled in Lac La Biche, north of Edmonton, Canada. He also served as president of the Lac La Biche Chamber of Commerce.[41] Subsequently, other Lebanese migrants settled in the lake country of Edmonton. Through the memoirs of some community leaders, we know of the observance of Muharram rituals by these early Shiʻis.[42] It is also probable that other Shiʻis had already so integrated themselves in American culture that they chose not to participate in these annual commemorations.

By the 1950s, there were clusters of Shiʻi families located in quite a few different cities in Canada and America.[43] To mark such important events in the Shiʻi calendar as the birth and death anniversaries of the Prophet and the Imams, Shiʻi students and professionals would often meet in rented facilities or houses. It is important to note that not all Shiʻis came from the Middle East. Some Shiʻis from India settled in Trinidad in the nineteenth century. These Indian Shiʻis organized ceremonial processions to commemorate the martyrdom of Imam Husayn, the grandson of the Prophet Muhammad, who was brutally killed in Kerbala, Iraq. In India, Shiʻis had been holding parades to mark the martyrdom of Husayn for some time. The practice was exported to the Caribbean by Indian Shiʻis in the middle of the nineteenth century. By 1884, the Hosay parade, as it came to be called, had created sufficient incidents for police to even fire upon the procession.[44]

While the earliest Shiʻi migrants were primarily Lebanese, according to Youssef M'roueh, between 1920 and 1938 thousands of Shiʻi Muslims from Lebanon, Syria, Iraq, Bahrain, Saudi Arabia, Azerbaijan, Iran, Afghanistan, and India migrated to America.[45] He also claims that in the

1940s, hundreds of Shi'is in New York City celebrated the *eid al-adha* in Harlem and on Broadway in a dazzling parade. M'roueh does not cite any specific source to substantiate his claims, but given the Shi'i penchant to mark their major religious holidays in a public setting, his claims are quite plausible.[46]

Immigration Laws and Their Impact on the American Shi'i Community

As with all immigrants, Shi'i immigration to America was contingent on United States immigration laws. In view of the rapid increase of immigrants from different parts of the world in the early part of the twentieth century, after World War I the U.S. government closed its borders to all but northwestern Europeans under the National Origins Act of 1924. The act effectively separated many immigrants from their homeland and reduced the flow of immigrants to the United States. For example, after 1924 Syrian immigrants, who had arrived by the thousands, were soon reduced to a few hundred under the new quota system.

After the end of World War II, however, the United States encouraged students from newly independent Arab states to study at American universities, but they were expected to return to their home countries after completing their studies. These students were predominantly of middle- and upper-class urban backgrounds who had had intimate experiences of living in pluralistic settings. According to Yvonne Haddad, a large number of these immigrants were graduates of foreign educational institutions run by secular and missionary groups in the Arab world. Two-thirds of the students married Americans, and a large number of them decided to settle in the United States.[47]

Although U.S. immigration laws were stricter after World War II, the Nationality Act of 1953 gave each country an annual quota of immigrants. Under this new system, Muslims came now not only from the Middle East but also from other parts of the world including India and Pakistan (after partition of the subcontinent in 1947), Eastern Europe (mainly from Albania and Yugoslavia), and the Soviet Union. Among these arrivals were Shi'is who now settled in places like Chicago and New York. Unlike their earlier counterparts, many of these Shi'i immigrants were students who hoped to continue their education or receive advanced technical training. Now, because of the increasingly friendly relations between the United States and Muhammad Pahlavi Shah's regime in Iran, an increasing number of Iranian students and professionals came to study or settle here in the 1950s and 1960s. Consequently, the ethnic composition of the Shi'i population became more diverse.

That the United States opened its doors to Muslims from different countries in this era meant, in the Shi'i case, the ethnicization of American Shi'ism. As we shall see in chapter 2, the diverse ethnic Shi'i groups later established distinctive ethnic centers. The granting of scholarships and financial aid to Asian, African, and Middle Eastern students further enhanced the ethnic diversity within the Shi'i community in America.

The size and composition of the Shi'i community in America was to change drastically in the 1960s. In 1965 President Lyndon Johnson signed the Hart-Celler Act, aimed at repealing the quotas based on national diversity within the United States. The act had the effect of reversing the historic preference for European immigrants. It also abolished the earlier law based on quotas from specific countries and reversed decades of discrimination, initiating preferential admission of immigrants especially from the Third World. For the first time since the early part of the century, immigration to America was no longer contingent on a person's national or ethnic origin. This change had dramatic effects on immigration patterns: immigration from Europe declined, while that from the Middle East and Asia increased.

The new immigration act changed the American religious landscape. The number of Muslims more than doubled in the next two decades, increasing from 4 percent of all immigrants in 1968 to 10.5 percent in 1986.[48] The new law also had the effect of increasing the ethnic diversity of the Muslim population in America. Post-1965 Muslim immigrants are racially, ethnically, linguistically, and religiously more heterogeneous than earlier immigrants, having come from more than one hundred different countries.[49]

For the Shi'is, as with other immigrants, the 1965 act dramatically altered the makeup and composition of the American Shi'i population. It meant that Shi'is ranging from students to factory workers and professionals could immigrate to America with their families. Those Shi'is who had settled here could now be joined by their families living abroad. According to Haddad:

> The new immigrants were more representative of the ethnic, national, and religious diversity of the Muslim world. They included a large number

of highly educated, socially mobile, professional Muslims—part of the Arab and South Asian "brain drain"—and more women. Meanwhile, the opening of the doors of emigration, the changes in immigration laws, and the lottery system that gave visas to winners from all over the world, brought a different "kind" of immigrants. All social and economic classes from villages, towns, and cities stretching from Morocco to Yemen were represented.[50]

The majority of these new Shi'i immigrants came from the Asian subcontinent—India, Pakistan, and Bangladesh. The latest arrivals included a substantial number of refugees from countries affected by civil wars and often suffering the results of Western presence in their home countries and from dictatorial regimes. Increased migration and conversion have led to Shi'is settling not only in the major cities but also in smaller ones. It would not be an exaggeration to state that today, there is a Shi'i community or family in virtually every major American city.

The 1965 act helped not only new immigrants but also had the important affect of helping single Shi'is who had settled here and wanted to get married. This is because Shi'i law differs fundamentally from Sunni law on the question of marriage with the "People of the Book" (Christians and Jews). Although the Qur'an allows Muslim men to marry non-Muslim women (5:5), most Shi'i jurists allow only temporary marriages (*mut'a*) with Christians and Jews. Basing their rulings on precautionary obligation, they prohibit permanent marriages with them.[51]

The prominent Shi'i religious leader, Ayatullah Seestani, is seen by many Shi'is to be the most distinguished and knowledgeable scholar of the time. He states in his juridical treatise (*al-risala al-'amaliyya*), "A Muslim woman cannot marry a non-Muslim, and a male Muslim also cannot marry a non-Muslim woman who [is] not Ahlul Kitab [Jews and Christians]. However, there is no harm in contracting temporary marriage with Jewish and Christian women, but the obligatory precaution is that a Muslim should not take them in permanent marriage."[52]

For many Shi'is living in the States, such a ruling meant that they had a choice of marrying Muslim women in America, converts to Islam, or returning to their home countries to find a spouse. The situation was compounded by the fact that there were few Shi'i women of their own ethnic background whom Shi'i men could marry. The 1965 act was important for Shi'i men because it gave them the opportunity to return home, marry, and bring their spouses back to the United States.

The Current Shi'i Population in America

Since the American census does not ask for religious affiliation, scholars have differed as to how many Muslims are in America. A conservative figure would be around seven million. One attempt to categorize and count Muslim Americans put African Americans at 42 percent, South Asians at 24.4 percent, Arabs at 12.4 percent, Africans at 6.2 percent, Iranians at 3.6 percent, Southeast Asians at 2 percent, European Americans at 1.6 percent, and "others" at 5.4 percent.[53] It is estimated that 20 percent of the Muslim population now lives in California and 16 percent lives in New York.[54]

Similarly, there is no reliable estimate as to the numbers of Shi'is in America. According to Jane Smith, the Twelver Shi'is, together with the Ismai'lis, form about one-fifth of the American Muslim community.[55] The Shi'i population is also growing rapidly in Canada. In the past twenty-five years, the number of Canadian Shi'is increased fivefold to 132,000 in 1996, the fastest growth any religion has experienced in Canada.[56] During the same period (1971–96), the total Muslim population in Canada increased from 93,000 to about 450,000.[57]

Lois Gottesman's contention that there are no more than 300,000 Shi'is in North America is noticeably outdated.[58] However, Ilyas Ba-Yunus and Kassim Kone estimate that there are 786,000 Shi'is in America, a figure that appears to be exceptionally low especially as thousands of Shi'is have migrated from a wide array of places since the 1970s.[59] M'roueh, on the other hand, claims that of the 9.6 million Muslims in America in 1995, 2 million are Shi'is. He further maintains that there are 256 Shi'i mosques in America, a figure that appears to be exaggerated.[60] Yasin al-Jibouri's estimate that the Shi'i community in the United States forms about 15 to 20 percent of the total population of 7 million Muslims in America appears more tenable.[61] In the absence of accurate statistical data, however, it is impossible to verify the figures cited.

In his important work on the American Muslim community and Muslim proselytization in America, Larry Poston claims that the Shi'is are confined to certain coastal areas.[62] This observation was probably based on the settlement of Shi'is in the 1980s. In fact, Shi'i communities are now located in virtually all the major cities of America, particularly given the rapid increase in immigration since 1965.

In contrast to the early twentieth century when there was a predominance of Lebanese Shi'is, the present American Shi'i community is composed of highly diverse ethnic and cultural groups, most of whom have moved and relocated from their initial locations since the 1970s. They originate from Iran, Iraq, Lebanon, the Indian subcontinent, the Gulf States, East Africa, and parts of North Africa. A growing number of African Americans are now converting to Shi'ism after having initially converted to Sunnism or to the Nation of Islam. Some Sufi groups with Shi'i proclivities have also been established in the United States. There are at least three Sufi Shi'i organizations within the Iranian community in California.[63]

Various factors have led to the proliferation of Shi'i migrants, partly as a response to changes in American immigration laws. Other factors have also precipitated increased migration to America. Adverse sociopolitical conditions in the Middle East, Pakistan, and India have occasioned increased migration to the West. Moreover, the Islamic revolution in Iran,[64] the inimical sociopolitical conditions in Iraq, civil strife in Pakistan, the breakup of Pakistan into Bangladesh, anti-Muslim pogroms in India, the civil war in Lebanon, adverse socioeconomic conditions in East Africa, the exodus of East African Asians during the regime of Idi Amin in Uganda, and the persecution of Hazara Shi'is by the Taliban regime in Afghanistan have all contributed to the increased Shi'i presence here.

Shi'is have also come from a large number of African nations, including Kenya, Uganda, Madagascar, Tanzania, Mozambique, Congo, Burundi, and many others. Thus, the Shi'i community in America is now comprised of a variety of people from many nations who represent diverse linguistic, national, ethnic, and racial backgrounds. Like other Muslims, Shi'is came to America in pursuit of political, religious, and economic freedom, or educational and professional opportunities. These immigrants represent a great range of Islamic thoughts and ideologies.

Given the relaxation of immigration laws in the 1960s and the increasing number of newly arriving Iranian, Iraqi, Lebanese, and South Asian Shi'is, it is reasonable to estimate that Shi'is now make up at least 20 percent of the total Muslim population of America. In the following section, I briefly examine the main Shi'i groups, their origins, and settlement in America in more depth.

The Iraqi Shi'is

In the 1950s and 1960s, many Shi'is from Iraq came to the United States as students. The establishment of the Baath party in 1958 and the ensuing volatile socioeconomic conditions meant that some of the Iraqis chose not to return home. Other Iraqis sought asylum in America after 1979 when Saddam Hussein came to power. Dispersed in different parts of the country, these Iraqis are well educated, highly skilled, and quite affluent, having established businesses or secured well-paid employment. Most Iraqi Shi'is come from cities like Baghdad, Najaf, Kerbala, or Basra.

According to imam Hisham Husainy, the imam of the Kerbala Center in Dearborn, it is necessary to differentiate between Iraqis who came before 1991 and those who arrived afterward. After the failed uprising against Saddam in 1991, many Iraqis escaped to Saudi Arabia where they were kept in refugee camps, some for as long as ten years. A number of other refugees escaped from Iraq during the eight-year war with Iran. Other Iraqis were captured by the allied forces during the first Gulf War, and some arrived here after the American invasion in 2003. These Iraqis came from Basra, al-Nasiriyya, al-Amarahand, and Hawr al-Hammar.[65]

Many of these refugees were granted asylum in America: of the 20,000 or so refugees who immigrated to America after 1991, about 10,000 settled in Dearborn. Many of these refugees came from the Southern Marshlands, where their chief occupations were agriculture and fishing, so they lacked the technical skills and educational background to join American industries. Some complain that their Iraqi degrees are not accepted by American institutions.

In February 2007, the U.S. government announced that it would accept seven thousand refugees from Iraq over the following year. This will likely increase the number of Iraqi Shi'is in America.[66] Since 2003 Iraqis have settled in different parts of the country from New York, Detroit, Chicago, Phoenix, and Denver to Nashville, Omaha, and Los Angeles forming tightly knit and close communities wherever they have settled.

Compared to all the other Shi'i groups, it is not an exaggeration to state that the Iraqi Shi'is (especially the recently arrived refugees) harbor the "myth of return" the most. Many of these Iraqis see themselves in exile, a term that suggests a desire and the possibility for a return to one's homeland. In exile, nostalgia for the homeland and the sense of loss that accompanies it often continues for extended periods of time. Thus, while in the United States, many Iraqis continue to speak their native languages and restrict interaction to members of their own ethnic or faith groups, establishing in the process ethnic islands within this country. Iraqi immigrants who still entertain the possibility of returning home do not engage in the necessary cultural and political adjustment in their local communities, and do not encourage interaction with the larger American society. The myth of return also encourages first-generation immigrants to cling to traditional norms and values of their homeland; they generally make little or no effort to adjust to their adopted homeland. In some cases, Iraqi refugees did indeed return home after the removal of Saddam Hussein's regime in 2003.

In contrast to the Iraqis who migrated in the 1970s and 1980s, most of the recent arrivals from Iraq form an unskilled labor force with little knowledge of English. Consequently, they tend to work in factories, gas stations, and perform other manual work. Due to their recent arrival and strong religious background, Iraqi refugees are in general more ritualistic and strict in their religious observances. Having lived in the Shi'i "holy cities" ('*atabat*) like Najaf and Kerbala where the Shi'i leadership (*maraji'*) reside,[67] Iraqi Shi'is bring with them a deep sense of religious commitment and a desire to replicate religious services in America, which is not always shared by Iranian and Lebanese Shi'is.[68] Some cling to home customs such as hitting themselves on the head and using iron chains when flagellating during the month of Muharram.[69] Many emphasize the public demonstration of Islamic practices, segregation of sexes, strict adherence to Islamic law including the Islamic dress code and following the edicts of the *marji'* to the letter of the law. On the other hand, the Lebanese originate from a more pluralistic and "open" background, while many Iranians have been influenced by the shah's modernization and Westernization programs. Hence, the outlook and vision of Shi'is from other cultures and background are quite different.

Because Iraqis are recent immigrants, they have not established their own religious institutions. Thus, in many cities, they have had to share centers with the Lebanese and Iranian communities, leading to quite a few altercations and resentment between the different groups. In one city, for example, Iraqi and Iranian Shi'is established a place of worship, but disputes soon arose on such issues as the use of vernacular in the sermons, the types of food to be served, performance of rituals, gender segregation, and other internal points of disagreement. In order to cater specifically to the increasing Dearborn Iraqi community, a separate center (appropriately called the Kerbala Center) was established in 1994 after the end of the Gulf War. While many Iraqi Shi'is are very traditional, some Iraqi mosques have a distinctly variant outlook. In an Iraqi-based mosque in Pomona, California (near Los Angeles), there is no gender segregation and women are encouraged to participate in the services and address the congregation.[70] Other Iraqis are quite liberal in their outlook and promote a full integration into American society.

The Iranian Shi'i Community

Iranians form the largest Shi'i group in America. Some estimates place the population of the Iranian community at close to 1 million, a number that is increasing every year.[71] A large majority of these are Shi'is although many do not visit Shi'i religious centers. The number of Iranians migrating to America has increased dramatically during the last three decades. In fact, Iranians account for 52 percent of Middle Eastern Muslim immigrants in America. In addition, one fourth of all Muslim immigrants from around the world are Iranians, outnumbering immigrants from all other Muslim-populated countries.[72]

Most of these Iranians came to the United States after the Iranian revolution in 1979 and settled in California, which has an estimated population of about 400,000 Iranians.[73] Of these, approximately 45,000 to 60,000 Iranians live in San Diego alone.[74] Iranian exiles decided to abandon their homeland primarily because of the revolution and transformation of Iranian society. For some, it was a matter of life and death, while for others it was a response to the new limitations on civil liberties and dress code, the restrictions imposed on universities, and the decline of the Iranian economy. Still others fled Iran in the 1980s to avoid conscription in the eight-year war with Iraq.

Iranians in America hold a broad spectrum of political views. They range from those who support the current regime in Iran to socialist movements like the Mojahedin-Khalq Organization (MEK). Other groups include the Iranian constitutionalists, who support the reinstatement of the monarchy in Iran.

The Iranian Shi'i community in America can be divided into three distinct groups. The first group comprises Iranian professionals and unskilled workers, many of whom left their native land fearing the policies of the new regime after the 1979 revolution. Having been influenced by the shah's white revolution and modernization policies that infused Western culture and lifestyle in Iran, many Iranians have adopted a secular outlook and have thus become estranged from Islam due to their bitterness toward the current regime in Iran. They come from the educated and more cultured class in Iran, a perspective that is indexed into mainstream American culture. A number of Iranians settled in Los Angeles and adopted the United States as their homeland.[75] They tend to exhibit the no religion preference, and choose to distance themselves from any affiliation with institutional religion, especially with Shi'ism.[76] It is not an exaggeration to state that among the various American Shiʻi communities, these Iranians have assimilated themselves most to American culture.

In contrast to the Iraqis, many assimilated Iranians have minimal contact with the religion of their home country, attending mosques only when a close family member or friend dies. In a survey conducted by George Sabadh and Mehdi Bozorgmehr, 54.7 percent of Iranians surveyed reported that they did not observe religious practices, and 48.2 percent of their spouses also affirmed that they did not observe Islam even when they lived in Iran.[77] In fact, many young Iranians have become so influenced by the West that they openly consume alcohol and pork, and eschew all affiliation with the religious community. For many of these secular Iranians, Iranian culture, rather than Islam, is the primary source of their definition and identity. Therefore, cultural identity is preponderant to their identity as Muslims.

Instead of visiting mosques these secular Iranians often attend Iranian cultural centers and commemorate important cultural events like *nawruz*, the beginning of the Iranian New Year. Few of this genre of Iranians would mark distinctive Shiʻi events such as the death anniversary of ʻAli b. Abi Talib or the day of ʻ*Ashura*' when Husayn was killed in Kerbala. For example, in Los Angeles, a Persian beauty contest—minus the swimsuit competition—was held during the emotionally charged Shiʻi mourning month of Muharram.[78] In March 2006, the day of *Arbaʻin* (the fortieth day after the martyrdom of Husayn) coincided with the day of *nawruz*. Many secular Iranians celebrated rather than mourned on that day.

For these Iranians, Islam with its dietary and other restrictions is seen as an impediment to full integration into American society. In the Sabadh and Bozorgmehr survey, only 4.3 percent of respondents and 9.0 percent of their spouses said they always or often observed their religious practices in America,[79] whereas only 3 percent were involved in a religious organization.[80] Another study shows that only 2 percent of Los Angeles' Iranian Muslims said they were religiously observant.[81]

When asked "what do you consider yourself primarily," 27 percent of respondents stated "Iranian Muslim," whereas 67 percent said just "Iranian." Only 2 out of 117 respondents identified themselves as Muslims.[82] Hardly any Iranian Muslims associate with non-Iranian Muslims, indicating again the ethnic ties that bind the Iranian community in Los Angeles.[83] The figures also indicate the low level of religious observance of Iranian Muslims in Los Angeles. Their secularism is probably explained by the fact that they were fleeing a religious revolution.

The secular orientation of this Muslim group, combined with the absence of an already thriving Shi'i community in Los Angeles, largely accounts for the group's scattered settlement patterns. Without an established institution such as an Iranian Shi'i mosque, these immigrants did not have a geographical point to draw them together.[84] They were all located in the enormous Los Angeles area, but were spread out among various neighborhoods. As a result, social interaction with other Iranian-Muslims was problematic. To form a collective identity they had to rely on cultural and political organizations such as Rotary clubs, which were less effective at reinforcing religious identity. Consequently, the children of these immigrants have become more susceptible to adopting the cultural norms of the host country and are less likely to maintain those of their parents.

By minimizing and hiding their beliefs and practices, making themselves as inconspicuous as possible, some Iranians hope to have an "invisible presence." Through such measures, they hope to assimilate into American society, often at the cost of their religious and social values. Assimilation also means to live in America, blend in, and leave different customs at home. Assimilation is another name for oneness—shedding differences and "be assimilated into the normative culture."[85] Assimilation also implies the absorption of values of the dominant culture and denotes a process through which members of a particular religious, ethnic, cultural, or minority group become similar to or adopt characteristics of the dominant community.

Assimilation occurs when a cultural or ethnic group consciously changes its identity to accord with another group, recognizing the latter's cultural superiority, so that the merged group may advance socially or politically by partially or totally giving up its original ethnic and racial identity. Assimilation may lead to changes in one's religious and cultural outlook or even disintegration of one's own identity. Those who favor assimilation try to distance themselves from elements of their own identity that would differentiate them from mainstream American society. For them, living in the West also means a commitment to full integration into American society.

Assimilation is also intertwined with cultural integration, a phenomenon that occurs when a culture increasingly upholds universalistic standards; thus stimulating intimate interaction among people of diverse cultural orientations. Cultural integration occurs more readily in the liberal religious sphere in terms of multifaith communication and cooperation with the "other." The effects of assimilation and merger into an American culture are evinced from the changing of names to the de-emphasizing of customs that would set people apart. Anglicization of names is a common phenomenon of new migrants who want to integrate themselves to the mainstream society. It is an important survival mechanism that helps alleviate racial or cultural prejudices.

Iranian-Americans employ secular publications and organizations to establish cultural ties and interconnectivity among community members. Targeting a broad Iranian American audience and encouraging engagement with, and preservation of, an Iranian cultural identity these institutions nevertheless endorse biculturalism and approve of an American cultural identity.[86] Due to technological advancements like the Internet, Iranian Americans have enjoyed increased access to these organizations.

Since 1980 Iranians have reportedly published at least eighty periodicals in Los Angeles alone; they have also produced dozens of Iranian television programs, radio programs, films, music videos, and theatrical and musical performances. Most of these secular programs aim to maintain Iranian ethnic and national identity. With time, this group has emerged as the dominant voice of Iranian exiles in Los Angeles.

In contrast to the secular Iranians are those who also came to the States after the revolution but who fully support the revolution and share its ideals. Many of them are students at various universities and promote the ideology of the current Iranian regime in Islamic centers. Hostility is evident between the diverse Iranian groups as anger is directed at those who propagate Iranian ideology. Because of their pro-government political stance, these Iranians are alienated not only from the larger American society but also from secular Iranians.

Devout Iranians regularly attend and participate in the religious activities of Islamic centers and are fully committed to bringing up their children as practicing Muslims. In areas where there are no centers, they hold religious festivals in their basements, teach Sunday schools, and reach out to Shi'is from different ethnic backgrounds. Some of these Iranians also participate in the Muslim Student Organization Persian-Speaking Group (MSA-PSG), an organization of predominantly Iranian students and ex-students who were a part of the Muslim Student Association (MSA) in the 1970s. The MSA-PSG holds gatherings at various college and university campuses and sometimes in the houses of individual members.

The third group is made up of those immigrants who are alarmed by the dissolution of religious values, especially among their younger generation, but who are not affiliated with the regime currently in power in Iran. To imbibe their youth with religious instruction, they organize events like Sunday classes, weekly lectures, and monthly Qur'anic classes in their houses. Many have also established Islamic centers. Their views differ radically from those propagated by the government in Iran and the MSA-PSG.[87]

Since they prefer to distance themselves from Iranian politics, these Iranians do not, generally speaking, directly ally themselves with the various Iranian centers. Instead, they join Shi'is from other parts of the world like the Khoja or Pakistani Shi'is to commemorate Shi'i religious holidays. Various factors certainly discouraged a number of highly qualified students from affiliation with or returning to Iran. The Iranian revolution, the imposition of strict Islamic laws, and the deterioration of the economic situation in the aftermath of the Iran-Iraq war meant that many Iranian students chose to remain in the States after completing their studies. Some of them married American women who would find it difficult to go to Iran and follow the strict moral codes introduced under the "Islamization" program. Furthermore, tensions between Iran and the United States regarding uranium enrichment and the possibility of American air strikes against Iranian targets have also deterred some Iranians from returning to their homeland.

The presence of different Iranian groups combined with their polarized perspectives regarding the regime in Iran have engendered controversy and lasting hostility within the Iranian community. There are, in fact, many instances of disputes and even violence between them. Supporters of the shah have, at times, equated the *hijab* with empathy for the regime in Iran.[88] Two Iranian Muslim women, who identified themselves as Venus and Soheil, described some of the discrimination they endured in Los Angeles for wearing the *hijab* stating that "walking down the street, people spit at me. . . . Especially Iranians . . . they just want to kill you! They look at you and they hate your guts!"[89] For younger women, veiling is considered not only a religious statement but also a political (primarily anti-Western or pro-Iranian) one. Disturbances between rival Iranian groups have also been reported in places like San Diego, which has a large Iranian population.[90]

To distance themselves from the regime in Iran, pro-shah and anti-Khumayni activists took to the streets in Los Angeles after the Iranian revolution. Pro-Khumayni supporters, in response, arranged counter-demonstrations, often in the same locations.[91] These protests sometimes resulted in violent scuffles between the pro- and anti-Khumayni groups. The antagonism is not confined along political lines. Animosity is also prevalent between pro-monarchists and the secular leftists who took part in the overthrow of the shah, but who later were marginalized by the mainstream Islamic movement. Leftists' involvement in the revolution was viewed by other exiles, especially the shah's supporters, as treason; however, some of these exiles did very little publicly to try to prevent the revolution from occurring.

Besides the Iranian groups, we should also mention Afghani Shi'is. When the Taliban, who were heavily influenced by Wahhabi ideology, came to power, they persecuted the Hazara Shi'is in Afghanistan, especially those living in Bamyan province. This led many Afghani Shi'is to seek asylum in the United States. Other Afghani Shi'is came to America when the Soviet Union invaded Afghanistan in 1979. Although not as significant in numbers as the other Shi'i groups, Afghani Shi'is have settled in different parts of the country. Since they are small in numbers, have limited financial resources, and share cultural and linguistic ties with the Iranians, Afghani Shi'is tend to blend in with Iranians and often visit Iranian centers. In larger cities Afghani Shi'is have been able to build their own mosques in order to preserve their distinctive culture.

The Lebanese Shi'is

Almost the entire first-, second-, and third-generation Muslims in the United States were of Lebanese ancestry and were among the first immigrants to settle in America in substantial numbers.[92] Yet not all Lebanese in Detroit are descendants of early immigrants. Between 1983 and 1990, soon after the Lebanese civil war ended, more than 30,000 immigrants came to Detroit directly from Lebanon.[93]

Like other Muslims living in America at that time, the early Lebanese immigrants, "seemed content, or at least constrained, to keep Islam within the parameters of their ethnic associations."[94] The early Lebanese found no large Muslim community present. They were quite liberal in their lifestyles and often quickly assimilated themselves to the American way of life, as corroborated by a survey conducted by Haddad and Lummis, which indicates that Americans born of Lebanese parents tend to be among the most liberal Muslims in America.[95] Their survey also found that midwestern Muslims, a large portion of whom are Lebanese, are above all the most liberal in their interpretation of Islam, especially when it comes to the question of women's clothing. They are also less likely to participate in regular Islamic obligations such as prayers and fasting.[96]

Compared to the other Shi'i groups, the challenges confronting the Lebanese community are quite different. Since many of the Lebanese are third- or fourth-generation citizens, transmission of Islam to future generation has already appropriated a distinctive American coloring. As such, many Lebanese centers have devised novel ways to attract the youth back to the mosques. In many centers, women play a greater role in religious services, and there is less emphasis on gender segregation in some centers in Dearborn. In addition, there are more youth-friendly programs held in many centers in Dearborn.

Protracted experience in the American environment has made the Lebanese realize the need to reach out to the American community. The genre of religious programs offered at their centers has been restructured to be more ecumenical in outlook. For example, there is a greater emphasis on interfaith dialogue at the Islamic House of Wisdom (IHW) and Islamic Center of America (ICA) in Dearborn. The IHW's advertisement book of 2001 carries a message from the imam of the center, Muhammad 'Ali Ilahi. In this he states:

> Our friends and co-workers, the classmates of our children, our neighbors, our bosses, our elected officials – all these need to be educated to the truth and beauty of Islam in order that the Muslim community be effectively integrated into American life. We need to be educated ourselves, in order that we may distinguish between insulating ourselves from the secular influences of American society and isolating ourselves from the rest of the world. That we cannot do, because we have a responsibility to propagate our faith, which isolation makes impossible.

Many programs offered at the Lebanese centers are broadcast on local television stations, and there is more emphasis on communicating with the media. Moreover, local politicians are frequently invited to participate in the programs and address the audience. Members of the Lebanese community, both Muslims and Christians, are increasingly playing more active roles in American civil life. It should be noted, however, that some Lebanese centers are more introverted and insist on replicating traditional Shi'i services and rituals. The Dearborn-based Majma', for example, advocates a strict and, at times, literalist interpretation of Islamic law, strictly enforcing gender segregation and eschewing dialogue with the non-Muslim community.[97]

Whereas in the last century, Lebanese Shi'is were concentrated in areas like Dearborn, today they are to be found in different parts of the United States. In cities like Austin, Cleveland, and Denver where they are not in great numbers, Lebanese Shi'is congregate with Shi'is from other ethnic and cultural backgrounds to mark important holidays in the Shi'i calendar.

Although the Lebanese and Iraqis share the same language, they are culturally dissimilar. The Lebanese in America tend to adopt a less rigorous approach to legalistic Islam, probably because the Lebanese have been more exposed to a Western lifestyle and because they originate from a more pluralistic background. For example, during their weddings, the Lebanese tend to have mixed-gendered gatherings accompanied by music. The Iraqis, on the other hand, abstain from entertainment that involves music and enforce strict gender segregation.

Given the pluralistic milieu in Lebanon, the Lebanese have become a more open and outward-looking community fostering closer interaction with members of other-faith groups. Having recently immigrated from religious cities ('*atabat*), the Iraqis, on the other hand, are more entrenched in religious practices and tend to emphasize rituals and a more rigid expression of Islam. The diverse cultural backgrounds and religious outlooks between the Lebanese and Iraqi Shi'is have meant that there is tension and conflict between the two groups.

Apart from Iraq and Lebanon, there are small groups of Arab Shi'is from Saudi Arabia, Kuwait, Bahrain, and Egypt. However, since they are small in number, these Shi'is tend to frequent the centers of other Arab Shi'is.

The South Asian Shi'is

The South Asian Muslim community in America is composed of migrants from Pakistan, India, and a lesser number from Bangladesh. They tend to share many cultural traditions, although the Bangladeshis speak Bengali in addition to Urdu. Immigrants from India, mostly from the Punjab, began to arrive in the United States in 1900,[98] the majority of whom were farm laborers and unskilled workers.[99] Toward the beginning of the twentieth century, many of them had moved south to settle in the

Stockton Valley in California.[100] By the late 1920s there were about one thousand South Asian Muslims living on the West Coast. Many of them married Mexican women and created a new type of ethnic identity. In all probability, there were a number of Shi'is present among these early migrants. These Muslims from the Indian coastal area are reported to have settled in California, Oregon, Washington, and Vancouver. Stories of their successes and the distinct possibilities of employment opportunities encouraged other Muslims from the same area to migrate to America. Other accounts further suggest Punjabi Muslims settled in San Diego from around 1912.[101]

Members of the South Asian community also migrated to America after World War II when the U.S. government sponsored students from different parts of the world. Other immigrants came seeking education and economic empowerment. A greater number of South Asian immigrants started arriving only after 1965. These immigrants benefited from the relaxation of American immigration laws at this time, for it meant that students who had settled here could, in turn, sponsor family members to join them. Among the South Asian migrants were Shi'is who, like the Sunnis, took advantage of the favorable immigration laws by settling here. Presently, nearly six thousand Pakistani Muslims immigrate annually.[102]

Immigration statistics and the census show a sharp increase in the numbers immigrating from India and Pakistan in the late 1960s, from Bangladesh after 1971 (after it split from West Pakistan), and from Afghanistan after the Soviets invaded it in 1979.[103] In fact, immigration of Pakistanis is reported to have increased ninefold since 1968.[104] Other statistics indicate that the South Asian community increased dramatically between 1970/71 and 1990—from 32,000 to almost 910,000.[105]

South Asian Shi'is are concentrated in Chicago, Atlanta, New York, Washington, D.C., Houston, and Los Angeles. These Shi'is are relatively more advanced in terms of their education and socioeconomic status; many of them are highly skilled, setting them apart from Iraqi refugees, who, although qualified in their own countries, have not had their certificates accredited here.

A distinctive feature of the South Asian Shi'i community is its close affinity to its culture and ethnicity. Although prayers and other traditional religious services are held to be important, ritualized services in Muharram, lectures, and the symbolic representation of Kerbala are also held in high esteem. Many of these Shi'is, for example, visit their centers only during the month of Muharram. The majority of services and liturgies are conducted in Urdu in highly ritualized forms resonating with the services in their countries of origins, and many South Asian Shi'is also perpetuate certain traditional Muharram rituals of public flagellation and inflicting wounds on their bodies.

The Khoja Shi'is

Little is known of the provenance and activities of the Khoja Twelver Shi'i Muslims. Khojas trace their ancestry to India, more specifically to Sind, Punjab, Gujarat, and Kutch where their ancestors were converted to Islam in the twelfth and thirteenth centuries. A Persian Isma'ili missionary, Pir Sadr al-Din (d. 1369 or 1416) was an Isma'ili *da'i* (proselyte) who is credited with the mass conversion of the Khojas from the Lohanas, a Hindu caste living predominantly in the Gujarat province in India.

The name *Khoja* is a phonetic corruption of the Persian word *khwaja* (master, teacher, honored). The name was given by Pir Sadr al-Din to Hindu Indian converts to Islam in the fourteenth century. Before their conversion, the Khojas reportedly formed the Lohana community, having descended from the mythic Indian king, Rama's son, Lav. Due to this, they were known as *thakkar,* which is also a phonetic corruption of the Indian title *thakor* (lord, master). The word is a close Indian approximation to the title given by Pir Sadr al-Din, *khwaja.*

Pir Sadr al-Din laid the basis for the communal organization of the Khojas by building the first three Jamaat Khanas (assembly or prayer halls) and appointing their *mukhis* (leaders).[106] Over a period of time, several pirs or spiritual leaders came after Sadr al-Din, and gradually the beliefs crystallized to those of the Isma'ili Nizari faith; particularly after the arrival of the Aga Khan Hasan 'Ali Shah from Iran to India in 1840. By this time, the Khojas had spread over Kutch and Gujarat; some had also moved to Mumbai and Muscat. They paid their dues to the Isma'ili Jamaat Khana and lived harmoniously within their society.

The arrival of the Agha Khan Hasan 'Ali Shah in India led to an escalation of earlier disputes within the Khoja community about the rights of the imam. The genesis of the split probably goes back to 1829 when a rich merchant, Habib Ibrahim, refused to pay a religious tax known as *dasond* (the tenth) to the Isma'ili administrative authorities. In 1866 a group of disenchanted members filed a suit against the Agha Khan regarding the usage of community finances. The judgment of Sir Joseph Arnold in a lawsuit fully upheld the rights and authority of the Agha Khan, leading to the dissidents separating themselves from the Isma'ili community. They were known as Sunni Khojas. Later dissidents, seceding in 1877 and 1901, formed the Ithna-asheri (Twelver) Khoja communities in Mumbai and East Africa.

In 1899 the Agha Khan issued a *farmaan* (religious decree) stating that those who did *not* wish to follow his policies and edicts could no longer consider themselves Isma'ilis. Consequently, three subgroups were created in India: those who continued to follow the Agha Khan and comprised the largest of Khojas (called Isma'ilis), while Bar Bhaya from the influential family of Habib Ibrahim and his followers were later influenced by Sunni scholars and became Sunnis. A third group converted to Twelver Shi'ism.

In the early 1900s, some Twelver Shi'i Khojas went to visit the holy sites in Iraq. During their discussions with a prominent scholar of the time, Shaykh Zayn al-'Abidin al-Mazandarani, they asked him to send a scholar to India to teach them the basic principles of Islam. At the request of Shaykh al-Mazandarani, Mulla Qadir Hussein arrived in India and taught several Khoja families the essentials of Twelver Shi'i faith. From these few families the community has now grown globally to more than 100,000 members.

An important figure in the conversion to and dissemination of Twelver Shi'i teachings was Haji Gulamali Haji Isma'il, popularly known as Haji Naji. He is credited with translating Arabic and Persian religious texts to Gujarati, a language spoken by most Khoja Shi'is of the time. Many of these texts articulated Shi'i beliefs and practices. His translation of *Mi'raj al-Sa'ada* (a manual of Islamic ethics) is known to have transformed the lives of many Khoja Shi'is in Africa.

Many Khojas living in India migrated to East Africa in the 1840s. They left India due famine and poverty and by the prospect of better financial opportunities in Africa. In a census carried out by the Khoja community in the late 1950s and then repeated during the 1960s, the Khoja Shi'is in East Africa, Somalia, Congo, Mauritius, Reunion Island, and Madagascar numbered around 20,000.[107] Not all Shi'is in East Africa came from India. Shi'is from Bahrain and Iran came to serve the Sultans of Zanzibar after they had made the island their headquarters from 1832 on.

During the 1950s, the Khoja community in America was comprised primarily of a few students who lived in isolated areas where there was no sizable Muslim community; thus, it is difficult to speak of a distinct Khoja presence in America before the 1960s. The majority of the

Khoja Shiʻis migrated to the West in 1972/3, a result of the East African governments' policies that favored Africans in the social, economic, and educational spheres. These measures included the nationalization of Asian-owned enterprises and buildings. The measures also stressed better education for Africans, often at the expense of the Indian community. Increased immigration by the Khoja community was also precipitated by the revolution in Zanzibar in 1964 and the expulsion of Ugandan Asians by Idi Amin in 1972. Khoja Shiʻis from Tanzania and Kenya also migrated due to the inimical sociopolitical conditions in their homeland countries.

Khoja Shiʻis have a multiplicity of complex identities. Khojas migrating from East Africa brought some African culture with them. Khojas coming from Tanzania, for example, often communicate with each other in their native language, Kiswahili. Yet, due to their Indian origins, they also speak Urdu or Gujarati and have appropriated the culture and values of the South Asian community. Living in the United States has also led them to adopt elements of American identity and culture. Their centers are structured along the same lines as the Pakistani and Indian mosques, and their places of worship contain icons that are exhibited in South Asian centers, thus retaining some of their South Asian culture.

Khoja Shiʻis are known for their sense of discipline and organization. In 1976, under the astute leadership of Asghar M. M. Jaffer (d. 2000), they established a world body called the World Federation of Khoja Shiʻa Ithnaʻasheri Jamaat in England. With the help of this institution, they have established centers of worship throughout the world. The federation's stated aim is to act as an umbrella organization, catering to the needs of the world Khoja community. The largest Khoja congregation in the States is in New York, and there are other Khoja centers in Los Angeles, Orlando, Minneapolis, and Allentown.

In an attempt to unite the diverse ethnic Shiʻi groups in North America, the Khoja community in Toronto established the North American Shiʻa Ithnaasheri Muslim Communities (NASIMCO) in 1980. Twenty-four Canadian and American Shiʻi communities consisting of nearly 20,000 people are currently members of NASIMCO, which helps coordinate Shiʻi religious and social activities throughout North America. Open to all Shiʻi organizations regardless of their ethnic or cultural background, it is predominately made up of members of East-African derivation. Its stated aim is to propagate Islam according to the Twelver Shiʻi school of law (called the Jaʻfari school).

Among the goals of NASIMCO is to establish religious schools for community members, assist in publishing books and journals, and educate non-Muslims regarding the tenets, doctrines, and practices of Islam. It is responsible for providing necessary religious guidance through regular contact with Shi'i centers of learning in Iran and Iraq, as well as financial support for capital projects undertaken by individual member communities. By acting as an umbrella organization, NASIMCO attempts to foster unity and promote religious, educational, social, and economic amelioration of the communities; in addition it also supports financially the establishment of new centers in North America.

NASIMCO collects and remits funds to sponsor indigent families and to build local hospitals and houses in India. The primary source of funding for NASIMCO are individual donations, subscriptions from member groups, and a portion of the religious tax of the *khumus* collected with the permission of the *marji'*.[108] In recent years, some non–East African Shi'i groups have also joined NASIMCO in order to benefit from its financial and religious resources and its various services.

Khoja Shi'is created an efficient religious education system. The most active wing of NASIMCO is the Islamic Education Board (IEB), which hosted biannual conferences and updated the syllabi for the *madaris* (pl. of *madrasa*, religious schools) in the 1990s. It coordinated educational activities between the different Sunday schools in North America, held regular workshops, and published newsletters for the benefit of *madrasa* teachers. The IEB also introduced teaching techniques and newer courses such as comparative religion and Islam in modern times.

Most of NASIMCO's subgroups are not very active, meaning that the organization has had little or no impact in the American Shi'i community. NASIMCO also failed to unite the diverse ethnic Shi'i communities because few non-Khoja institutions actually joined the organization. Lack of financial resources and internal disputes have further undermined the activities of NASIMCO. Apart from Shi'is from different ethnic backgrounds, there are also some Shi'is, like the Sufi Shi'is, who have a more spiritual orientation.

Sufism in the American Context

Islamic mysticism (also called Sufism) advocates an approach to the worship of God that is not constricted to the exoteric or legalistic expression of Islam. It was during the Umayyad Dynasty in the eighth century that a distinct group of mystics emerged. The worldly outlook of the Umayyad rulers, the rapid expansion of the Islamic empire in the first century of Islam, and a general disdain of religious principles led many Muslims to believe that the ideals and values established by the Prophet Muhammad had been compromised or destroyed by the ruling elite. These were major factors that precipitated the rise of a group of piety-minded people, the early mystics of Islam.

Sufism is premised on the need to purify the soul through an elaborate exercise of *dhikr* (remembrance of the names of God) and other devotional practices. Sufis demonstrate many of the hallmarks characteristic of holy men in other religious traditions. They perform a wide range of devotional exercises ranging from self-mortification, vigils, protracted prayers, and meditation to emulating the spiritual exercises of the Prophet Muhammad.

Sufis are often derided by more legalistic groups of Muslims, whose Islam is built around the observation of explicit commandments of Islamic law (*shariʿa*) and on a rejection of the esoteric dimension of Islam, especially that of the veneration of saints. Due to this conflict, many tracts from Wahhabi and Salafi groups in America criticize Sufism as an aberration from the "true" Islam.[109]

Sufism was brought to and established in America by various Sufi masters. Sufi groups originating from abroad have attracted many converts to their *tariqa*s (orders) not only because of their willingness to welcome non-Muslims to participate in their *dhikr* sessions but they also do not stress the more formal elements of Islamic devotions. For American converts to Islam, the lure of Sufism is the inner, spiritual journey to God and its promotion of asceticism, which, they believe, reflects the essence of Islamic revelation.[110]

Sufism cuts across the racial, ethnic, and cultural lines that characterize much of American Islam and accentuates the egalitarian dimension of Islam. Because of this factor, it draws adherents from all over the world. Sufism also appeals to American women because of its more lenient regulations on gender mixing during the times and places of worship. Some orders even allow female leaders or *shaykha*s to conduct their *dhikr* sessions in contrast to many American mosques in which women are either secluded or excluded.

Sufi orders found in the United States today include the Naqshbandiyya, the Qadiriyya, the Jerahiyya, the Muridiyya, the Tijaniyya, the Chistiyya, and others. The writings of Sufi teachers like Hazrat Inayat Khan

(d. 1927), Idries Shah (d. 1997), and Fadlallah Haeri, with their emphasis on the inner life over the outer forms of religion have been influential on American travelers on the *tariqa* (path). Inayat Khan, for example, was one of the first to teach Sufi doctrines in the West when he visited there in 1910.[111] He also initiated a number of disciples and founded a Sufi order in England. His teachings are contained in the voluminous series, *The Sufi Message of Hazrat Inayat Khan*. In the 1960s, his son Pir Vilayat Khan emerged as an important Sufi leader in the West. It was not until the late 1960s, when immigration to the United States became more feasible, that a new generation of Sufi teachers was born in Muslim societies. Since that time, Sufi movements in the United States have proliferated.

Esoteric Shi'ism

Shi'is embrace the mystical tradition that developed in the classical period of Islam. Shi'i mysticism shares many features with mainstream Sufism, such as the development of powers of self-denial, acts of devotion, and asceticism. Like Sufism, the very heart of Shi'i mysticism is the distinction between subject and object and an experience of the world in which the seer and the seen are one.[112]

Shi'i esotericism is centered on the spiritual powers and teachings of the Prophet and the Imams. For the Shi'is, the Imams possess comprehensive authority (*al-wilaya al-mutlaqa*) in the sense of temporal and spiritual authority over the lives of the believers. The *wilaya*, it is believed, was transmitted by the Prophet to 'Ali and subsequently to the rest of the Imams. This *wilaya* enables the Imam to guide his followers in both the exoteric and esoteric sense.

For the Shi'is, the Imams not only possessed esoteric truths, they embodied, lived, and taught them to some of their closest disciples. The gnostic teachings of the Imams encouraged their disciples and even contemporary Shi'is to engage in this field. Traditions cited in Shi'i sources indicate that the Imams would often share spiritual secrets with some of their close disciples. In a tradition that accentuates the close relationship between Ja'far al-Sadiq, the sixth Imam, and his disciple, Mu'alla b. Khunays (n.d.), the Imam is quoted as warning him to, "[C]onceal our secrets, for one who conceals our secrets, God creates for him a light between his eyes and gives him strength among the people."[113] They believe that these secretive teachings are often difficult to handle as only those whose hearts have been purified can accept them.[114]

The importance of the Imams as spiritual guides extends beyond eso-teric Shi'ism. The Imams feature prominently in Sufi literature too, not as Imams in the Shi'i theological sense but as great mystical, esoteric figures. This coalescing of Shi'i and Sufi tendencies in the figure of the Imams can be discerned from a study of 'Ali b. Abi Talib. For the Shi'is, 'Ali is the first divinely appointed Imam, having inherited the Prophet's spiritual and temporal authority and his extraordinary powers. For the Sufis, he is a prominent ascetic and an archetype of spirituality in the early period of Islam. Many Sufi orders are traced to him since he appears as the spiritual authority par excellence after the Prophet.[115]

The special sanctity of the Imams and their descendants is also ac-knowledged by Sufis; like the Shi'is, they also revere the family of the Prophet.[116] Sufis include one or more of the first eight Imams among their spiritual ancestors because these eight Imams formed the "golden chain," linking subsequent generations to the Prophet himself.[117] For example, 'Ali al-Rida (d. 818), the eighth Shi'i Imam, taught Ma'ruf al-Karkhi (d. 815), who then brought Sufism to Baghdad. Ma'ruf had reportedly converted to Islam due to the pervasive influence of al-Rida.[118]

Sufi groups like the Bektashi, Kubrawiya, and Ni'matullah trace their lineage to 'Ali b. Abi Talib through 'Ali al-Rida and Ma'ruf al-Karkhi.[119] Naqshbandi Sufis believe that all twelve Imams deserve reverence and can function as spiritual guides after their deaths.[120] Naqshbandi genealogies normally include at least one of the following Shi'i Imams: Ja'far al-Sadiq, 'Ali al-Rida, or 'Ali b. Abi Talib.[121]

The Sufi Shi'is of the United States

The discussion on esoteric Shi'ism and the sanctity and authority of the Imams suggests that there is much conceptual convergence between Sufism and Shi'ism. Among the Shi'i population in the United States are various Sufi Shi'i groups, the majority of whom have been active here since the 1970s. Sufi movements among the Shi'i community are certainly not widespread or diverse; most of the movements are established within the Iranian community in California where there are at least three Sufi meet-ing places in Los Angeles.[122] Many Iranians prefer the esoteric dimension to the rigid and more strict Iranian mosques, some of which subscribe to the ideology of the Iranian regime or emphasize a legalistic interpretation of Shi'i Islam.

One of the largest Sufi Shiʻi orders is the Nimatullahi. The word *Nimatullah* is derived from its founder, Shah Nimatullah Wali, who established the order at the end of the fourteenth century and was one of the great Sufi masters of Iran. Shah Nimatullah was born in 1330 in Aleppo, Syria; he traveled extensively in the Islamic world and became acquainted with the important ideas of his time, especially the philosophical views of Ibn al-ʻArabi.

Until recently, the Nimatullahi order was based primarily in Iran, and the majority of Nimatullahi Sufis were Iranians. Nimatullahi centers can be found in more than one hundred Iranian cities; it is estimated that 30,000 members belong to the order. An Iranian psychiatrist, Dr. Javad Nurbakhsh, became the leader of the Nimatullahi order in 1953, when his master, Munis ʻAli Shah Dhu al-Riyasatain, passed away.

For the last thirty-five years Dr. Nurbakhsh has established more than a hundred *khaniqas* or places of worship, and numerous libraries and museums throughout Iran. In the 1970s, a number of Americans and Europeans visited Iran and were initiated into the Nimatullahi order. On their return to their home countries they sensed the need for a place to congregate and perform the *dhikr*. When Nurbakhsh first came to America in 1974 he became aware of the interest in Sufism in America and the need to establish a place of worship.[123] The first Nimatullahi *khaniqa* (place of worship) outside Iran was founded in San Francisco in 1975.

In 1975 Nurbakhsh sent his deputy, the shaykh of Shiraz, Niktab, to the United States. *Khaniqas* were opened in San Francisco and New York. After the Iranian revolution in 1979, Nurbakhsh moved to Los Angeles before moving to England in 1983. The Nimatullahi order has since reached a global audience as a great number of *khaniqas* have been built in North America, Western Europe, Africa, and Australia.[124] There are Nimatullahi centers in nine American cities including New York, Washington, D.C., and Boston. The majority of the disciples are Anglo American, but a significant number, perhaps as many as 50 percent of West Coast disciples, are Iranians.[125] Nurbakhsh stresses a Sufism concerned with actions and observation rather than with thinking and talking. He emphasizes the realization of the truth through love and devotion.

Another branch of the Nimatullahis is led by Nasir ʻAli Shah, who is based in Istanbul and Paris. *Murids* (followers) of this order are to be found in various cities like New York, Boulder, Colorado, and in North Carolina.[126] Followers of the branch are required to convert to Islam.[127] Ron Kelley describes a typical meeting of this order:

Under the leadership of the organization's only shaykh in America, Dalavar Karaien, members first sit in meditative postures against the walls of the center, listening to traditional Iranian music in dim light. Next, about half the members turn to traditional prostration prayers toward Mecca; others choose to leave the room. Another tape is played, this time a lecture by the Nimatullahi master, Javad Nurbakhsh and an English translation tape follows. Finally, on occasion, a dinner is placed on the floor. The food is served and eaten in total silence except for the shaykh's brief directives to begin and conclude the meal. As the leader leaves, the congregation rises in homage and he meets with members for private consultation behind a curtain in another area.[128]

Nimatullahi-Gunabadi

The Nimatullahi-Gunabadi Sufi order was established by Sultan Husayn Tabandah, Rida Ali Shah (b. 1914) with branches in Orange County, California, and Toronto, Canada. The current leader succeeded his father and was appointed *khalifa* (leader) of the order in 1960. Like other Sufi Shi'i groups, most of the followers of the order in North America are members of the Iranian community.

Recently, followers of Nimatullahi-Gonabadi Sufi order complained of harassment by the Iranian government. In 2007, it was reported their gathering and prayer center in Qum was seized. Followers of the order resisted the attacks by the authorities, which resulted in the wounding and injuring of several members of the order.[129] However, the Associate Press reported differing versions as to the source of the conflict.

Ja'fari-Shadhili Order

Shaykh Fadlallah Haeri, an Iraqi engineer and a Shi'i Muslim, was affiliated with 'Abd al-Qadir's Sufi group, the Habibiyya, during the 1970s. In 1980 he and a group of followers established a Sufi community, the Zahra Trust, in Blanco, Texas, near San Antonio. In 1981 they built a mosque and *madrasa* (religious school), which became the nucleus of a community known as the *Bayt al-Deen* (home of religion), modeled on the first Islamic community at Medina. By the late 1980s, however, Haeri had decided to move his organization to England.[130] Zahra Publications, a part of the Zahra Trust, has published many books on Islam and Sufism since 1981 in Europe and America; most of these publications focus on spiritual and transformative teachings.

Oveyssi-Shahmaghsoudi

Another Sufi movement of Iranian origin is the Uwaysi order, a Shi'i branch of the Kubrawiya brought to the West by its shaykh, Shah Maghsoud Angha (d. 1980).[131] It has since divided into two Sufi movements functioning in the United States, both descended from Shah Maghsoud Angha.[132] The larger movement, known as the Shah Maghsoudi order, is headed by his son, Mawlana Salaheddin Ali Nader Shah Angha, known to his followers as "Hazrat Pir."[133] The order, which is also known as Maktab Tariqat Uwaysi or as the School of Islamic Sufism, has many centers throughout the world, including the United States, Canada, Europe, the Middle East, and Asia.[134] This order is currently spread over nineteen states with a high concentration in San Francisco and Los Angeles. While the order is based on Islamic principles, no formal conversion to Islam is required to join the movement. Neither the Shi'i underpinnings of the order nor the role of the Imams on the *tariqa* are accentuated. Hence, it is the spiritual rather than the sectarian element that shines within the movement.

Meetings held by Mawlana Salaheddin Angha and his deputies often attract audiences, mainly Iranians, of hundreds for *dhikr* and meditative practices. At the centers in Burbank and Concord, California, meetings are held on alternate evenings to accommodate large crowds. Activities within the *tariqa* are not confined to devotional services. Various educational and community service programs, such as meditation classes, children's programs, and prison outreach, are offered through the various centers. This group has attracted thousands of followers in the States and is much larger than that of the Nimatullahis. In 1990, between three thousand and five thousand people are reported to have gathered for the birthday of Oveyssi Shahmaghsoud in the desert city of Lancaster, California.[135]

International Association of Sufism

Another movement derived from the teachings of Shahmaghsoud is headed by his daughter, Dr. Nahid Angha, and the wife of another Sufi, Dr. Ali Kianfar.[136] Together, they founded the International Association of Sufism, based in San Rafael, California, which aims to facilitate communication and cooperation across many Sufi orders. The movement began in 1983 to introduce Sufism to the public, provide a forum for dialogue among Sufi orders, and to propagate the message of Sufism. Its member-ship is predominantly American, and the formal practice of Islam is not required of its members.

Seyida Nahid Angha is also the founder of the Sufi Women Organiza-tion and the co-director of the International Association of Sufism. She was appointed to teach in her father's Uwaysi tradition, becoming the first woman given this honor. An internationally published author, she is one of the most influential Sufi women and contributors to the world of Sufi doctrine and a major Sufi writer and translator of Sufi literature.

The International Association of Sufism has worked to achieve its goals through different ways including an extensive publication program, which has brought Sufi masters together with writers, translators, editors, and other members of the English-speaking intellectual community. Among its many publications and productions are *Sufism: An Inquiry*, a quarterly journal and *Insight*, an IAS newsletter.[137]

The two movements that emerged from Shah Maghsoud Angha's line, the International Association of Sufism and the MTO (*Maktaba Tarigha Oveysiyya*), have established their own Associations for Sufi Psychology. Representatives teach in psychology programs such as the California In-stitute of Integral Studies and hold academic conferences under the rubric of "Sufi Psychology."

Conclusion

This chapter has traced the provenance, migration, and settlement of the Shi'i community in America. The early Shi'i immigrants arrived in the United States at about the same time the Sunnis did. Initially, the two groups ignored their sectarian differences and focused on their Islamic identity. They worshiped together, often intermarried, and met at various social func-tions; they also represented the Muslim community as a singular group.

Shi'is in America come from different countries. While in the early years most Shi'is were of Lebanese origins, now, the majority are from Iran. There are many Shi'is of Iraqi, Khoja, and South Asian descent, as well as Sufi Shi'i groups, composed primarily of Iranians in California. As a generation of Shi'is was coming of age in America, the elders soon realized that they would not be returning home. Consequently, Leba-non, Iran, or Pakistan became more of a "spiritual" than a "geographical" homeland. Many Shi'is imported their homeland culture and rituals to the States whereas others sought novel methods to adapt to living here.

In the following chapters, we will see that, with time, the Shi'i community in America became diverse and segmented, which led to communal fragmentation as each community chose different ways to adapt to the American ambience. In many instances, communities now express their faith and beliefs in culturally conditioned forms, leading many Shi'is to minoritization within the Shi'i community.

2

The American Shi'i Community: Ethnicity and Identity

Immigrant Muslims who came to the United States in the early twentieth century sensed the need to create communal prayer spaces and mark important religious holidays. By 1920 Muslim spaces or associations existed in New York, North Dakota, Iowa, Indiana, Michigan, Maine, and Ohio. These were informal gathering places frequently located in coffee shops, the homes of community leaders, or, on rare occasions, in the workplace. In most cases, the communities left little or no documentation of where they conducted their religious services, making it difficult to trace the activities of the early Muslim community.

The first mosque built in America specifically as a house of worship was, in all probability, the Moslem Mosque in Highland Park, Michigan. Its grand opening was celebrated on *eid al-fitr* in 1921.[1] The mosque was built to encourage Muslims to pray regularly, to facilitate the celebration of Islamic holidays, and to serve as an outpost and architectural symbol of Islam in the West.[2] Mohammed Karoub, a wealthy real estate developer, designed and financed the mosque. His brother, Hussein Karoub, oversaw construction and acted as its spiritual leader, or imam. The Highland Park mosque attracted the attention of the local press; its opening day parade and holiday celebration drew a crowd of several hundred worshipers and was presided over by three imams: Hussein Karoub, Khalil Bazzy, and Mufti Mohammed Sadiq, each representing a different tradition of Islamic practice.[3]

Most of those frequenting the mosque were Sunnis. The Shi'is who remained in Highland Park were loyal to their imam, Sheikh Khalil Bazzy, and refused to give the mosque (under the leadership of Hussein Karoub) any financial backing. In 1926, after much contention, the building was sold to the city of Highland Park.[4]

In 1924 the Shi'is in Michigan City, Indiana, were among the first to construct a specifically Shi'i mosque in the United States. According to a booklet published by the Islamic Center of Michigan City, the center was first incorporated on April 26, 1914, under the name of the Bader Elmoneer Society of Michigan City, Indiana.⁵ The main purpose of the organization was to engage in and teach the history and practice of the Islamic faith as founded by the Prophet. Thus, it was supposed to be primarily a religious rather than social institution. The founder and first president was Hussein Boudeeb Mohamed (d. 1914) who was also the community's religious leader.

In the early 1920s, the Bader Elmoneer Society purchased land across from the existing Michigan City Police Station and erected a building that became the first Shi'i mosque built in America. On May 10, 1924,⁶ under the name of the Asser El Jadeed (the new generation) Arabian Islamic Society, the organization reorganized itself as a nonprofit religious entity. The Asser El Jadeed predated the mosque in Cedar Rapids by more than ten years and the Hashemite hall in Detroit by sixteen years. This corroborates my point that there was an active and vibrant Shi'i community in Michigan City in the early part of the twentieth century.

The Asser El Jadeed became a social and religious center that sponsored religious events, conventions, and meetings for friends and relatives from Detroit, Toledo, and Chicago. As with other religious organizations in Michigan City, in 1929 the Asser El Jadeed purchased a section in a local cemetery for the burial of Muslims who were members of the congregation. The Asser El Jadeed Masjid, with its familiar minaret and façade, remained in existence on Second Street in Michigan City until 1969 when the Michigan City Redevelopment Department purchased the building as part of the Michigan City Urban Renewal Program. On October 24, 1969, the Asser El Jadeed Arabian Islamic Society adopted its present name, The Islamic Center of Michigan City, Indiana, Inc. In 1971 the center bought another building on the outskirts of Michigan City and converted it into a mosque with a familiar minaret and dome.

The establishment of and services offered at Asser El Jadeed are confirmed by Julia Harajali, who was born in Michigan City in 1920 and now lives in Dearborn. She recalls attending religious and social events at the mosque. Jacob Hussein Abraham was born in Michigan City in 1927. The mosque, he states, was used primarily for social rather than religious gatherings. On certain festive occasions, alcohol was served in the compounds of the mosque, counter to Islamic tradition, which led Jacob's father to break away from the mosque community. For him, the mosque was not "religious enough." In the 1920s and 1930s, there were no special services offered in the Islamic month of Muharram or the day of 'Ashura'. In fact,

The New Islamic Center of America in Dearborn, Michigan. Courtesy of Islamic Center of America, Dearborn, Michigan.

no Friday prayers were offered at all. Hussein Hakim, who migrated to Michigan City in 1948, recalls that most Shi'is lived close to the mosque even though there was no religious leader until 1950, when imam Chirri arrived from Dearborn.

The Lebanese Shi'is in Detroit bought a bank and converted it into a hall in the 1940s. The Hashemite hall, which could barely accommodate 150 people, was used for both religious and social purposes. Services were held on Sundays until the 1950s. Arriving in Detroit in 1949, imam Muhammad Jawad Chirri sought to transform a community that had almost assimilated into mainstream American culture into a community that was solidly established along religious lines. Initially, Chirri served the Shi'i community at the Hashemite hall. As the community increased in number, he had a vision of a proper, permanent *masjid* (mosque). On his travels to Egypt in 1959, Chirri was able to meet and persuade President Jamel 'Abd al-Nasser to donate a sum of money for the center. His goal was to spread Islam to an American community that had no knowledge of the religion. The result was the Islamic Center of America, which opened its doors in 1963. Shaykh Chirri served as the imam of the center until the early 1990s. In 2005 the center relocated to Ford Road in Dearborn, where a magnificent multipurpose building was opened.

The Establishment of Shi'i Centers

As the number of Shi'i migrants increased in the 1960s, Shi'is in other American cities realized the need to establish their own centers. In 1973 the Iraqi-born Yasin al-Jibouri founded the Islamic Society of Georgia after he left a local Islamic center in Atlanta when members of the community realized that he was a Shi'i. Al-Jibouri also began publishing a newsletter called *Islamic Affairs*, which was, in the view of the author, "the mouthpiece of Shi'a Islam and the most powerful advocate of Shi'ism in America."[7]

In 1976 the eminent Shi'i spiritual leader of the time, Ayatullah Abu al-Qasim al-Khu'i (d. 1992), residing in Iraq, sent a representative, Shaykh Muhammad Sarwar from Quetta, Pakistan, to establish al-Khoei Foundation in America. The center was to provide guidance, conduct religious services, commemorate important religious occasions, and provide literature to the Shi'i community. Clearly, the Shi'i religious leadership abroad was responding to the needs of the growing American Shi'i community. Eleven years later in 1987, Ayatullah al-Khu'i asked Ayatullah al-Sayyid Fadhil Milani, a prominent scholar from Iraq, to establish a similar center in London, England.

As more Shi'i immigrants migrated in the late 1970s and 1980s, they soon realized that the United States would be their permanent home especially as social, economic, and political turmoil in their own countries made it highly unlikely that they would return to their native lands. In addition to the centers, facilities for teaching the Qur'an, establishing Sunday schools, performing marriages, burial, and circumcision rites were arranged. When their families joined them, immigrant workers now had to come into contact with representatives from the school system, social workers, and public housing officials. The community realized it could not afford to remain invisible in America any longer.

Gradually, the Shi'i community built infrastructures that would protect and perpetuate the identity of its members and ensure the transmission of its teachings to the future generation. Before the revolution in the Islamic republic, the Alawi Foundation (then called the Pahlavi Foundation) looked after Iranian financial interests in America. After the revolution, the foundation was placed under the direct management of the Mostaza-fan Foundation in Tehran. Subsequently, its name was changed to Alawi. The Alawi Foundation has also helped to establish Shiʻi religious centers in Houston, Washington, and New York. Since the 1980s, the World Federation of Khoja Shiʻa Ithnaʼasheri Communities, based in London, England, has also helped construct both Khoja and non-Khoja centers in America. By 2006 there were some two hundred Shiʻi institutions established in America and Canada.[8]

Table 1 (see appendix for all tables) shows that more than 45 percent of the centers were established in the 1990s, suggesting that the majority of the Shiʻi community in North America is relatively young (29 percent of the centers were established in the 1980s and 16 percent in the 2000s). Another significant point is that only 9 percent of the centers were established in the 1970s. Instead of building centers of worship, the early Shiʻi communities met in people's houses. It was only when more Shiʻis arrived in the 1980s that Islamic centers were constructed. Many centers hold programs in languages reflecting their countries of origins (Urdu, Farsi, or Arabic). Thus, Shiʻis from different ethnic backgrounds generally feel excluded from partaking in programs held at a different ethnic center.

Many centers are still in the process of consolidation, building up their membership, meeting the various needs of their members, and paying off debts. Many centers are more concerned with meeting their financial obligations than with establishing links and engaging in dialogue with non-Muslims. In my survey, I raise a question concerning the current and future challenges of the centers. The results further corroborate that since the centers were established quite recently, most are engaged in an ongoing struggle to meet their financial obligations. Table 2 indicates that more than 50 percent of the centers surveyed identified financial stability as the most important current challenge. Seventy percent of the centers stated that acquiring a facility and/or adding to the current facility were the most important challenges. These two factors were also identified as future challenges.

One center stated, "Until recently, we had only 10–15 families from India and Pakistan. In the last 3–4 years, many families arrived from Iran, Iraq, and Afghanistan. Many are students from Iran and others are refugees from Iraq. Most of the population is young and struggling economically." The arrival of newer immigrants puts a major strain on the financial resources of a center, especially if these immigrants are students or refugees. Clearly, this is an important challenge that centers are seeking to overcome.

Table 3 indicates that most Shi'i centers provide only the basic services. Thus, most programs are held on Thursday nights.[9] The centers also celebrate the birth and death anniversaries of the Imams (table 4) and hold Friday prayers. Since most of the centers are quite new, they do not provide funeral services or open their mosques to non-Muslims. Sixty-eight percent engage in interfaith dialogue (table 5). In response to a question about *da'wa* (proselytization) work (table 8), nearly 38 percent of the centers did not respond at all; however, 90 percent of the organizations that did respond reported positively about engaging in some form of *da'wa* activities indicating that the Shi'i community is still in a state of transition and growth.

A recent report published by the Council on American-Islamic Relations (CAIR) indicates that the founding year of Sunni mosques ranges from 1925 to 2000: just 2 percent were founded prior to 1950; half the mosques surveyed were founded by 1980, and the other half were founded after that. The vast majority of existing mosques (87 percent) have been established since 1970.[10] Since they were established earlier and have more members, Sunni mosques are better organized, tend to have more resources, and are better equipped to cater to the increasing needs of their community.

As more Shi'is immigrate here and as the younger generation matures, the centers are gradually evolving to reflect the various needs of the community. It is essential, therefore, to discuss the main factors that shape and impact the Shi'i centers: immigration, ethnicization, and the quest for cultural and religious identity.

Immigration and Its Impact on the Shi'i Community

In their native countries, most Shi'is experienced a monolithic Shi'ism, one that was not informed by ethnic and cultural diversity. This monolithic, homeland Shi'ism is challenged in America where immigrant Shi'is have to contend with American pluralism, a multiethnic Shi'ism, and an Islam defined primarily by Sunnism.[11] Furthermore, Shi'is need to contend with increasing attacks against Islam by the media and Christian fundamentalists. These factors create additional challenges for the immigrant Shi'i community.

We should note that the Shi'i community has a greater composition of an immigrant component than its Sunni counterpart. This is because of the lack of indigenous Shi'is and because most converts accept Sunni rather than Shi'i Islam. In contrast to the Shi'i community, the Sunni community is composed of a large percentage of African Americans, and a smaller number of Caucasians, Latinos, and Native Americans. Due to this factor, in the American Shi'i community, tensions are felt more within the immigrant community than between immigrants and converts.

How does immigration impact the American Shi'i community? The immigrant psyche is shaped by the memory of a homeland, by images carried across the oceans as well as the visions they would like to transmit to their children. Once in America, immigrants often witness the dilution of a pristine, homeland Islam where religion was embedded in a given culture and society. Faced with this possible threat, they often respond by renewing ties with the homeland, reviving traditional norms, and imposing a conservative and extraneous expression of Islam. As they find themselves in situations of cultural displacement and marginality, immigrants mediate Islam in a culturally conditioned form, one that is highly resistant to change.

Most Shi'i immigrants try to impose the homeland culture in America by determining how the mosques are run, or what is an acceptable dress code, language, and behavior. Newer immigrants also tend to have their own predispositions on issues such as gender integration, political activism in a non-Muslim country, engagement with different ethnic groups, interfaith dialogue, joint activities with Sunnis, and the like. In many cases, Shi'i immigrants tend to emphasize the public expression of their religious beliefs and practices and are thus less likely to assimilate.

Immigrants also challenge the American expression of Islam, precipitating a crisis and even splits within certain mosques. They bring with them a more intense form of Shi'ism, one whose discourse is frequently more aggressive and polemic, reasserting thereby the traditional demarcating lines between Shi'ism and Sunnism.[12] Thus, immigration has enhanced tensions between the Sunnis and Shi'is in America.[13] Such measures are often resisted by those members who have lived in America for a long period or by those Shi'is who come from a different culture. As they try to impose a homogenized, monolithic Shi'ism in America, immigrant Shi'is often clash with the Shi'ism of different ethnic groups. Immigrant Shi'ism is also challenged by the youth in the community. According to Najjah Bazzy, a prominent member of the Islamic Center of America in Dearborn, the Iraqis brought with them an intense form of Shi'ism and expression of devotion to the family of the Prophet and have impacted the Lebanese community who relinquished some of their religious laxity and became more strict. More specifically, she notes, the

Iraqis carried to the States the intensity of '*Ashura*'. The Lebanese were too lax; the Iraqis, on the other hand, were too stringent, leading to much altercation between the two groups. Due to such disparities, there has been considerable resistance to the Iraqi presence in some Lebanese centers in Dearborn.[14]

The American Shi'i community is constituted in a different environment in which Shi'is form a conglomerate of disparate ethnic groups. This confluence of Shi'is sharing common space has proved to be problematic. Increased immigration from various parts of the world has resulted in the Shi'i community in America becoming more fragmented as bonds of common faith have been replaced by ties to common origins, ethnicity, and culture.

The Ethnic Factor in American Shi'ism

The transcultural phenomenon of American Shi'ism means that the Shi'i community spans the entire world, one that encompasses various cultures and outlooks. To re-create and live out their distinct cultures, immigrants tend to divide themselves along ethnic lines. Ethnicity, broadly defined, refers to a social identification based on a set of shared cultural characteristics and a sense, at a group level, of being distinct from other cultural groupings. The identity of an ethnic group is premised on a wide conglomeration of beliefs and behaviors that reflect distinctiveness from the dominant culture, such as ethnic language, retention, use of ethnic clothing and other cultural products, as well as one's attachment to the ethnic group. Ethnic identification begins with the application of a label to oneself in a cognitive process of self-categorization, involving not only a claim to membership in a group or category but also a contrast of one's group or category with other groups or categories.[15]

The notion of affiliation to an ethnic community essentially creates boundaries between groups of people based on perceived differences. Jimmy M. Sanders defines ethnic boundaries as "patterns of social interaction that give rise to, and subsequently reinforce, in-group members' self-identification and outsiders' confirmation of group distinctions."[16] These boundaries encourage the formation of groups based on ethnic differences. In this dichotomous relationship, ethnic identification among individuals form groups based on ethnicity, and ethnic groups also reinforce individual ethnicities. Ethnic boundaries are neither fixed nor permanent; rather, they are continuously negotiated.

The ethnic identity that accompanies boundary construction helps to militate against assimilation to the pervasive influence of American culture. Although present even in homeland countries, ethnic identity manifests itself as the number of immigrants from abroad increases, and the process of self-identification and self-differentiation begins to be felt. Ethnic boundaries and differentiation from other ethnic groups are expressed in many ways, one of the most common being the formation of ethnic institutions.

The establishment of religious institution along ethnic lines is a common phenomenon among American immigrant communities. Sociologists Yang and Ebaugh note that "Historically, religious institutions were among the most important resources that immigrant groups used to reproduce their ethno-religious identity in new surroundings and to help them adjust to the challenges of surviving in a demanding and often threatening environment."[17]

Why do members coalesce around mosques that are frequented by people from the same background? Ethnic institutions are important for the psychological survival of new immigrants since they perpetuate customs and rituals that resonate with the home environment. They create the physical and social spaces in which those who share the same traditions, customs, and languages can reproduce aspects of their native cultures for themselves and attempt to pass them on to their children. Ethnic institutions also provide stability and comfort in an alien world, preserving rites that have been established since time immemorial, strengthening, in the process, religious convictions in a culturally acceptable manner. Stated differently, ethnic institutions create cultural buffers, and reaffirm ethnic and cultural ties.[18] Due to these factors, Shi'i institutions, whether in the form of mosques, Islamic schools, or centers, have tended to fragment along ethnic lines and remain loyal to customs fermented in home states.

Moreover, especially after the events of September 11, 2001, many Shi'i immigrants have felt ostracized and alienated from American society. The experience of marginalization creates binary and essentialist categories with the dominant culture. Formation of ethnic based organizations helps offset the isolation and threat that many migrants have perceived since 9/11. Contact with and usage of the culture of origin and ethnic solidarity helps Shi'is sustain their self-identity under difficult and, at times, hostile circumstances.

Despite the common beliefs and practices that characterize the global Shi'i community, the unity of the community evaporates in the face of ethnic, linguistic, and national differences. The diversity emasculates the vision of an egalitarian circle of believers coalescing around Islamic principles. Indeed, more than any other factor, it is the ethnic factor that seems to have kept Shi'ism from becoming a dominant and shared source of identity.

Nowhere in the world is the ethnic diversity in the Shi'i community as evident as it is in America. Major cities like New York, Los Angeles, Houston, Detroit, Washington, and Chicago are characterized by disparate Shi'i centers established along ethnic lines. Thus, in many of these cities, it is possible to find Lebanese, Iranian, South Asian, and Khoja mosques without these being linked or affiliated in any coherent way. In Los Angeles, for example, Lebanese and Pakistani Shi'i centers are one mile apart, and an Iranian and Iraqi-based mosque are less than five miles from either of them. All are in Hispanic neighborhoods.[19] Similarly, in the Queens borough of New York, there are three Shi'i centers within a five-mile radius. In Houston, Pakistani and Arab centers are located virtually opposite each other.

In Dearborn, the Islamic Center of America is frequented primarily by the Lebanese. Within a few miles lies the Kerbala Center, which was established in 1995 to cater especially to the Iraqis. In my discussions with them, a few members of the Lebanese community in Dearborn restated the view that the relationship with the Iraqis in Dearborn was not very strong; in fact, there was some resistance to the Iraqi presence at the Islamic Center of America. Shaykh Hisham Husainy of the Kerbala Center in Dearborn admitted that a cultural chasm existed between the Lebanese and Iraqi Shi'is. The former, he observed, are more lax and do not observe a rigid interpretation of Islam. According to him, only a few Lebanese frequent the Kerbala Center.[20]

In some cities, members from the same ethnic background establish separate centers due to "mosque politics" and the struggle for power within the centers. According to Garbi Schmidt, by the late 1990s, there were five Shi'i centers in Chicago, three of them serving the South Asian community.[21] Others served the Iranian and Iraqi communities. Table 6 of my survey substantiates this point. It shows that most of the centers are ethnically defined, marginalizing, in the process, those from different ethnic backgrounds. Some centers identify themselves as primarily of East African or South Asian origins, whereas others are classified as of Iranian or Arab origins.

The predominance of Shi'i ethnic centers is supported by the survey. Table 6 indicates that of all the institutes surveyed, almost 65 percent of the attendees were from Iran; 50 percent of the centers surveyed were frequented by members from India, 53 percent from Pakistan, and 35 percent from Iraq. The survey confirms that the pervasive influence of ethnicity means that instead of a mosque being a focal point for all Shi'is, it has brought together Shi'is from the same ethnic community. The uniting factor within individual groups often seems to be a common language and cultural ties rather than religious affiliation. Shi'i centers have become a home away from home, and as such are crucial in perpetuating an immigrant identity. The great variety of national, ethnic, and cultural backgrounds of Shi'is living in a non-Muslim country is unprecedented in their history. However, the existence of variant cultural traditions means that each ethnic group imposes its own distinctive understanding of how it experiences Shi'i Islam and firmly believes it to be the most authentic expression of Shi'ism, even, at times, disparaging the experiences and praxis of other ethnic groups that share the same faith.

Many centers hold programs in languages that reflect their countries of origins (Urdu, Persian, or Arabic), thus alienating them from Shi'is originating from a different cultural or linguistic background. The linguistic and cultural bias of programs held at the centers also means that identification and interaction with Shi'is from a different ethnic background is rare. In large cities, there are often concentrations of Shi'is in particular areas. This concentration, together with regular contact with the culture of the country of origin (through telephones, Internet, visitation), support separatist identifications within Shi'i Islam. The ethnic division within the Shi'i community in America has been further accentuated by the absence of a singular, centralized authority that could provide religious identity to encompass ethnic affiliations. To date, there is no institution that can act as a unifying factor for all the diverse Shi'i groups.

Due to the predominance of ethnic centers, there are few interethnic marriages, and few Shi'is have friends outside their own ethnic background. As I discuss in chapter five, African American converts often complain that having converted to Shi'ism, they are discriminated against by Sunnis and fellow Shi'is alike. When traditional values and religious identity are under threat from both the West and the Wahhabis, Shi'is construct additional borders to protect themselves. As territorial borders are fading away in the wake of globalization and immigration, ethnic and religious borders are constructed, especially by those who feel most threatened by the American diaspora. In the past, Shi'ism was embedded in particular territorial and regional cultures. Migration to America has put an end to that. For the Shi'is, the challenge is no longer to protect territorial boundaries; it is the ethnic, cultural, and religious borders that need to be protected.

It is important to bear in mind that the ethnic factor is more accentuated in Shi'ism than in Sunnism. This is because the Shi'i notion of sanctity and holiness is markedly differently from that of other Muslims. Sunni religious events are confined to daily or weekly prayers and annual events in which Muslims from different ethnic backgrounds congregate. The Shi'is, on the other hand, have their own calendar of days wherein venerated Imams and holidays are clearly marked as distinct from profane time. Besides holding daily, Friday, and *eid* prayers, Shi'i communities across America hold functions to commemorate the martyrdom of Husayn, the birth and death anniversaries of other Imams and events like *eid al-Ghadir*, when the Prophet is reported to have designated 'Ali b. Abi Talib as his successor. Other holidays include the day of *Arba'in* (the fortieth day after the death of Husayn) and *Mubahila*. It is reported that, on this day, the Prophet brought his family when challenged to an imprecation by a Christian community. The Christians reportedly preferred to sign a peace agreement than imprecate against the *ahl al-bayt*.[22]

Such religious events are marked in different ways. South Asian Shi'is who congregate at the *Husayniyya*[23] mark events like the martyrdom of Husayn differently from the way that Iraqi or Iranian Shi'is do. South Asian and Khoja Shi'is reenact and commemorate the events of Kerbala with their own culturally generated symbols and modes of expressions. Thus, Muharram rituals construct additional boundaries that further segment the Shi'i community.

The view that Sunni mosques are more ethnically diverse than Shi'i centers is corroborated by a report issued by the Council on American-Islamic Relations (CAIR). The report is primarily focused on Sunni mosques. According to the report's primary researcher, Ihsan Bagby, "One of the most significant findings in this survey is that mosques are quite ethnically diverse." Bagby noted that 93 percent of all mosques nationwide are attended by more than one ethnic group. Only 7 percent of mosques are attended by only one ethnic group and almost 90 percent of all mosques have some South Asians, African Americans, and Arabs.[24] Thirty one percent of the mosques were attended by two major ethnic groups, the most frequent combination being South Asian and Arab.[25] In addition, one of three regular attendees in Sunni mosques is a convert.[26] These figures further highlight the difference between the Sunni and Shi'i experience in America. They indicate that ethnicity is a more pervasive phenomenon in the American Shi'i community.

The ethnic division dissipates in communities where Shi'is of different ethnic and cultural backgrounds come together to share limited resources and form multiethnic centers. In communities like Cleveland, Indianapolis, Seattle, Nashville, Phoenix, and Austin, the ethnic divide is almost nonexistent as different ethnic Shi'i groups coalesce under the common banner of the Prophet and his progeny. Others may even hold joint religious programs with local Sunni communities. However, even in such multiethnic centers, there is much tension as different groups try to impose their peculiar understanding and articulation of Shi'ism. Occasionally, there are disputes regarding which speakers to invite, what kind of food to serve, whether men and women should be seated in the same hall, whether and how to perform acts of flagellations, and the like. I observed much tension in one center engendered by a debate as to whether *tabarri'* (which was understood by some to refer to the explicit cursing of the enemies of the *ahl al-bayt*), was to be undertaken during the programs or not. Some clearly felt that the center should replicate the old tradition of cursing the enemies of the family of the Prophet whereas other members favored accentuating the more positive *tawalli* (stressing the virtues and following the examples of the Prophet and his family).

The Cultural Factor in American Shi'ism

The discussion on the pervasiveness of ethnicity in the American Shi'i community indicates that the community is too diffuse to be singularized, too ethnically diverse to be considered monolithic. In many instances, there are more points of divergence than convergence within the Shi'i community as different ethnic groups import and impose their cultures in America.

Religion is linked to culture, for the structures and practices as well as the rituals of any religious community are affected by the cultural markings of its members.[27] At the same time, culture isolates and differentiates. It emphasizes certain traits that separate one group from another. As such, culture often becomes an ideological battleground within a religious community.

Immigration and ethnicization mean that, like other Muslim immigrants, many recent Shi'i arrivals see Islam through a cultural prism, a lens that they have been accustomed to. Hence, to practice Shi'ism in any other way is often seen as an aberration or construed as cultural heresy. Living in an American pluralistic society means that Shi'is encounter and participate in multiple cultures through their professional and personal contacts. They encounter fellow Shi'is, fellow Muslims, and non-Muslim Americans, all of whom have different cultures and worldviews. From a predominantly homogeneous society in their own countries, Shi'is find themselves in a multicultural, multilingual, and multireligious setting in America.

For many new immigrants, the dominant American culture is perceived as a religious and cultural threat. The response has generally been a mixture of cultural insularity and distinctiveness. Resistance to the dominant culture is equated by many with being more Islamic and authentic. This resistance takes the form of upholding the virtues and preponderance of one's own culture and the cultural reproduction of old country forms. However, attachment to one's culture further impedes the growth of transnational Shi'i consciousness and militates against interaction with other forms of cultural Shi'ism. This leads to the juxtaposition of different expressions of Shi'ism in America.

Cultural differences within the Shi'i community are most visible in the running of and genres of programs held in the centers. They are also discernable in the symbols displayed, rituals enacted, and in how marriages are conducted and celebrated. For example, Khoja marriages are usually solemnized in the *Husayniyya* or, as they are called in the South Asian culture, *Imambargah*, whereas other Shi'i groups solemnize marriages in their homes or at a banquet hall. Khoja marriages exhibit many traits of Hindu culture. These range from the types of clothes worn during the ceremonies (many Khoja women wear the *saree*, a traditional Hindu dressing) to the ceremonies that welcome the bride to her new home. A ceremony called *khobo* marks the bride and groom's arrival at his home after the marriage ceremony. The bride's in-laws welcome the couple at the door of her new home with milk mixed with almonds, pistachios, and saffron. Coins are placed on a plate in front of the bride. The father-in-law, in conjunction with the bride, scoop as many coins as they can.[28] This, it is popularly believed, will bring prosperity to the groom's family.

Iranian weddings, on the other hand are distinctly different. At the time of the solemnization of the marriage, a spread or *sofreh* is prepared for the bride and groom. They sit facing the spread, which contains food and traditional items to share their new life together. Items on the *sofreh* include *ayneh* and *shumdan* (mirror and candles), signifying prosperity, light, and fire. *Sini-ye Aatel O Batel,* herbs, spices and incense, are kept to guard against evil spirits. Eggs are decorated with colorful designs to symbolize fertility. Included in the *sofreh* are pomegranates (fruits of heaven), apples (symbolizing the divine creation of mankind), *termeh* (a traditional silk or gold embroidered cloth handed down from generations symbolizing family values), a flat bread (to bring food and feasts in the couple's life), and many other items.[29]

Pakistani weddings also tend to be very colorful. A head ornament called *sehra* that covers the face, usually made of flowers, is tied to the groom's head. The *sehra* is initially placed on the foreheads of five married men by a grandfather or an uncle. Once the custom of *sehra bandi* (tying of the *sehra*) is completed, this group, called *Barat,* goes to the venue where the bride and her family waits.

The groom sits on a raised stage while an imam goes to the bride and asks if she consents to the marriage. Once the agreement is obtained, the imam returns to the groom to conduct the religious ceremony. After the ceremony, the bride is brought and seated next to the groom. She is clad in red and is usually covered with a veil. The groom first sees her reflection in a mirror and writes a Qur'anic verse on her forehead with his finger, and puts sandalwood powder on her hair.

Before she leaves, the bride throws a fistful of rice back to where her family is standing. The custom is called *ghar bharna* (filling of the house). The intent is to symbolically cover the emptiness left by her departure. The bride and groom are brought into his house and another set of customs are performed. Five women of the family take rice in their hands and touch it to the bride's feet, knees, and shoulders, and throw it over the groom. Then the groom washes the bride's feet with milk or water in a pan; the milk or water is then sprinkled in four corners of the house. Although these customs have no religious significance, they are performed to invoke God's blessings.[30] Such cultural variations among the different ethnic groups mean that even at the time of weddings, there is limited interaction among them.

In Dearborn, problems between Iraqi and Lebanese Arabs have also arisen due to cultural and economic differences. Disparities between the two groups have led to the alienation of the Iraqi community. Many members of the Lebanese community are well educated and skilled, whereas most Iraqis are refugees who fled Iraq after the Gulf War. Such variations indicate that American Shi'ism comprises a kaleidoscope of cultural perspectives. Cultural diversity between Shi'i groups means they are different from each other while, at the same time, they are different from the non-Muslim and non-Shi'i other.

The imposition of an alien and imported culture in the centers has estranged the youth in the Shi'i community. More significantly, programs held at the centers do not seem to be capable of generating or sustaining interest even within their own ethnic members, especially among the younger generation. This is due to linguistic barriers and the ritualization of religious practices, a point that alienates many members of the community.

The "intellectually inclined" adults and the younger generation reject the ancestral traditions and demand changes in the format of the programs offered. This observation is corroborated by the fact that the average crowd for Thursday night lectures in many centers is normally only twenty to thirty people. Thus, the division is not only among the different centers but also within the centers as different groups impose their vision and expression of Islam. Significantly, my survey indicates that many centers are slowly adapting to English as a medium of communication (table 7). Eighty-nine percent of the centers now use English as one of their primary languages. The older the institutions, the more they try to incorporate English in their services. Most centers use more than one language. We need to note, though, that younger centers still adhere to the "mother languages." Cultural variations are most evident when community members gather to mark important religious holidays. These differences become apparent because most Shi'is mark these events with their own culturally generated rituals, which often clash with rituals that originate from a different background.

Muharram Rituals in Shi'i Centers

Most Shi'is have encountered some kind of religious diversity in their homeland. However, in America they face a new kind of diversity, one that is more challenging to deal with. American Shi'is encounter the internal, cultural diversity in their sacred places, the mosque or the *Husayniyya*. The external diversity, on the other hand, is met outside these boundaries.

Instead of meeting Shi'is from other parts of the world when they go to the holy places for *ziyarat*[31] or when they go for pilgrimage to Mecca, they now run into them on a regular basis in the local mosque. Dealing with this internal cultural diversity is a great challenge. In fact, the internal diversity can be more difficult to handle than the external one because the former is encountered inside the mosque where Shi'is engage in their religious practices. Internal diversity impacts how Shi'is enact their rituals, what they eat, and with whom they socialize and engage in the mosques. It also impacts the genres of programs offered at the mosque and how the programs are formatted. The external diversity, on the other hand, is encountered at work places, schools, and colleges. In this instance, Shi'is do not have to make any compromises in their rituals and eating habits; they can choose to ignore the "external other."

Despite the diversity of Shi'i ethnic groups, a single thread links these groups to the larger tapestry of Shi'ism—their love for the Prophet and his family. All Shi'i groups share the essential rituals of Islam, including the performance of daily prayers, fasting, and the pilgrimage to Mecca. An inherent element in the Shi'i religious experience is the commemoration of the martyrdom of Husayn. This experience is marked annually with a series of lectures and the performance of various Muharram rituals in the *Husayniyya*. By facilitating the performance of rituals endemic to a particular ethnic group, the *Husayniyyas* tend to strengthen and amplify religious values in a secular society. At the same time, they highlight the differences that characterize the cultural expression of Muharram rituals.

American Shi'is express their Islamic praxis in a form that is often culturally conditioned to the new environment. Since the rituals are practiced in different ways by the various religious groups, they tend to accentuate ethnic disparities. South Asian and Khoja Shi'is, for example, commemorate events like the death of Husayn differently from the way that Iraqi or Iranian Shi'is do. The former reenact the events in Kerbala with their own culturally generated symbols and modes of expressions. They insist on having replicas or symbols of Kerbala in their centers. These include a special *dharih* room, which often contains a depiction of the horse of Husayn and his sword. Included among the replicas are the symbolic representation of the *'alam* of 'Abbas[32] (lit. a flag symbolizing the bravery and courage of 'Abbas) in the form of a palm, a cradle that symbolizes Husayn's six-month-old child who was also killed in Kerbala, and other traditional replicas of shrines. Like the other rituals performed in the shrine complex, the purpose of the symbols is to encourage weeping and engender a sense of commitment and devotion to the Imams. Through the symbols, the Shi'i is able to identify with the Imams and the suffering they endured.

In many Khoja centers, symbols that evoke stories of the martyrs of Kerbala are carried through the crowd in the hall after the main lecture. These take the form of a coffin draped in a white cloth colored with red dye, as if bloodstained, and the *'alam*. A cradle is also paraded to remind the faithful of the innocent youthfulness of 'Ali Asghar, the infant son of Husayn. The Khojas often decorate these symbols with garlands of flowers. Many attendees will even consume parts of the flowers, believing them to contain *baraka* (blessings) and curative powers. The importance that some Shi'is attach to the *'alams* and other symbols can be discerned from a question posed to Ayatullah Fadhil Milani, a prominent Iraqi-born *mujtahid* residing in England.[33] He was asked if one can prostrate to an *'alam* as a mark of respect. Milani states unequivocally that such an act is not permissible.[34]

Symbolic representations like the *'alam* draw attention to the central paradigm of Shi'i piety—the Prophet and his family, and they also evoke memories of the martyrdom of Husayn. However, such acts of reverence and symbolic representations are alien to Arab and Iranian Shi'is. Some even see them as subtle forms of *shirk* (polytheism). The symbolic representations described earlier are absent in Iranian and Arab centers,

The *alams* as displayed in the *dharih* room. Courtesy of Ja'ffari Islamic Center, Toronto, photo by Nisar Sheraly.

Miniature shrines of Ja'far al-Sadiq (*left*) and Masuma (sister of the eighth Imam) on the *right*. These shrines are displayed in the *dharih* room at the Ja'ffari Islamic Center in Toronto, Canada. Courtesy of Ja'ffari Islamic Center, Toronto, photo by Nisar Sheraly.

which instead display slogans and certain utterances attributed to Husayn. Frequently, these slogans are aimed at evoking the political and moral consciousness of Shi'is. Iranian centers will often display paintings of the Imams, especially of the first and eighth Imams, 'Ali b. Abi Talib and 'Ali b. Musa al-Rida (d. 818) respectively. South Asian and Khoja Shi'is frown upon such pictorial representations of the Imams.

The Ritual of Flagellation

An important ritual in the month of Muharram is that of flagellation. In Shi'ism, flagellation is a composite term that includes the use of swords and knives to cut the head (*tatbir*), chains (*zanjir*), as well as striking of the chest (*matam*). *Tatbir* is the most violent of these acts practiced by only a small portion of the Shi'i community. *Matam* or *latmiyya* designates the formal ritual acts of breast-beating and self-flagellation generally undertaken by all Shi'i groups. However, the methods and forms of flagellation vary between

The *alams* in the background and the cradle of 'Ali Asghar in the foreground. Courtesy of Ja'ffari Islamic Center, Toronto, photo by Nisar Sheraly.

the groups. The Khojas, who share many rituals with South Asian Shi'is, often perform their *matam* in a rhythmic, circular movement call *saff*. This form of flagellation is foreign to South Asian, Iranian, and Arab Shi'is who often stand in straight lines while striking their chests. The diverse ways of flagellating that are practiced by the disparate ethnic groups means that they will not feel comfortable engaging in this ritual together.

Together with other rituals, flagellation is important as it helps induce a state of altered awareness in which ordinary restraints of prudence are removed. The flagellant loses not only his sense of self-protection but also his sense of separateness from the Imam as the flagellations generate a mood of identification with sacred Shi'i figures. The flagellant breaks the boundary between himself and his fellow flagellants and even between himself and the model he seeks to imitate.[35]

Flagellation performs different functions. For many flagellants, the induced physical sensations help in the attainment of spiritual states. Blows to the body stimulate identification with the blows inflicted on

Husayn and allow the historical tradition not only to be intellectually apprehended but also emotionally and physically experienced.[36] Shedding blood is seen as the pilgrim's way of demonstrating grief for Husayn's suffering and identification with the mortal wounds of the Imam. Symbolically, it is also his way of stating *had I been in Kerbala, I would have protected the Imam with my blood.*[37] Flagellation also helps to propagate Shi'i beliefs and reminds both Shi'is and non-Shi'is of the atrocities committed against the family of the Prophet.

Emotions are also aroused by the recitation of poetry. As poetry is able to touch the hearts of listeners and make people weep, poets have played an important role in Shi'i mourning ceremonies. Although not as popular or widespread as the other rituals, poetry gives a different expression to the proceedings, using symbolic language to express love and devotion to the Imams.[38] Besides poetry, the *marathiya* (eulogies) are recited to emotionally arouse the listeners. South Asians have their own brand of *nawahi* (pl. of *nawha*, lamentations), which are emotionally charged and take certain rhythmic tones. These are very different from Iranian *nawahi*, which are more somber. The Khojas, on the other hand, tend to shy away from poetry and concentrate more on the *marathiya* and *nawahi*.

Like many other religions, Shi'ism has taken on distinctly indigenous forms in the different lands that it has spread. The practices of "popular Shi'ism" are where the differences are most pronounced. Popular practices are often the most important agents in spreading a religion in lands where it is foreign and must be understood through a reconstructed native understanding. After the establishment of the Safawid empire in Iran in 1501, Iranians created a popular ritual called the *taziyeh*, a dramatic reenactment of the events at Kerbala. Subsequently, the *taziyeh* has assumed different forms as various Shi'i groups have expressed their devotion to Husayn in a myriad of culturally conditioned forms. In the Indo-Pakistani subcontinent, for example, *taziyeh* refers to a replica of the tomb of Husayn that is constructed, paraded in processions, and then kept in special sanctuaries within the precincts of the mosque. In Iran the same term signifies passion plays that depict the events in Kerbala. In Lebanon *taziyeh* refers to a gathering to mark Husayn's martyrdom.

Taziyeh productions in Iran were held throughout the country as a medium of profound religious expression. During the reign of the third Safawid Shah, 'Abbas (1576–1616 CE), Muharram ceremonies, "which, had until then been apparently rather limited to their devotional and folkloric aspects, became a great festival, both civil and religious."[39] During the drama, different figures act as the heroes and villains of Kerbala. The plays reenact the events of Kerbala and remind the audience of the issues of martyrdom, intercession, and the pivotal role of the Imams in the lives of the Shi'is. Passion plays are often held after a procession passes through the town, especially during the month of Muharram. Men and women flock to the streets to witness and weep over the plays. Such acts of representations of holy figures are seen by South Asian and Khoja Shi'is as sacrilegious. These groups do not hold passion plays since they believe that no ordinary mortal should play the role of the Imams.

Tensions between the communities arise sometimes due to differences as to what is respectful and what is not. Iranian and Arab Shi'is often serve tea and light refreshments during the Muharram lectures. Such acts are seen as highly disrespectful and disruptive by South Asian and Khoja Shi'is, who insist on complete silence and discipline during the lectures.

Another aspect of the Muharram rituals are processions. As in Iran, Indian Shi'is had to nativize and indigenize Shi'ism in India by engaging in cultural syncretism and exchange. This is most visibly seen in the large Muharram processions commemorating '*Ashura*' in major Shi'i centers of India like Lucknow and Hyderabad. These processions often took on a festive theme as people of all confessional backgrounds joined in the commemoration of the martyrs of Kerbala. The employment of *tassa* (drums), the adoption of richly adorned elephants, and the creation of elaborate *taziyehs* (unlike Iran, this term refers to the manufactured miniature replicas of the Imams' shrines that are paraded in these processions) were all part of the distinctly Indian contribution to popular Shi'ism. One of the most distinctly Indian aspects of the Muharram observations is the participation of both Hindus and Sunnis.

The Muharram processions have been brought to America by members of the South Asian community. In major cities like New York and Chicago, some South Asian communities hold a procession (*julus*) in which the icons and symbols are displayed and carried in the streets. Especially in the South Asian community, *'alams* and biers are paraded to remind the crowd of the suffering that Husayn had to endure. In India and Pakistan, a horse representing Husayn's horse in Kerbala is a focal point in some Muharram processions.[40] As it is paraded among the crowd, the horse triggers an outburst of grief and initiates wailing.

For many South Asian Shi'is, holding a *julus* procession in the United States is a statement of their faith and identity. It is a potent form of conveying the message of Islam to an American audience. The processions specifically assert the legitimacy of a particular Islamic approach—that focused on the Imams and their suffering. The processions also highlight political and social grievances and represent protests against the homeland government. It is because of this factor that some Sunni regimes have tried to stop the processions in their countries. By marching and even flagellating in public, the Shi'is assert pride in their beliefs and practices. Whether explicit or implicit, once people have marched openly in a place, they have shown that they are willing to expose themselves and their bodies to possible outside ridicule for the sake of their faith. Marching through the streets is also an assertion of power and confidence.[41] As they participate especially in the large processions that take place during the mourning season, they also become the public face of the community to the wider society.

Muharram processions are also interwoven to asserting a Shi'i identity in America. In my survey, one of the institutions clearly linked fashioning a Shi'i identity with observing Muharram rituals. When asked how it expressed its Shi'i identity, a center responded: "We were the first to take out *julus* in North America." During the processions, Shi'is will often distribute literature to non-Muslim onlookers regarding their faith and beliefs. In this way, a reenactment of a historical event is used to remove Western misconceptions of Islam. By observing the Muharram festivities in public, Shi'is utilize the occasion to foster a better understanding with their non-Muslim neighbors and at the same time making a statement of who they are. Not only have the Shi'is preserved and affirmed their identity, they have done it in public. By displaying icons and writings on Kerbala and the family of the Prophet in public, they assert both their Islamic and sectarian identity. The various rituals performed by American Shi'is engender a closer relationship with the Imam and reflect the love for and devotion to him. Collectively, these rituals further cultivate the legacy of the deceased Imam.

The *Majlis* in America

Besides the rituals and symbols, a key element in the commemorative gatherings is a lecture and recollection of the martyrdom of Husayn in Kerbala, called *majlis*. Historically, the Kerbala narrative was transmitted to different generations through prose and poetry including the *majlis*.[42] The *majalis* (pl. of *majlis*) are lamentation assemblies where the stories of the martyrs of Kerbala are recited for the evocation of grief. Narratives associated with the Imams are often heard in the *majlis*. These gatherings have also been used to recount the persecution endured by the Shi'i

Imams, evoking thereby the emotions of the audience. In addition, their virtues, miracles, and valor are recounted. In this way, the human and supernatural qualities of the Imams are enshrined in the hearts and minds of the attendees.

The lectures or sermons delivered at the *Husayniyya* seek to prove the verities of Shiʻi beliefs and liturgical practices, thereby reaffirming the authority of the Imams over the populace. The *majlis* becomes a statement of Shiʻi piety and reinforces the emotional attachment and devotion to the Imams. In the process, due to the remembrance of their virtuous and heroic conduct, the Imams become the compelling paradigm of correct demeanor and upright human conduct.

With time, participation in the *majlis* congregation became an important medium to reinforce Shiʻi beliefs and identity. The role of these gatherings in regulating the sociopolitical and religious lives of Shiʻi Muslims in America must be properly understood. Although lectures are held at the *Husayniyyas* throughout the year, the Shiʻi faithful congregate in large numbers during the month of Muharram. The *majlis* is an important ritual as it helps mediate Shiʻi Islam to the community.

It is in the *majlis* that the preachers (*khutabaʼ*) often relate the events of Kerbala, reaffirm allegiance to the family of the Prophet, and discuss the challenges of living in a secularized Western society. As Schubel states:

> The remembrance of the battle of Kerbala as a significant historical and religious event is crucial to the way in which Shiʻi Muslims maintain their unique identity within the larger *umma* [the community]. The importation of rituals for the remembrance of Kerbala has also facilitated the community's adaptation to the Canadian environment. The remembrance and re-creation of Kerbala allows the Shiʻi community to claim space in North America that is both North American and Islamic: they thus Islamize elements of North American culture while creatively adapting Islam to the North American environment.[43]

The *majlis* is important to the American Shiʻis for different reasons. In many centers, it has become a vehicle for educating and edifying the community. It speaks to the specific needs of the American audience and imbibes core values to resist assimilation to American culture. At the same time, the Muharram *majalis* are important in helping Shiʻis adapt to the American milieu, especially as many of the lectures deal with issues relevant to their lives as American Muslims. By linking events in Kerbala with the challenges of living an Islamic-oriented life in America, the *majlis*, although imported from abroad, acts as a source of moral edification, teaching young American Shi'is that their sacred history demands devotion to the family of the Prophet even in a non-Muslim environment. Thus, the *majlis* becomes an important tool in perpetuating Shi'i heritage and ethos. The *majlis* also provides the leadership with an important vehicle to bring about the reformations necessary as this religious minority strives to assert its identity in the midst of living through the challenges of a pluralistic society.

The *majlis* also seeks to prove the verities of Shi'i beliefs and liturgical practices so as to forge and perpetuate a distinct Shi'i identity in America. This didactic function is indispensable to a religious minority that seeks to transmit and inculcate the universal values as articulated by the Prophet and the Imams. The didactic portions of the *majlis* are reinforced by the emotional power of the lamentations and *matam* that follow. Through the various forms, the commemorative gatherings challenge the community to live up to the ideals of Husayn and his companions.[44]

Women and children also attend Muharram lectures. They do not normally attend daily or Friday prayers; hence the *majlis* provides an additional source of education for an important segment of the Shi'i community. The *majlis* has been a source of perpetuating the corporal identity of the Shi'is as a minority within the larger Muslim community. Thus, wherever the Shi'is have gone, they have taken the *majlis* with them.

It must be remembered that Shi'is are often signified by some members within the Sunni community who refer to them by derogatory terms such as *Rafidis*[45] and *kafirs* (nonbelievers). Such signification is to obviate the threat of conversion to Shi'ism and to assert the preponderance of Sunni beliefs. Polemical disputations between the sects have resurfaced in America (see chap. 3). For the Shi'is, the *majlis* provides the forum for resistance and opposition to such forms of signification.[46]

Shi'ism in America manifests diversity within an overarching unity, a diversity that is reflected in the ethnic variances within the Shi'i institutions. Within the fractured ethnic communities, it is possible to speak of a wide array of diasporic religious practices. It is the Muharram rites that give American Islam a distinctly Shi'i coloring for they differentiate Shi'is from Sunnis and all other Muslim sects. Paradoxically, the very institution that is supposed to unite Shi'i Muslims (the mosque and the rituals) has become a catalyst for the perpetuation of a distinctive ethnic ethos.

The Role of the *Khutaba'* in the *Majlis*

Most Shi'i groups tend to import imams and *khutaba'* from their home-land. The *khutaba'* are often itinerant preachers who use the mosques as bases for inculcating Islamic values, bringing forth what they perceive to be normative Islam, encouraging public demonstrations of piety, and seeking to reinforce such established patterns of behaviors as communal segregation of sexes. The *khutaba'* have been specifically trained to re-cite eulogies of the Imams, recounting their sufferings and persecution through history, and evoking the feelings of their audience by delivering emotionally charged sermons.

A prominent theme in *majlis* discourses in Awadh, India, preached at the end of nineteenth and the beginning of the twentieth centuries, was what is known in Urdu as *munazara* (argument or polemic, understood generally in the Shi'i context as being against Sunni Islam). Within the South Asian context, *munazara* has been a part of Shi'i discourse the-ology since the beginning, and it was incorporated into the new *majlis* preaching. Even in America, South Asian *khutaba'* or, as they are known in Urdu, *zakirs*, regularly engage in *munazara* in emotionally charged lec-tures that are delivered in the month of Muharram.

The *zakirs* articulate and delineate the orthodox position (stating what is and what is not acceptable to the Shi'is) and reflect the community's at-tempts at self-identification and differentiation from the Sunnis. Through their lectures, Shi'i preachers construct boundaries of identity and exclu-sion and establish the basis for Shi'i differentiation from Sunnism. The exposition of highly polemicized and politicized discourses and repeated affirmation of the historical injustices endured by the progeny of the Prophet helps mediate Shi'i Islam to the community in America. These lectures further seek to assert the verity and preponderance of Shi'i be-liefs and liturgical practices. Although this genre of preachers is able to cater to the immigrant adult population by appealing to their emotions and reinforcing long-held views on history, it has alienated the younger generation and other adults within the community who view such topics as irrelevant to their contemporary needs in America.

Ironically, these imported preachers tend to amplify the ethnic factor in the services they render. Since they are not acquainted with American sociopolitical issues and do not comprehend the challenges that Muslim youth encounter in America, the *khutaba's* discourses are often confined to issues that are germane to the elder generation within their particular ethnic community creating, in the process, an obstacle to the allegiance to universal Islam. It is not an exaggeration to state that the South Asian Shi'i community seems to be the most resistant to initiate transformation in their centers, resulting in many youth being alienated from the community.

Within many Shi'i American communities, there is an increasing concern that the contents of the lectures be connected to the needs of that community. To cater to the needs of the increasing number of youth, some centers have sought native or English-speaking young imams who can talk about religious and social issues relevant to young people, like peer pressure, alcohol, and dating. The centers want religious leaders who can advise them on day-to-day American topics like how to set up a 401(k) plan to funnel charitable donations and the Islamic perspective on euthanasia and organ donation.

While different ethnic Shi'is can offer the Friday prayers together with little difficulty, there is a greater challenge to hold the Muharram *majlis* together due to the diverse rituals it entails. Even the *majlis* and the events of Kerbala are recounted in different ways. In South Asian and Khoja centers an anecdote describing each martyr is reserved for a particular night. For example, recitation of the heroics of 'Abbas, the half-brother of Husayn, is reserved for the seventh day, when water was no longer available to the family of the Prophet. On the eve of '*Ashura*', the sufferings of 'Ali al-Asghar ('Abd Allah), the six-month-old infant son of Husayn, are recounted. *Marathi* (eulogies) and lamentations devoted to these persons are recited on "their nights." However, Arab and Iranian Shi'is do not abide by such arrangements. Sometimes they recount the death of 'Abbas on the first night of Muharram.

The tensions that Muharram rituals can generate can be discerned from the following anecdote that occurred in Denver, Colorado, at a multiethnic center in 2005. In the morning on the day of '*Ashura*', Arab Shi'is normally recite the *majlis* recounting the death of Husayn. After the noon prayers, they eat, and then disperse. South Asian and Khoja Shi'is, on the other hand, commemorate the day of '*Ashura*' very differently. Their morning session is marked with special supplications and prayers, followed by noon prayers and the *majlis* marking the martyrdom of Husayn. The *majlis* is followed by a flagellation session. Many South Asian Shi'is will abstain from food until late afternoon. At the incident in Denver, a clash followed as the Arabs and South Asian Shi'is sought to mark the same event differently. The conflict arose as the Arabs wanted to eat after the noon prayers whereas the South Asians sought to mourn the death of Husayn at the same time. In the same mosque and at the same time, while the South Asians were fasting, the Arabs were feasting. The distinctive cultural modes of expressing the Muharram rituals have engendered much tension among the diverse ethnic groups leading to the fragmentation of the Shi'i community.[47]

The division that such rituals can create was further highlighted by the Shi'i proselyte Yasin al-Jibouri in 1993. He states in his *Memoirs:*

> The negative role these *majalis* have played in the lives of American and Canadian Shi'as is that they deepened the ethnic divisions among them; they exhaust their financial resources (though for a worthy cause, yet it would be better if some funds are spent on *Tabligh* (proselytization)); and many youth and children do not benefit much from them because the latter are not versed in their mother tongue. When Indian, Arab, or Iranian Shi'as assemble to commemorate '*Ashura*', for example, they like to do so in Urdu, Arabic, or Farsi, respectively. This creates barriers among our small communities. American Muslim converts have expressed frustration about such a situation, and some of them have gone as far as establishing organizations of their own to cater to their own particular needs. . . . Unless you know the language spoken at a *majlis,* there is no sense in going there.[48]

These rituals allow the believer to experience Kerbala in America, precipitating individual and communal reflection insofar as it challenges the believers to base their demeanor on the paradigmatic actions of the Shi'i Imams. At the same time, the various Shi'i rituals demonstrate a great deal of diversity within the overarching unity of devotion to the *ahl al-bayt.* They are traditionally generated, cultural specific rituals that have no textual basis in Shi'ism.

There is no *hadith*[49] from the Prophet or an Imam stating which symbols to display in Muharram or the forms that flagellations should take. Each immigrant Shi'i group brought its symbols, methods of enacting rituals, and culturally conditioned ways of running their centers. These were bound to clash with other immigrant Shi'i groups. Paradoxically, the ritual practices draw boundaries within the Shi'i community as they separate different Shi'i ethnic groups. The struggle for the Shi'is is to maintain unity while they continue to be affiliated to their cultural and ethnic identity.

We need to remember that the Muharram rituals are intrinsic to Shi'i piety and expressions of love for the family of the Prophet. The differences outlined should not disguise the fact that Shi'is are united in their belief in the Qur'an, the Prophet, and the Imams as the sources of authority. As Vernon Schubel states, "While all Shi'a may agree that allegiance to the *ahl al-bayt* is crucial, there is a great deal of disagreement over precisely how to manifest that allegiance. While the virtues of the Kerbala martyrs—courage, self-sacrifice, piety, devotion—are agreed upon, the proper means of articulating them are more controversial."[50]

These practices give the Shi'i community a distinctive identity, one that sets it apart from the Sunni community. For the Sunnis, despite ethnic differences, their rituals do not engender differences the way they do in Shi'i Islam as most Sunni rituals take the form of prayers and sermons. For the Shi'is, rituals, especially those that are performed in Muharram, can augment or even be the cause of differences since they are often culturally conditioned.

Rituals pertaining to a particular culture or religion may lose their significance when transferred into a new context. Frequently, they are adjusted and adapted to suit the new environment. Some Shi'i communities have modified their rituals in the American milieu. Instead of shedding blood on the day of '*Ashura*', some Shi'i communities, for example, will frequently donate blood to the Red Cross in the name of Husayn. Most centers now deliver a portion of their lectures in English. Many supplications are displayed in PowerPoint format so that they can be easily comprehended. In Minneapolis, the imam often delivers the *majlis* by deploying such a presentation in order to engage and captivate the audience. In some centers, even the *marathiya* and *matam* are conducted in English. By modifying and adapting these rituals, the Shi'is have paved the way for the future generation to relate to the rituals and what they mean in a different, American way. The modified version enables the younger generation to relate to the rituals and to incorporate a distinctly Shi'i identity in America.

The Shi'i Identity in America

A corollary to the discussion on ethnicity, culture, and rituals is the formation of a distinct Shi'i identity. Identity refers to a set of characteristics that collectively serve to distinguish a group or individual from others as a distinct and recognizable entity. Identity also defines and describes an individual's sense of self, group affiliations, structural positions, and ascribed and achieved statuses.[51] It is one of the most important elements for an immigrant community settling in a culturally diverse environment. Identity is created, maintained, and often promoted primarily through institutions that identify and singularize those who hold it. It is often fluid and negotiated; there are shifts that take place within the individual between different identities.

Identities are shaped and structured by different factors. In the case of Muslims in America, these may include prejudice against Muslims, the need to preserve one's culture and language, the perceived threat from fellow Muslims or non-Muslims, resistance to assimilation to mainstream American culture, and so forth. Besides religion, other indices compete as an identity marker in America. In fact, one can talk of various diasporic identities that are constructed by an immigrant community. These identities are multiple and often contested, sometimes within the same immigrant community. A person can be defined politically, linguistically, culturally, and ethnically. We can have multiple identities at one particular time. Overlapping identities allow us to identify with overlapping communities. As an immigrant from Zanzibar, when I meet a Christian from Kenya and we converse in Kiswahili, for example, we draw on our common cultural and linguistic rather than religious, ethnic, or national identities.

Drawing upon different identities, a person can identify him or herself as a Muslim, South Asian, or as an American at the same time. Other identities include ethnicity, sectarian affiliation, race and/or class. America has become an arena where different cultural, ethnic, and religious identities are contested. It is therefore necessary to move away from the notion of a single, rigid, ethnic/religious identity.

There has been much discussion about the relationship between religious and ethnic identities. Some immigrant religious communities emphasize their religious identities more than their ethnic foundation, whereas others stress ethnic identity and rely on religious institutions primarily to preserve cultural traditions and ethnic boundaries.[52] For new immigrants, religious identity is often interwoven with ethnic or national identity. This identity is affirmed and expressed in different ways, from the mode of dressings to the religious symbols displayed, the language of communication, and the rhetoric in the speeches delivered.

The emergence of a distinctly Muslim American identity is a relatively recent phenomenon. As we have seen, Muslims who migrated here before the 1950s had, in many cases, assimilated into American culture. The influx of Muslims from different parts of the world since the 1970s has nurtured the sense of identity formation around Islam. The preservation of an Islamic identity was important due to the spatial disconnectedness of the immigrants from their Muslim homelands during the period of their residence in a non-Muslim country. The clear implication was that the Islamic identity that was brought from the original home countries was authentic. Many immigrants also assumed that living in an American environment would inevitably lead to cultural assimilation and moral decay. The obvious way to obviate this perceived threat was to accentuate their Islamic identity.

For the Shi'is, living in a secular, non-Muslim society impels them to cling to their homeland identity even more.[53] As we have seen in the previous chapter, the majority of the Shi'is are first- or second-generation immigrants. Their challenges center on the preservation of their faith and religious identity in an American milieu that is not only informed by Judeo-Christian values but often hostile to a public expression of Islamic values. Shi'i identity is further challenged by Wahhabi or Salafi verbal attacks, which can often be more invidious than those experienced from non-Muslims. Hence, for the Shi'is, the preservation of their identity in America becomes even more important.

Traditionally, in their own countries, Shi'is have defined themselves in opposition to the majority Sunnis. This Shi'i self-identity and differentiation from the Sunni other is evident in the vast amount of polemic literature that has proliferated from both sides. It is also evident from the numerous lectures and religious practices to assert a distinct Shi'i identity. In America, however, Sunni dominance has become less and less relevant as a reference point. Now, "the other" is both the Sunnis and mainstream American culture. The Shi'is go through a process of crystallizing a Shi'i identity against the Western and Sunni other. Since Sunni dominance is less obvious in the diaspora, it is easier for the Shi'is to self identify and express themselves in the diaspora than in many Muslim countries. The American environment has provided a context of freedom of religious expression that many Shi'is have not experienced before. Indeed, many Shi'is have remarked that they have to practice *taqiyya* (dissimulation) in countries like Saudi Arabia rather than in America where they are free to express their religious affiliation and convictions. America has enabled the Shi'i community to nurture its identity in a context independent of the supervision from Muslim governments or Islamic institutions, features that Shi'is have had to deal with in their own countries for a long time.

Identity construction involves the construction of symbols and boundaries that differentiate one group from another. In this, religion is often used as a mode of expression of identity within the community. In America, the expression of a distinctly Shiʻi identity is most visible in the *Husayniyya*. In my classes on Islam, I take my students to both Sunni and Shiʻi centers of worship and ask them to write a report comparing and contrasting their experience in the two centers. In their reports, they invariably remark on how very different the two centers appear. The calligraphy, symbols, openness to non-Muslims, and genres of services are very different. In fact, even the form and number of prayers offered vary. This is because Shiʻis combine their prayers whereas Sunnis separate them.[54] Shiʻis also prostrate on clay tablets (called *turba*); even the call to prayer (*adhan*) is different as Shiʻis insert "ʻAli is the friend of God" after bearing witness to the prophecy of Muhammad.[55] The students also note that these differences are indicative of the Shiʻi desire to promote their own distinctive identity, one that is independent of the Sunni other. Yet, as I discussed earlier, even within the *Husayniyya*, Shiʻi identity is often interwoven to a distinct ethnic identity. Thus, we can talk of two simultaneous forms of identities that are constructed in many centers, a Shiʻi, and an ethnic identity. Shiʻis are differentiated not only from Sunnis and non-Muslims but also from fellow Shiʻis.

Religious institutions provide a conducive environment to articulate and affirm identity. Articulation of a distinct Shiʻi identity is most evident in the Shiʻi centers. The calligraphy in the *Husayniyya*, for example, is a mixture of Qurʼanic verses and salutations to or names of those killed in Kerbala. Many of them will have the *hadith al-thaqalayn*[56] or narrate the virtues of ʻAli and the other Imams. Drawings in the Shiʻi centers may depict Lahiq, the horse of Husayn,[57] or mention the names of the members of the Prophet's immediate family, i.e., Muhammad, ʻAli, Fatima, Hasan, and Husayn. Pictorial representations of the Kaʻaba are fixed next to the domes and shrines of the Imams in Kerbala, Najaf, or Mashad. Some Iranian and Arab centers will also have the pictures of ʻAli, Husayn, or ʻAbbas. Sunni centers prohibit such depictions.

It is these genres of distinctive Shiʻi symbols and icons that create Shiʻi space and identity in America. These visual words and symbols convey the message that distinguishes Shiʻi from Sunni Islam; they also affirm the charismatic authority of ʻAli and his descendants, the Imams, and that salvation is attained through the recognition of the *wilaya* (authority) of the

Imams. These icons and engravings link the local Shi'i center to the universal Shi'i message; yet, since they are culturally conditioned, they often particularize that message. In this way, Shi'i identity is asserted vis-à-vis the West and Sunni Islam simultaneously. Collectively, these features are also important in transmitting Shi'ism to the next generation.

Shi'i identity is also visible in the names given to many centers. Anjumane Asghari, Idara Ja'fariyya, Ahl al-Bayt Center, al-Mahdi Center, Ja'fari Islamic Center, Kerbala Center, and al-Zahra Center indicate in no uncertain terms that these are Shi'i places of worship where services will be conducted based on the Ja'fari school of law.[58] Such identity expression also fosters a sense of shared spirituality of and love for the Imams.

Many Shi'is take great pride in asserting and affirming their cultural identity. Fatima Haji-Taki, a student at the University of Minnesota, conducted a survey of Khoja Shi'is in Minneapolis in 2004. She found that for most of the respondents, being a Khoja Shi'i is a great source of pride because of the rich culture and heritage it represents. One woman indicated that the Khoja culture is special to her because it is a unique blend of various countries, an evolved religious tradition and many languages, while another said the term Khoja Shi'i summed up both her cultural (Khoja) and religious identity (Shi'i). A young father believed his Khoja Shi'i identity became more important after he had children because it would be important for them to have a sense of identity and not "get lost" in the chaos of the world. He gave the example of Hindu immigrants who are losing their identity and values under Western influence. A young woman pointed out that being a Khoja Shi'i was a big part of her identity, even if she tried to deny some of the norms and traditions at times. Another respondent mentioned that he was comforted by the fact that he could go around the world and find a Khoja Shi'i community to settle in, although it might be limiting at times.[59] For many Shi'is, the conflation of religious and cultural identity is the only way that they can conceive of themselves. In many instances, they affirm their identity by visiting places of worship that resonate with their culture. This is an important way to offset the marginalization that many Shi'is experience in America.

Not all Shi'i centers affirm their Shi'i identity. While they are engaged in Shi'i practices, some centers prefer to stress their Islamic identity, and their affiliation to their Sunni brethren. Although they are known as Shi'i centers, few explicitly Shi'i symbols are displayed in the Islamic Center of America, Islamic House of Wisdom, or at the Majma' in Dearborn. In my survey I asked a question related to the tension experienced between maintaining a distinct Shiʻi identity and being a Muslim in America. It is noticeable that centers located in areas where there is a small Shiʻi population are more willing to identify themselves with the larger Muslim community than those Shiʻis living in places like New York or Washington where support from the community is much greater. Thus, a respondent stated: "While our mosque is Shiʻa, our doors are always open to all Muslims. This is necessary in such a small community." While not denying their Shiʻi penchant, smaller communities are more likely to downplay their Shiʻi predilections than larger ones. This is also done to overcome the disadvantage of being in a double minority status, that is, Shiʻi Muslims are not only disadvantaged (and thus in a minority) because they are Muslims but are also further marginalized because they are Shiʻis.

The issue of identity is important not only because it connotes who one is, it also indicates who one is *not*. Thus, not conforming to or expressing Shiʻi identity can lead to a charge of not being a true or proper Shiʻi by fellow Shiʻis. A Shiʻi, for example, who does not dissociate him or herself from the enemies of the family of the Prophet, or does not engage in the ritual of flagellation, or does not attend a center in Muharram could be ridiculed as a "Sushi" Muslim, meaning a Sunni-Shiʻi Muslim. This might lead to the Shiʻi being ostracized and even ridiculed within the Shiʻi community.

Besides the Shiʻi centers, Shiʻi identity is often cultivated at home. This takes the form of displaying Shiʻi icons (names of Imams), supplications for the reappearance of the twelfth Imam, pictures of ʻAli or another Imam, representation of Lahiq, the horse of Husayn in Kerbala, and in some South Asian and Khoja families, special rooms where the ʻalams, cradles, and miniature representations of the shrines of the Imams are displayed. In this way, Shiʻi homes are sacralized as it is popularly believed that *baraka* (blessings) descend on homes that contain such relics. Home-centered devotion supplements or at times even replaces devotions in the mosque. The home space is where religion is articulated through mnemonic visual discourse. The sacred is invoked at home and links the private and public memories and practices.[60]

The problem of identity confronting the Shiʻis in America is indeed greater than that facing the Sunnis. This is because the Shiʻis seek not only to assert their Islamic identity in the West but also to maintain their own distinct Shiʻi identity.

Shi'i Youth in America

Like other immigrant youth, Shi'i youth were either born or raised here. They seek American cultural citizenship, not just economic and political rights.[61] They accept American political values, such as liberty and democracy, while questioning or rejecting American foreign policies. At the same time, they identify themselves locally, listen to American music, and watch MTV. In short, second-generation Shi'is have adopted an American culture. Gradually, Pakistani, Iranian, and Lebanese Shi'is have become American Shi'is.

Younger generation Shi'is embrace a broader spectrum of American life than their parents do. In his *American Jihad*, Steve Baraboza quotes an American Muslim youth as saying, "We are less likely to identify with the homesick mosque culture and more likely to assert a very active political role for the Islamic center, and to do it as an American Muslim community—not as Egyptian, Pakistani, or Malaysian Expatriates, but as Americans."[62] Thus, most youth want to dissociate from the sectarian and ethnic identities that are a source of divisiveness and fragmentation.

As the younger generation matures, Islam frames their primary identity especially as they have little affiliation with the home country and do not identify with American secular values and customs. The youth seek a global Islamic identity, replacing a local culture in favor of a transnational or universal culture. Ethnic, cultural, and linguistic particularities give way to broader religious ones. Pakistani, Iranian, and Lebanese Shi'is will simply become American Shi'is.

Gradually, a chasm has developed between immigrants, who attempt to impose their homeland culture, and the youth, who have adopted a distinctly American culture. Youth identification with American culture is visible in their modes of dressing, the type of food they eat, the language they speak, and the peers they choose. Furthermore, Shi'i youth often challenge their parents' cultural articulation of Islam especially where there is no Islamic basis for such practices. Many youth question practices such as the *matam*, especially when they are done with iron chains (*zanjir*). Other youth also question the religious basis of some of the Shi'i icons, especially the *dharih* room and some wedding practices. The affirmation of an American Shi'i identity within the younger generation is significant since it indicates a paradigm shift. Like other Muslims, Shi'is are transitioning from being the absolute other to becoming a visible minority. They are also shifting from being Muslims in America to becoming American Muslims. From this, they can negotiate their social and political spaces in America.

The struggle between homeland and American culture is not confined to devout or observant Shi'is. Even secular Iranian youth in Los Angeles, who have little or no affiliation to religion, experience such struggles. They express interest in Iranian affairs, but their transnational ties with Iran are predominantly driven by their parents and the media. In the words of Hamid Naficy, the second generation has "a deepening engagement with the here and now."[63] Iran is distant and the experience of their parents is not their own. Cultural transfer to the second generation is evident in their continued interest in Iranian identity, the political affairs of Iran, and ethnic intermarriage; however, their bicultural identity is revealed by the deterioration of patriarchal family structures, traditional values, and the Persian language (Farsi). The patriarchal family structure of Iranian families is one of the traditions being challenged by the second generation. Culturally generated values and practices in Iran are no longer unchallenged in America.[64]

Articles posted at websites like Iranian.com document the efforts of the second-generation Iranian Shi'is to extricate themselves from their parents' exilic baggage, political views, and unrealistic expectations. Iranian Americans express their own identity by modifying and challenging some of their parents' values in discussions about sexuality, dating, and politics. This reveals ongoing intense cultural conflicts in Los Angeles that second-generation Iranians are dealing with as they remake and negotiate a bicultural identity.

Ethnicity among the Shi'i Youth

Shi'i youth are brought up in an American milieu yet they are encouraged by parents, various Islamic groups, imams, and extended family to dis-identify with American culture and politics, and to position themselves somewhere in the Middle East or South Asia. This reductive dichotomy is tantamount to stating that the parent's way is God's way, however cultured that way is. Pakistani youth often complain that their parents want to raise not only Shi'i children in America but also Pakistani ones. A similar complaint is heard from Iranian or Lebanese youth. Some Pakistani youth even complain that their parents send them back home in the summer to become "more Pakistani."

Like other Muslim youth, Shi'i youth reject the ethnic Islam phenomenon particularly as they experience and live in a post-ethnic world. They
have voluntary rather than involuntary affiliations, meaning that they
can negotiate and move between different ethnic, religious, national, and
racial groups. On campuses they can choose to affiliate with Muslim or
non-Muslim friends. This is an example of post-ethnicity rather than the
ethnic-racial groups they are affiliated with by descent.[65]

The trans-ethnic form of Shi'i Islam has emerged primarily because
the ethnicized version is alien and isolationist to the younger generation. Greater engagement with rather than separation from mainstream
American culture has further nurtured the trans-ethnic phenomenon. It
is the younger generation who, due to their interaction with fellow Shi'is,
Muslims, and non-Muslims, are becoming homogenized. Non-American
traits, whether they be cultural, ethnic, or linguistic, are gradually but
surely flattened out. Stated differently, Shi'i youth are engaged in the de-
ethnicization of ethnic Islam, an Islam that is radically different from the
one known to their parents. This growing trend is changing the face of
Shi'ism in America.

Post-ethnicity, or what I have called de-ethnicization, occurs within
Shi'i youth in several ways. As an ethnic *Husayniyya* devotes a portion of
its *majlis* to English, youth from other ethnic backgrounds are attracted
to the center, especially if a powerful or charismatic speaker delivers the
majlis in Muharram. Paradoxically, de-ethnicization occurs within the
same premises that promoted ethnicity in the first place.

De-ethnicization also takes place on Internet sites and the *ahl al-bayt*
chat group where Shi'i youth from different ethnic backgrounds exchange
views on a wide range of topics. The desire by Shi'i youth to use the Internet to transcend cultural peculiarities can be discerned from a new project initiated by Alqaem Youth Society. Its websites, http://www.alqaim.
info/aqyouth and http://alqaim.info/unity state,

> [This] is a project that has been launched by dedicated members of the
> Shi'i Community, in an attempt to bring together individuals belonging
> to various different religious, ethnic and cultural backgrounds, via the
> method of discussion. I am sure this blog *http://smma59.wordpress.com*
> shall soon prove a great center of knowledge, as we are having full sup-
> port of five Muslim scholars from different part of the world. All the dis-
> cussion will be published in one of our blogs and website *www.alqaem.
> org* also.

Such statements evince increasing attempts by Shi'i youth to challenge and transcend the ethnic boundaries that their immigrant parents had constructed and imposed. In their discussions on chat groups such as the *Ahl al-Bayt Discussion Group* (ABDG), Shi'i youth from diverse ethnic backgrounds connect and communicate with each other, breaking down ethnic barriers that often divide their parents.

De-ethnicization also occurs on university campuses and at youth events like retreats, debates, and special discussion groups. At these venues, the youth try to reclaim their religious heritage and identity replacing, in the process, the parents' ethnically identified religious congregations. Shi'i national institutions like the Universal Muslim Association of America (UMAA) and the recently formed Muslim Congress also provide a forum where Shi'is from different ethnic backgrounds can convene and discuss local issues.[66] Participation in such events facilitates the reclamation of a de-ethnicized Islamic identity. The theme of the fourth annual Muslim Congress conference in July 2008 was the reclamation of "a pure Islam" of the *ahl al-bayt*. The focus on pure Islam in the conference was an attempt at essentializing the religion and purging it of cultural and American accretions.[67]

A good example of a post-ethnic institution is the Yaseen Educational Foundation. The institution was established in 1999 by three Shi'i youth from the Los Angeles area. Yaseen was established because other Shi'i centers held their programs in their native languages. (i.e., Arabic, Perisan, Urdu, etc.) The youth were not able to identify or relate to the centers their parents attended. Thus, Yaseen was formed as one of the few only-English-speaking centers. The youth meet on Thursday nights to recite the supplication of Kumayl in their apartment close to the university campus. The supplication of Kumayl is recited at Yaseen in Arabic but it has a line-by-line translation so that it can be understood by all.

After some time, students from nearby campuses began attending the event. Gradually, Yaseen grew into a diverse community comprising of Muslims (primarily Shi'is) from various backgrounds and ethnicities ranging from American, Arab, South Asian, and Afghan to Iranian, Senegalese, Chechnyan, and others. All of the speeches and programs are conducted in English; it is one of the few only English-speaking centers in the Los Angeles area. Yaseen is unique in that it consists of second-generation Muslims and converts who have tried to perpetuate Shi'ism in the American milieu.[68] When I spoke to some members of the Yaseen community in January 2008, it was clear that they felt estranged both from other Shi'i centers and the adult community.

Members of Yaseen stated that, initially, there was tension at some centers because the adults insisted on holding programs in their native language even when the youth asked that programs be held simultaneously in different languages. The adults resisted by not allowing an English speaker to attend or by blocking the use of empty halls in the center, which could be used for a simultaneous program, or even by claiming that speaking about Imam Husayn in English was prohibited (*haram*).

The quest for a trans-ethnic identity is interwoven to the quest for a Shi'i Islam that is not informed by the parents' culture. Young Shi'is are no longer tied to their parent's homeland to direct their cultural identity; rather, they foster a consciousness that is distinctively American. Shi'i youth see America as a platform where they can assert the essence of Islam more clearly. Their practice of Islam, however, does not simply represent a spiritual return to the religion of their parents. Preferring to distance themselves from parental practices that seem more superstitious than informed, they pursue what they call the "real Islam," however that may be defined.[69]

Shi'i youth also reject what is posited as "normative Islam" imposed by the adult immigrant community. In my discussion with several Shi'i youth, I found that they distinguish between "our Islam" and "the true Islam." The youth feel that the adults cling to an Islam that is culturally conditioned, one that is formed by the "back-home mentality" and one with which the youth cannot identify and often reject. For many youth, the shift from the cultural to the "real Islam" is a return to the "true" tenets of Islam; they feel they can lead a better Islamic life in America where they are extricated from the homeland culture.

Shi'i youth must navigate between two worlds of which neither is wholly comfortable or accepting. They are removed from the traditional culture of their parents, while at the same time they live in an American secular society that does not fully accept them. They are exposed to the negative images of a religion into which they were born and a country that they feel is exclusivist. While the youth have negotiated differences between Muslim, ethnic Shi'ism, and American, being a Shi'i Muslim is the identity most important to them. This is evident not only in the values and structure that Shi'i Islam provides for them, but also in their desire to marry within the sect and to raise their children as Shi'i Muslims in the future. In many ways, it is the Shi'i youth who are changing the face of American Shi'ism.

The Pressures on the Youth

Shi'i youth experience the pressures that other young people encounter in America. These include peer pressure, the temptation to dissolve into American culture, and the possible rejection of Islam. Many centers are very concerned about the religious values transmitted to the next generation. Parents too have expressed concern regarding the spiritual well-being and moral rectitude of their children. Before discussing how the centers have dealt with issues related to the youth, it is helpful to draw on the results of a survey that was conducted in Toronto, Canada, in 1995.[70] The sample features Shi'i youth, the majority of whom were born outside of Canada and, on average, have lived in the country for more than ten years.

One of the questions in the survey related to the youths' understanding of Islam and on how much religion regulated their lives. The survey shows that those who have lived in Canada longer do not see Islam to be a complete way of life. This is in contrast to Islamic belief, which maintains that Islam should regulate all parts of their lives. Twenty-nine percent of the youth surveyed felt that Islam is out of date.[71] Furthermore, those who have lived in Canada longer found it more difficult to adhere to Islamic practices.[72]

Perhaps the most startling statistics are that almost half the youth felt that alcohol consumption and premarital sex were widespread among the youth, whereas a third thought that casino gambling and drug use were widely prevalent.[73] Many of these youth personally knew peers who were engaged in such activities. This may be a reflection of some of the pressures that Muslim youth are confronted with in the North American milieu.

Another question concerned their level of involvement within the community. This was seen as an indicator of their willingness to help improve the institutions so that they better serve their needs. Only a little more than one-third were very or somewhat involved, but a quarter were very willing and another half (for a total of three-quarters) were somewhat willing to remain involved or to get involved. The involvement is higher among younger constituents and those who have attended a *madrasa* longer. The survey also suggests that youth who have been here for a longer period are more disillusioned with the community and do not feel a sense of obligation to contribute to it. They do not feel a sense of belonging to the centers. This corroborates the point made previously that many youth cannot relate to the centers and feel marginalized and even alienated from them.

The greatest challenge that the youth identified was the difficulty of abiding by Islamic values in the West. A question in the survey was connected to the more delicate issue of interaction with members of the opposite sex and, more specifically, to where the youth would draw a line in the development of a closer relationship. A substantial majority said they would freely interact with members of the other sex, though only about a third would go as far as dating and a fifth would want to become intimate.[74]

The survey suggests that the parents and Islamic centers have not been able to transmit Islamic norms to the next generation effectively. Even though the survey was conducted in 1995, most centers have done little to ameliorate the situation within the Shiʿi community.

The Centers and the Youth

My 2006 survey indicates that Shiʿi centers are clearly concerned about the youth within the community. Table 2 indicates that 70 percent identified the transmission of Islam to the next generation as a future challenge; an equal number saw the acquisition of a proper facility as an important future challenge. Significantly, cooperation with other Muslims (25 percent), developing literature for non-Muslims (25 percent), and having women involved in the programs (16 percent) were well below the priority list.

A question was posed in the survey regarding the needs of the centers. Most institutions view the establishment of youth-related programs to be among their most pressing needs. Seventy percent of the institutions interviewed said they plan to organize events that would attract the younger generation within the community. Significantly, many seem perplexed or unsure as to how to attract the youth to the centers. The lack of participation by the younger generation in the centers has concerned many parents, who have reexamined the types of programs offered in the centers and the genres of speakers invited in order to attract the youth to the centers. A remark in one of the responses is worth noting: "Muslim youth are more attracted by American rather than traditional Muslim events. Thus, they are more likely to be attracted to retreats, recreational camps, picnics, and debates than sermons and prayers." Most centers within the Shiʿi community do not hold events that could attract the youth on a regular basis.

In addition to there being no interaction with preachers in the centers, the lectures are either delivered in languages that are alien to the youth or they are in the form of repetitive and highly polemicized discourses, quite distinct from the intellectual discourses the youth are accustomed to in the universities. Some centers have tried to overcome the "ritualization" problem by providing appropriate translations of supplications, by encouraging youth to speak before the main lectures, and by facilitating question/answer sessions after the lectures. As noted above, some imams have even resorted to presenting their lectures in PowerPoint format to stimulate interest among the younger generation. In Los Angeles, imam Mustafa al-Qazwini holds special youth sessions on Friday nights where, after a lecture is delivered, youth are able to discuss the lecture and question the speakers. These interactive sessions have proved to be very popular weekly events.

In Dearborn, the Young Muslim Association (YMA), which was launched in 1999, is affiliated to the Islamic Center of America. With a membership of seven hundred, it has grown to become one of the largest Muslim youth organizations in America. It hosts a number of events, including fund-raising dinners and a thirty-day program during Ramadhan. These young people also promote Islamic awareness within the Muslim community, have food drives, and hold annual retreats with imams. Since the events of 9/11, YMA has become more active; they participate in interfaith programs and respond to newspaper articles.

ʻAli Dabaja, a member of the YMA, believes that American Shiʻis must cross ethnic lines. They must also reexamine the services offered in the centers. The youth have been turned off by the dogmatism prevalent in their centers. According to Dabaja, the Twelver Shiʻi Imams have been placed on too much of a pedestal for the youth to emulate. Devotion to the Imams has been limited to embellishing and praising them. The *majalis*, he continues, are too narrative and repetitive to provide for the intellect and spirit of the youth.

Dabaja further states that Islam is neither cool nor attractive to the youth. "Islam is not about bleeding chests and black and white turbans, it is more about role models. Faith, as preached in the centers, needs to be more pragmatic rather than narrative. Currently, the youth are not identifying with the faith," Dabaja says.[75] Another youth told me, "Our leaders are more concerned with building centers than with investing in the hearts and minds of the youth who will occupy those buildings." Such statements from Shiʻi youth indicate their growing dissatisfaction with the running of the centers and the genres of programs that are provided.

As with Sunni mosques, Shiʻi centers have had to adapt to the new environment to attract more members. Services and rituals in some centers have been adapted to facilitate an American articulation of Islam. Besides the incorporation of English, youth committees hold events that are more likely to appeal to the younger generation. A good example of the tension that many communities experience is provided by Shi'i centers in Chicago. There are three major Shi'i centers in the city, all of them of South Asian origin. What distinguishes Bait al-'Ilm from the other South Asian centers is that most of its lectures are in English, a fact that attracts a more ethnically diverse crowd. Attendees will, on most occasions, sit on chairs rather than on floors. Most sessions are interactive, and the subjects discussed are more pertinent to the Shi'i presence in America. The imam of the center, Shaykh Mukhtar Fyzee, consciously attempts to reach out to the Shi'i youth in Chicago.

At the Islamic House of Wisdom in Dearborn, members congregate in the auditorium and sit on pews during the services while the imam of the center, Muhammad 'Ali Ilahi, delivers his lectures standing at a podium rather than sitting on a pulpit. In some centers, traditional supplications on Thursday nights and during the months of Ramadhan are recited in the vernacular instead of the traditional Arabic language. At the Idara Ja'fariyya in Maryland, the youth conduct the *marathiya* and lamentations for the Imams in English while the adults perform the *marathiya* in Urdu in an adjacent hall. Such measures are a good indication of how centers are transforming their services to attract the youth.

Another notable feature of American Shi'i institutions is that more centers are building community centers rather than traditional places of worship. This is done with the explicit aim of incorporating recreational events to attract the younger generation to their activities. Al-Khoei Foundation in New York established a precedent in the late 1980s. Faced with the increasing needs of a growing Shi'i populace in New York, a new multipurpose center was built. It included a prayer hall, a gymnasium, a full-time Islamic school, and a functional library. Recognizing the need of servicing various "ethnic groups" within the Shi'i community, al-Khoei Foundation built separate lecture halls where *majalis* could be delivered in different languages simultaneously in the month of Muharram.

Differences with the Sunni Experience

While Shi'i youth share many of the challenges that Sunni youth encounter (ethnicization, the bifurcation of a cultural and "pure Islam," assimilation to American culture, peer pressure), there are fundamental differences between the experiences of the two groups. To assume that Muslim youth encounter similar challenges in America would be to homogenize their experience.

There are many points of divergence between the experiences of Shi'i and Sunni youth. They go to their own Islamic centers, visit Internet sites that speak to their specific religious needs, seek religious guidance from different sources, and practice Islam based on their distinct sectarian teachings. In the summer, Shi'i youth often attend their own summer retreat camps where they are instructed in matters pertaining to their school of law. When Shi'i and Sunni youth are together on campuses, there are frequent altercations between the two groups.

Shi'i youth will visit, for example, al-Islam.org, a Shi'i site that speaks to many Shi'i issues. Here, they are instructed on Shi'i differences with Sunni Islam and the preponderance of their faith. The site also has a large collection of online Islamic resources covering a variety of subjects in various media formats such as audio, video, presentations, image gallery, and short and full-length texts. Youth who want to hear the *nawahi, matam,* or *majlis* online visit sites like www.yahusain.org or other popular Shi'i sites where they can hear the latest *nawahi* (also called *nasheed*). Another internet site, http://www.shiatv.net, contains more than two thousand videos that address specifically Shi'i issues. The videos range from documentaries to *majalis* of various *khutaba'* and even *'Ashura'* processions in places like Bangkok and Afghanistan. Shi'i youth also subscribe to a popular Internet chat line, called ahlul bayt.org where many pertinent issues, Shi'i or otherwise, are debated and discussed. In the 1990s, the chat line had facilitated a network service whereby members of the community could pose questions to Shi'i scholars online.[76]

Contrary to the Sunni experience, there are no extraneous Shi'i movements that have established themselves in America. There is no Shi'i equivalent of Salafi, Wahhabi, Hizb al-Tahrir, or Tablighi movements. These movements have imposed their ideologies and influenced Muslim student bodies on many campuses. The Wahhabis and Salafis, in particular, have created much division within student bodies. Instead of the importation of extraneous movements, Shi'ism relies on a different form of religious authority. Authority in Twelver Shi'ism is distinctly hierarchical, meaning that Shi'is are required to imitate (*taqlid*) a *marji'* (source of reference).[77] Depending on who he or she imitates, a Shi'i youth can go online at, say, Seestani.org or Bayynat.org and post questions to or seek religious guidance from the office of a *marji'*. Some *maraji'* have representatives in America from whom religious guidance may be sought. In this way, Shiʿism is distinctly different from Sunnism since the concept of reference to the most learned authority does not exist in the latter.

One religious figure who has become increasingly popular among many Shiʿi youth is the Lebanese *marjiʿ*, Ayatullah Muhammad Hussein Fadlallah. His popularity in the West is based on his greater accessibility to the laity. In fact, it is even possible to converse with him directly over the telephone.[78] Fadlallah is more popular with the youth than other *ʿulamaʾ* because his religious edicts (*fatawa*) are deduced with an understanding of the importance of time and context rather than adopting a literalist reading of textual sources. Contrary to Ayatullah Seestani, for example, he allows the shaving of the beard. He argues that the ruling given by classical scholars regarding the requirement of keeping a beard has to be properly contextualized. Their edict was predicated on the need to differentiate between Muslims and Jews. This, Fadlallah says, is restricted to cases in which Muslims are in a minority and others in a majority. He further states: "It is understood from the *hadith* that the prohibition of shaving the beard was contingent on a time-related issue at the beginning of the Islamic message."[79] Fadlallah also differs from Seestani in that he allows playing chess.[80]

Fadlallah has written books that deal exclusively with youth and women, addressing issues that directly impact Muslims in the West. In his *World of Our Youth*, he quotes a tradition from the first Shiʿi Imam, ʿAli b. Abi Talib, exhorting parents to raise their children based on the needs of the time. He provides guidelines that outline the traits necessary for a happy marriage, whom to befriend, and the basis of a proper relationship with parents.

He also raises such sensitive issues as sex and alcohol in a manner more likely to appeal to the youth. Fadlallah further calls for a reevaluation of the traditional Muslim view on sex by stating that it is necessary to impart sex education to Muslim youth. Contrary to popular belief, he says, Islam does not regard it as dirty or an affront to a woman's dignity. He also maintains that gender inequalities in child rearing are predicated on cultural, not religious, constructs. Traditionally, he says, a girl is made to assume responsibility for the family's collective virtue in a manner that is not expected of a boy, "This kind of rearing is incorrect. Virtue is an Islamic requirement equally of the male and female. Individually, chastity is required of the boy and girl."[81]

The need to address the younger generation residing in the West is further illustrated by the title of a recently published book, *A Code of*

Practice for Muslims in the West in Accordance with the Edicts of Ayatullah al-Udhma as-Sayyid 'Ali al-Husaini as-Seestani. Here, such issues as masturbation, homosexuality, and viewing pornographic pictures and films are discussed quite explicitly.[82]

Conclusion

America is indeed a land of opportunity and freedom of religion of conscience, something that many immigrants have been denied in their homeland countries. Shi'is are freer to express themselves and practice their faith in America than in many Muslim countries where they frequently have to conceal their identity and religious practices. The religious freedom that Americans enjoy has given rise to religious diversity. Ironically, it is the diversity that has led to fragmentation rather than unification of the Shi'i community. In the processes of cultural negotiations, redefinitions, and reappropriation of a different culture, Shi'i immigrants have pursued different ways to adapt to the American milieu.

The new immigrants have deployed the most powerful weapons in the religious arsenal: institutions, rituals, and symbols. They have also used the most telling point in Shi'i history to gather the Shi'i populace in the American diaspora—the tragedy of Kerbala. It is this event that has brought the community together and ensured that members retain their unique identity.

Two levels of loyalty compete for the allegiance of the Shi'is—religious and ethnic. Shi'is identify themselves through religion that is interpreted ethnically. The net result has been the establishment of religious institutions along ethnic lines where Shi'ism is expressed in the form of variant extraneous cultural traditions. Ethnicity and rituals endemic to a particular community have become the main categories of identification in America. They are distinctive markers that despite doctrinal similarities, continue to segment the Shi'i community in America. Such diversity has made it difficult for Shi'i centers to create a common agenda to direct the lives of community members.

Like youth from other immigrant communities, Shi'i youth are engaged in a paradigm shift, forcing the adults to rethink their axioms. Young Shi'is are reconstructing their identities, ethnicities, and coalitions in America. They establish Shi'i organizations and try to carve a place for themselves within the American intellectual and sociopolitical spheres.

This repositioning has forced the parents to reassess their own attitudes and place in the American milieu.

For American Shi'is, the challenge is not only in defining the mode of interaction with the outside world but also how to engage Shi'is from other ethnic communities. Due to the challenges outlined above, a Shi'i can become "the other" even within his/her own community. Such dichotomization and differentiation within the Shi'i community suggests that their identity is framed sometimes with and at other times against fellow Shi'is.

3

Sunni–Shi'i Interaction in America

The Shi'i experience in America has to be understood within the context of the community's relationship with both non-Muslims and fellow Muslims, the Sunnis. This is because, from the very beginning, American Shi'is have had to contend with both groups. They have had to interact and cooperate with and, at times, respond to accusations from fellow Muslims.

Shi'i–Sunni dynamics in America have to be contextualized within the framework of the history of the early Muslim community, which, as we have seen, comprised both groups. Faced with the challenge of assimilation to American culture, the early Shi'is sought to keep their faith intact and perform their religious obligations. They also felt the need to socialize and maintain regular contact with their religious brethren. Since they were a minority in America, they stressed their Islamic, rather than sectarian identity. Despite their sectarian differences, Shi'i and Sunni Muslims often intermarried, worshiped in the same mosques, marked social occasions, and together represented Islam to the non-American community.

Julia Harajali, who was born in Michigan City in 1920 and lived there until 1935, recalls that she never heard of the Sunni–Shi'i divide when she resided there. She states that Sunnis would even worship in the Shi'i mosque. The first time she heard of differences between Sunnis and Shi'is was in 1942 when a family member wanted to marry a Sunni. Linda Walbridge further substantiates this point. According to her research, even in Detroit, where there were many Sunnis and Shi'is, each would attend the other's events. Muhammad Jawad Chirri, the Shi'i religious leader, was involved with both the Sunni and Shi'i communities.[1] His son, Adnan Chirri, confirmed that his father preferred to abstain from sectarian issues. Rather than discussing Sunni–Shi'i differences, he focused on introducing Islam to America. Marium 'Uthman, who was born in Michigan, does not recall hearing of the Sunni–Shi'i divide when she grew up in Dearborn. On the contrary, she remembers that Sunnis often spoke at

Shi'i events, and vice versa. Similarly, Shaykh Khalil Bazzy, another Shi'i religious leader in the 1930s and 1940s, served both the Shi'i and Sunni communities in Detroit.[2]

Paradoxically, Sunnis and Shi'is were able to coexist with and accept each other more in America than in their home countries. Realizing the need to unite with fellow Muslims in the face of an alien environment, Shi'is and Sunnis organized joint events for social interchange to maintain their sense of religious identity. Joint gatherings between the Shi'is and Sunnis in Detroit continued until the Shi'is purchased a meeting place, the Hashemite hall, in the 1940s. When the hall was purchased, many Sunnis left, as they felt a more Shi'i identity was being accentuated. Despite the parting of the ways, relations between the two communities continued to remain good.

Shi'is and Sunnis interacted in other parts of America as well. There was much cooperation between the two sects in Michigan City with Sunnis joining Shi'is in worship and other social events after the mosque was built in 1924. In the 1950s, however, sectarian tensions began to surface in other parts of the country. Abdo Elkholy states that differences between Shi'is and Sunnis surfaced soon after a mosque was built in Toledo in 1955. Although he does not delve into the source of the differences, his comment that Shi'is participated in social but not religious activities at the mosque suggests that there were significant religious differences between the two groups. Elkholy also indicates that the sectarian conflict was greater in Detroit than in Toledo. This was, according to him, due to the high concentration of Muslims in a small area of Detroit. Muslims in Toledo, on the other hand, were dispersed in different parts of the city.[3]

Sunnis and Shi'is in Quincy, Massachusetts, formed the Arab American Banner Society in 1937. Although this was an Arab rather than an Islamic institution, Sunnis and Shi'is cooperated to establish a society whose purpose was to "preserve the racial identity among the Arabs in the United States and its development in accordance with the highest principles and traditions of American life and education."[4] The Quincy Muslims also bought a house in 1937 as a meeting place to hear the recitation of the Qur'an and the lifestyle of the Prophet.[5] In the early days, there were few signs of tensions between Sunnis and Shi'is, which corroborates my previous observation that in the early part of the last century, the need to unite in an alien American environment tended to override sectarian considerations.

Shi'is were also closely affiliated with Sunni institutes. When the Federation of Islamic Association (FIA) was formed in Cedar Rapids in 1952, Shi'is attended and fully participated in the proceedings. Khalil (Chuck) Alwan, a member of the Shi'i community in Detroit, recalls that he was asked to chair the meeting when the FIA convention was held in Detroit in 1957. Imam Chirri led the prayers and spoke at the convention. Nayfee Krugler, who was born in Cedar Rapids in 1945, recalls that the Shi'is participated in the organization, and contributed to the social and religious activities. Krugler also remembers that there was little differentiation between Sunnis and Shi'is in either Cedar Rapids or Toledo. However, she cautions that it would be wrong to think that there were no sectarian tensions; on the contrary, differences between the two sects did exist but were not accentuated.

Shi'i and Sunni interaction was not confined to Michigan. Shi'i immigrants who arrived before the 1960s were generally young and single. The preexisting Shi'i communities in America were often isolated from college and university students and professional Shi'is. Hence, there was little if any interaction between the different Shi'i groups in America. The lack of Shi'i institutions and centers of worship meant that many Shi'is interacted more with Sunnis than with fellow Shi'is.

In 1963, the Muslim Student Association (MSA) was formed by students at the University of Illinois–Urbana. An important feature in the formative period of the organization was that commitment to Islam overrode sectarian considerations, with Sunnis and Shi'is worshiping together. In fact, some early MSA presidents were Shi'is.[6] A significant portion of this student body came from the followers of Ayatullah al-Khu'i (d. 1992) of Najaf, Iraq. Besides the Arab Shi'is, there were many Iranian Shi'is within the student body who joined and fully contributed to the activities of the MSA.

Until the late 1970s, Sunnis and Shi'is often worked together, holding joint programs in the MSAs and even in the mosques. Yasin al-Jibouri, a Shi'i proselyte, recalls that in the 1970s he could deliver sermons and lead prayers at a Sunni mosque, the Islamic Center of Atlanta, despite his Shi'i affiliations.[7] He also delivered many sermons at the Atlanta MSA, edited their newsletter, and was later asked to be the president of the institution, an offer that he declined.[8] Sectarianism in America had not reached a level of intensity that it had in other parts of the world; this did not mean, however, that it did not exist, or that its presence was not felt anywhere in the American religious landscape. In 1973, al-Jibouri was asked to stop leading prayers at the Islamic Center of Atlanta when the community realized that he was a Shi'i.[9] As more Muslim immigrants migrated to America in the 1970s and 1980s, sectarian differences within the American Muslim community began to surface.

The Iranian Revolution and the Sectarian Divide

To understand Sunni–Shi'i relations in contemporary America, it is essential to discuss, albeit briefly, the impact that the Iranian revolution had in the Muslim world. Relations between Shi'is and Sunnis in America have been contingent on religious and political considerations in the Middle East and other parts of the Muslim world, especially since the revolution.

The 1979 revolution in Iran awakened religious sentiment in the Muslim community in general, and among Shi'is in particular. It created religious awareness and inculcated a sense of pride in being a Muslim. An attitude of being a "reborn" Muslim was engendered among younger generations of Shi'is and Sunnis alike. Muslim women all over the world began wearing the *hijab*, men kept beards and took pride in asserting their Islamic identity.

The impact of the Iranian revolution has been felt in America in different ways: through the influx of pro-Iranian Shi'i immigrants, through the Internet, and the importation of foreign literature. Immigrants brought their impressions of the revolution and transmitted these to American Shi'is. In addition, a number of American Muslims were invited to the Islamic Republic of Iran after the revolution in 1979 and many returned with renewed zest for a more active expression of Islam in America. This activism has expressed itself in a number of ways, ranging from a ban on mixed swimming and music lessons in schools to the establishment of worship areas in some airports. The Iranian revolution also created heightened concern about how children were being raised in America.[10]

Iranian influence is also evident in the literature that is available in many Shi'i centers and bookstores. Literature regarding Iran is publicized mainly through Islamic centers that offer a variety of educational programs, bookstores, and sites for community gatherings. The thoughts and sermons of Ayatullah Khumayni and other Iranian scholars like Ayatullah Murtada Mutahhari are widely circulated in such gatherings and conferences.

The impact of the Iranian revolution has not been confined to Shi'i Muslims in America. According to Yvonne Haddad, 85 percent of those interviewed in her survey expressed joy at the passing of the shah's regime.[11] The revolution injected a sense of pride and provided a positive affirmation of identity, as it was viewed by many Muslims as a vindication of God's promise to grant victory to the believers.[12] The establishment of an Islamic government was interpreted as an empowering of the Islamic community by God and an indication that salvation in America could come only through a similar process, one in which Muslims take charge of their lives by eschewing Western values and returning to the Islam taught by the Prophet.[13]

The revolution also had a profound effect on some members of the Khoja community in America. In a survey conducted by Fatima Haji-Taki, a student at the University of Minneapolis, many respondents reported that they were glad that because of the revolution, Shi'ism had become a known entity globally and they were no longer ashamed or scared to reveal their Shi'i identity. Most respondents also stated that before the revolution, they had been following Islam without understanding it, while some said that they previously did not pray, fast, or follow any rules. They became ardent followers of Islam after the revolution. "I began to identify Islam as a dynamic rather than a stagnant religion," one woman said. For another woman, it reinstated her belief in the twelfth Imam and that "he could reappear during her lifetime."[14]

The Iranian revolution also had a major impact on the activities and modes of dressing among American Shi'is. At the Islamic Center of America in Dearborn, after the fall of the shah, Ayatullah Khumayni's picture appeared in the mosque's foyer, where it was hung for a number of years. Women entering the mosque were now asked to cover their hair. Even imam Chirri's appearance changed. He exchanged his Western suit in favor of the flowing robes of a traditional imam, and he grew a beard.[15]

Khumayni himself called for unity between Shi'is and Sunnis. He also called for Muslims all over the world to rise up against dictatorial regimes. The revolution also emboldened Saudi Shi'is, inspiring them to challenge the Saudi regime in the 1980s.[16] As the revolution galvanized Muslims all over the world, Sunni rulers and monarchs of Middle Eastern states like Jordan, Iraq, Egypt, and Saudi Arabia saw it as a threat to their own regimes.

The Saudi Response to the Revolution

Saudi Arabia is a theocratic state where all variant expressions of Islam and non-Muslims are precluded from the public square. Threatened by the Iranian revolution and its regime, the Saudis, who espouse Wahhabi ideology, felt a need to respond to the purported Shiʻi threat. They did this by disseminating Wahhabism in different parts of the world.

The Wahhabis base their ideology on the views of the fourteenth-century scholar Ibn Taymiyya. He saw the Shiʻis as the enemy within, guilty of corrupting Islam. Shiʻism, he believed, was a heretical movement that had to be combated, violently, if necessary. In his *Minhaj al-Sunna al-Nabawiyya fi Naqd Kalam al-Shiʻa al-Qadariyya* (The Way of the Prophetic Traditions in the Critique of the Theology of the Qadari Shiʻism), Ibn Taymiyya refuted key Shiʻi beliefs and practices. He argued against the Shiʻi belief in the divinely appointed Imams, maintaining that there was no basis for such a view either in the Qurʾan or the Prophetic traditions. Ibn Taymiyya also attacked the Shiʻi belief in the esoteric interpretation of revealed sources. He insisted that the Qurʾan and the Prophet's traditions had to be accepted literally, and that there was no room in Islam for esotericism.[17] Ibn Taymiyya also argued against the Shiʻi chiliastic belief of the messianism of the twelfth Imam. Faith in some hidden Imam, he continued, was irrational and simply underscored the Shiʻis' folly.

Ibn Taymiyya's arguments and works are important because they have been appropriated by the Wahhabis to discredit Shiʻism in present times. His works have also been popularized and promulgated by those who insist on puritanical and fundamentalist interpretations of Islam, like the Salafis.[18] As Vali Nasr states, "Indeed, it might not be going too far to say that the surge of extremist Sunnism that troubles the Muslim world and hence the globe today is unimaginable without this one long-dead jurist."[19]

The Wahhabis fully appropriated Ibn Taymiyya's arguments to vindicate their vitriolic attacks against the Shiʻis. The chief Wahhabi ʻulamaʾ, led by the chief state cleric, ʻAbd al-ʻAziz ibn Baz (d. 1999) issued proclamations stating that Shiʻis were infidels and prohibited Muslims from dealing with them.[20] In December 2006, a top Saudi Arabian Sunni cleric declared Shiʻis to be infidels who should be considered worse than Jews or Christians. ʻAbd al-Rahman al-Barak, one of the top several Wahhabi clerics in Saudi Arabia and considered close to that kingdom's royal family, also urged Sunnis worldwide to oppose reconciliation with Shiʻis. "By and large, the rejectionists (*Rafidis*)[21] are the most evil sect of the nation and they have all the ingredients of the infidels," 'Abd al-Rahman wrote in a *fatwa*, or religious edict, which was posted on his web site. "The general ruling is that they are infidels, apostates and hypocrites," he continued, which, 'Abd al-Rahman said, was in response to a question from a follower. He further claimed that the sect was the work of a Jewish conspiracy.[22]

Sectarian Discord in South Asia

The revolution in Iran was followed by a plethora of pro-Iranian and specifically Shi'i literature. Shi'i scholars, preachers, and *madaris* (religious schools) of Pakistan exalted Iran and its revolution.[23] In doing so, they produced works that glorified the revolution, often positing the Shi'i Imams as paradigmatic models of resistance to oppression. While such works could be traced to the classical period of Islamic history, their proliferation in a Sunni milieu antagonized many in Pakistan. Soon after the revolution, Sunni–Shi'i disputes and confrontation surfaced in other parts of the Muslim world, especially in India and Pakistan.

The Iranian regime wanted to win Sunni support for its revolution so that Muslims could rise against their own regimes. The Iranians stressed the Islamic rather than Shi'i basis of the revolution. Many Sunnis, especially those who were inspired by the Wahhabis, were concerned that the success of the revolution could lead to the exportation of Shi'ism. They sensed the need to confront the growing popularity of the revolution, especially among the Sunni laity. The only way to do this was to attack the ideological basis of the revolution, that of Twelver Shi'ism. In the process, centuries-old sectarian antagonism and acrimony were rekindled. These hostilities were then exported to different parts of the Muslim and non-Muslim world.

In South Asia, the main opposition to the Iranian revolution and Shi'ism came from the Deobandi movement, which was founded in 1867 and named after a town in Uttar Pradesh in northern India. The Deobandis developed as a reaction to British colonialism in India, which, they believed, would corrupt the Muslim community. A group of Indian '*ulama*', led by Mawlana Qasim Nanautavi, founded an Islamic seminary known as Darul Uloom Waqf Deoband. The center continues to serve as an active place for the teaching of the Islamic tradition. Since the center's creation, more than 65,000 Muslims are believed to have studied there, and it is estimated that there are an additional 5,000 or more Deobandi schools scattered throughout the Indian subcontinent.[24] The exponential growth of such *madaris* in Pakistan, especially in the last few decades, has been a major factor in precipitating sectarian feuds.

Ultimately, sectarian dispute is also a competition for religious legitimacy. Different groups contest for the right to speak for Islam and the right to decide who is a Muslim. Deobandi schools teach not only what Islam is, they also stress what it is not. They delineate sectarian boundaries and parameters, again emphasizing in the process who is and who is not a Muslim.

In response to the increasing threat from the Iranian revolution, in 1984 a senior Deobandi leader, Muhammad Manzour Nomani, of Lucknow, published a book titled *Irani Inqilab: Imam Khumayni awr Shi'iyyat* (Iranian Revolution: Imam Khomeini and Shiism). The preface to the book was written by a popular and erudite Indian religious scholar, Abu al-Hasan 'Ali Nadwi (d. 2000), one of the most senior religious leaders of India. Nadwi was an adviser to the Saudi Islamic World League.[25]

In the foreword to the book, Nadwi criticizes Khumayni for his derision of the companions of the Prophet. He says that after the revolution, he thought Khumayni would, for the sake of Muslim unity, "forget the past and begin a new chapter so that the resplendent picture of Islam should once again emerge."[26] However, Nadwi was disappointed that Khumayni had continued to promulgate Shi'ism in his writings, often at the expense of Sunni Islam.

Nadwi's complaints against Khumayni are replicated by Nomani. The latter complains in the preface of the work that after the revolution,

> conferences are regularly held to which such delegates from all over the world are invited as are expected to be ideologically converted to their way of thinking, and, in turn, can be used for the aforesaid cause. Apart from this, such a flood of books, pamphlets, folders, journals and newspapers is being let loose that, at least the present writer has not, during the seventy years of his cognitive life, witnessed a propaganda of this dimension and intensity carried out with such skill and ingenuity by any government, organization or political party. . . . I have learnt from reliable sources that such literature has reached even the rural areas of our country.[27]

The last sentence evinces Nomani's chief concern. The Iranian revolution was bound to appeal to many Muslims especially as it had defied a major superpower of the time and because Khumayni had characterized

America as the great Satan. For Nomani, the revolution was intertwined to the spread of Shi'ism. The subtitle of the work (*Khomeini, Iranian revolution and the Shi'ite Faith*) indicates those aspects that worried Nomani most. In fact, he starts his work with a critique of the revolution and then proceeds to refute various aspects of Shi'i beliefs and practices. He states, "Khomeini's revolution is based totally on the foundation of Shi'ite religion, i.e., upon its doctrines of Imamate, *Ghaibate Kubra* (major absence) of [the] Imam-i-Akhiruzzaman (the Imam of the last phase—the awaited Mehdi) and, during this absence, the establishment of *wilayat-ul-faqih* (the rule of the *mujtahid*)."[28]

Both Nomani and Nadwi felt threatened not only by the Iranian revolution but, more importantly, the appeal of Shi'ism, especially as its revolutionary message could attract the Sunni youth. Hence, they and other Sunni scholars sought to expose what they claimed to be the "real" face of Shi'ism, exporting, in the process, their writings and sectarian literature abroad. The book further attacked the Shi'is for their "unIslamic practices and beliefs." Soon, Nomani's book became a best seller throughout the Sunni world. With Saudi support, the book was translated from Urdu into English, Arabic, and Turkish, and made available for wide circulation.[29]

The dissemination of sectarian literature in South Asia was accompanied by a military component. The Sipah-I Sahaba (soldiers of the companions [of the Prophet]) was established under the regime of Zia al-Haqq in Pakistan in 1985. As the name indicates, the Sipah posited themselves as the vanguards of the companions, a position that inevitably entailed opposition to and confrontation with the Shi'is. The Sipah-I Sahaba tried to combat the Shi'is at different levels. They resorted to publishing anti-Shi'i literature highlighting elements in Shi'i texts that were bound to anger Sunnis. These include the denigration of the companions in general and the Prophet's wife, 'A'isha, in particular. They also quoted Shi'i *hadith* and *tafsir* literature that pronounced the Qur'an to be incomplete. This would vindicate their contention that Shi'ism has transgressed Islamic parameters. The Sipah further highlighted traditions that claimed that the Imams were superior to all Prophets apart from the last Prophet. What the Sipah failed to point out was that the Shi'is themselves do not consider their texts to be completely authentic. In fact, they reject many traditions such as those that suggest the present Qur'an is incomplete.[30]

For the Sipah, the danger of Shi'ism lay not only in its heretical beliefs and practices, but also in its proselytism, especially in urban areas. The Shi'is, the Sipah claim, are not only ignorant of true Islam but are responsible for disseminating their ignorance. This has led many Sunnis to stray from the "true Islam." For the Deobandis and Sipah, confronting and combating Shi'ism was not only necessary, it was a religious obligation.[31]

The Sipah has a more militant offshoot, the Lashkar-I Jhangawi, which was established in Jhang by Mawlana Haqq Nawaz Jhangawi (d. 1990). The most potent aspect of the Sipah movement was the militant attacks against the Shi'is and the subsequent Shi'i retaliation. Sipah and Lashkar, which later became a part of the al-Qa'ida network in Pakistan, attacked Shi'i targets especially in their holy places and mosques.[32]

The Shi'is responded by forming their own movement, Tahrik-I Ja'fari (initially called the Tahrik–Nifaz-I Fiqh-I Ja'fariyya movement for the implementation of Ja'fari law). Founded by Mufti Ja'far Husayn (d. 1983) in Pakistan, it was initially a movement that sought Shi'i representation at the highest levels of the state. The fact that the movement became more vociferous and demanded rights for the Shi'is after the Iranian revolution alarmed many Sunnis. Tahrik-I Ja'fari has tried to cultivate an image of moderation. However, it too has an offshoot, the Sipah-I Muhammad, which was established in 1991. The Sipah-i Muhammadi has, according to Zaman, been linked to much anti-Sunni violence in the Punjab, Karachi, and other areas.[33] It has claimed that it resorted to militancy in response to Sipah Sahaba attacks against the Shi'is.

Both the Sipah Muhammad and Sipah Sahaba have been involved in acts of sectarian violence in Pakistan. Bombings and assassinations since the 1980s have scarred the Sunni and the Shi'i communities. Since 1989 more than nine hundred clashes between the two groups have claimed more than four thousand lives. In August 2001, the Lashkar, together with the Sipah-I Muhammad, were banned by the Pakistani government.[34]

As sectarian violence and tension continue to proliferate in South Asia, Islam has been used to justify violence against fellow Muslims leading to gross violations of basic human rights. From January to May 1997, Sunni groups assassinated seventy-five Shi'i community leaders in a systematic attempt to remove Shi'is from positions of authority.[35] Such acts of violence have been endorsed by Wahhabi *fatwas* that continue to declare Shi'ism a heresy and portray Shi'ism as a "fifth column for the enemies of true Islam." In 2004, the Saudi Wahhabi cleric Nasir al-Umar, accused Iraqi Shi'is of being close to the United States and argued that both were enemies of Muslims everywhere.[36] Such proclamations are indicative of human capacity to fuel deadly conflicts under the guise of divine mandate.

Sunni–Shi'i conflicts have not been confined to South Asia.; they have in fact spread to many parts of the Muslim world. Forces in various Muslim countries ranging from Nigeria to Malaysia and Indonesia have sought to drive wedges between Sunnism and Shi'ism, positing the former as the "true" Islam while branding the latter as a Jewish-inspired aberration. In 1998, the Nigerian government of General Sani Abacha accused the Muslim Brotherhood leader Sheikh Ibrahim al-Zak Zaki of being a Shi'i just before he went on trial for antigovernment activism. In the 1990s, the government of Bahrain repeatedly dismissed calls for political reform by labeling them as Shi'i plots.[37] The Shi'is, it was claimed, were responsible for political unrest and a threat to the government.

Islamic Movements in America

The discussion on sectarian violence in South Asia is essential in order to comprehend the dynamics of Sunni–Shi'i relations in America. Since the 1980s, political and religious disputes in the Muslim world have been globalized, impinging on Muslims in America. Especially since the Iranian revolution, identity issues and sectarian interests have fragmented American Muslims into various groups, preventing them from interacting on a common platform.[38] Political and religious conflicts in the Middle East and elsewhere in the Muslim world have been transposed into Sunni–Shi'i religious disputes in America.

Sectarianism has been imported to America through various sources, one of the most important of these being in the form of foreign-based movements. Movements of Islamic affirmation are able to proliferate and grow more productively in America than in their own countries, where they are often oppressed. Movements such as the Wahhabis and Salafis in the Middle East have seen the West as potentially fertile ground for the growth, development, and expression of their ideas. Passage to the United States has allowed them more opportunity to spread sectarian ideas as there are fewer restrictions from the government as long as American law is not violated.

Through sources such as the Internet, the print media, and local *masajid* (mosques), Islamic movements can reach a wider and more diverse group of Muslims than they can in Pakistan or Saudi Arabia. Given the freedom they enjoy to express their religious beliefs and excoriate the views of others, both Sunnis and Shi'is have sought to reach a global *umma* and to spread their teachings throughout America. Islamic fundamentalist movements have sought to become axiomatic in America; they have tried to define their agenda and sought to delineate the "true Islam." Their voices tend to be heard most because of their extremist and often militant views.

An important movement is the Salafi, a term that means "predecessor" and is most often associated with "followers of the pious ancestors." The movement was founded in the late nineteenth century by Muslim reformers including Muhammad 'Abduh (d. 1905), Jamal al-Din al-Afghani (d. 1897), Muhammad Rashid Rida (d. 1935), and others. Although these early Salafi leaders advocated for a return to the revealed texts, they were not considered anti-intellectual and were even criticized for being progressive.

In the contemporary context, the term *Salafiyya* has come to connote a return to pristine Islam and to an understanding of faith as exemplified by the early generation of Muslims, i.e., the period of the Prophet, his companions, and their successors. For the Salafis, the earthly power and success of the first generation of Muslims were due to their strict adherence to the pure faith, the fundamentals of Islam. If Muslims want to regain their pristine purity, they must emulate their pious ancestors in all spheres of human activity, including governance. As such, the term *Salafi* (someone who follows the *salaf*) is appealing to many as it is denotes a return to a pure, pristine, and unadulterated Islam of the Prophet and his companions. This puritanical ideology has a considerable following all over the Islamic world.

Because of its emphasis on a return to a pure, golden past, Salafi ideology has been appropriated by various movements that seek legitimacy by claiming connection to the idealized Islam of the past. Militant groups such as Jama'at Islami in Britain, the Taliban in Afghanistan, and Ahl-I Hadith in Pakistan are all part of the Salafi network. In addition, various figures such as Abu Hamza al-Masri and Omar Bakri Muhammad in London have appropriated Salafi ideals to promote their movements.

Salafis and Wahhabis claim normative status for themselves and deny other Muslims the right to reject their interpretation because of the fear that dissension can challenge or destroy the identity and cohesiveness of the faith community. Their parochial and often literalist interpretation of Islamic texts, combined with exclusivist salvific claims, leaves little room for building intracommunal relationship between Sunni and Shi'i Muslims, much less between Muslims and the People of the Book, meaning Jews and Christians. This inevitably means that such movements clash with the Shi'is.

The structure of the Salafi movement is very fluid, and its ideology permeates many movements. Salafi thought is carried by movements such as the Qur'an and Sunna society.[39] Due to its fluidity, Wahhabism was able to co-opt the language and symbolisms of Salafism until the two had become practically coterminous.[40] The symbiosis of the two meant that Salafism became a vehicle that could transmit Wahhabi ideology abroad. By conflating its ideology with Wahhabism, Salafiyya was gradually transformed into a conservative theology. The *fatawa* (religious edicts) of Sheikh 'Abdul 'Aziz ibn Baz, the Grand Mufti of the Saudi Kingdom, and of Sheikh al-Albani have been utilized by their disciples in the West.[41] As Salafism has become imbedded within Wahhabism, their "societies" have been supported by the Saudi Arabian Embassy and Dar al-Iftah in Saudi Arabia, and the revival of Islamic Heritage Society in Kuwait.[42] Two main centers of Salafi organization developed in New Jersey and in Canada. The Canada-based Majliss of Al-Haqq Publication Society (Qur'an and Sunnah Society) has, through Mahmoud Murad, helped form strong Salafi centers in Los Angeles and Washington, D.C.[43]

Since the 1970s when the price of oil increased exponentially, the Saudis have propagated their ideology throughout the world. Thousands of preachers, Islamic scholars, and activists from Nigeria to Indonesia have gone to Saudi Arabia to study there.[44] Many of those who studied and worked in Saudi Arabia then spread throughout the Muslim world to teach and work at Saudi-funded universities, schools, mosques, and research institutions. Scholarships and pilgrimages to Mecca continue to provide new recruits for Saudi-sponsored networks.[45]

Saudi Arabia has distributed Wahhabi literature all over the world, provided funding for publishers, mosques, organizations, schools, and individuals, as well as translating their version of the Qur'an into all major languages of the world. Saudi television channels that promote Wahhabi thoughts can now be viewed in America by satellite television. To reach a Western audience, one of the channels is broadcast in English. Each Saudi embassy has a department of religious affairs responsible for funding Islamic institutions. These measures, together with the increase in the number of Internet sites, facilitate access to Wahhabi teachings and help promote Wahhabism as the sole guardian of Islamic thought. Through these channels, Wahhabi ideology is offered as a heuristic device or strategy for confirming God's will and the ensuing salvation.

Wahhabism is also propagated by learned sheikhs or teachers based in the Gulf states. Their impact is felt by the issuance of *fatwas* or juridical edicts. They extend their influence through conferences or lectures, the Internet, television stations, or via booklets. Through informal networks of disciples and former students, they reach a lay audience far larger than the *madaris* in which they teach.[46]

The Saudis have also spread their ideology to the West by contributing to various projects. In 1978 Saudi Arabia announced that it was contributing grants of up to three million dollars for religious projects in North America.[47] Saudi Arabia has sponsored expensive Islamic exhibitions in many cities, published a colorful introductory booklet on Islam, and supported the activities of the Muslim World League (MWL) in America. The MWL reflects Saudi religious interests in America and, through various means, disseminates views attributed to the Wahhabis. In 1990, for example, the MWL reached out to African American organizations to seek support for the American-led invasion of Iraq.[48]

MWL provides funding for the construction of mosques, distribution of the Qur'an, and other educational information.[49] The MWL has also provided fellowships and grants for Muslim university professors. The diverse nature of the league's activities in America becomes evident from the fact that at their 1977 meeting in Newark, New Jersey, Ahmad Sakr, the former director of the MWL office to the United Nations and North America, reported that the MWL had helped to broadcast Islamic television and radio programs.[50] Apart from supporting the plenitude of newspapers and Muslim journals, MWL has also published a considerable amount of Islamic literature for distribution.[51]

Prior to the events of 9/11, the MWL exerted its influence by remunerating imams. According to Yvonne Haddad and Jane Smith, twenty-six imams in the United States were supported by the MWL in the 1980s. Many of the imams were trained in the traditional Islamic sciences in the Middle East.[52] These imams' interpretation of Islam is often parochial and out of touch with the reality of Muslim life in America.[53] Hiring imams paid for by foreign countries also carries the additional burden of attached strings.

Wahhabism is the most powerful Islamic movement that has come to America. As Gilles Kippel asserts, Wahhabism's goal is "to make Islam a factor in the forefront on the international stage, substituting it for defeated nationalism, and reducing the pluralistic forms of expressions of the religion to the credo of the lords of Mecca."[54] In South Asia, Wahhabi thought was disseminated by movements like the Deobandis. In the process, they created much sectarian discord. A similar process has occurred in the United States where the Wahhabis have a network for promulgating their version of Islam. They have both embassies and transnational organizations such as the Organization of the Islamic Conference, the Muslim World League (MWL), and the World Association of Muslim Youth (WAMY).

Another movement that has been influential in the American religious landscape is the Tablighi Jamaat, which originated in India seventy years ago. A subsect within the larger Deobandi movement, the Tablighi movement was founded in 1927 by Mawlana Muhammad Ilyas (d. 1944). The essential principle of the movement states that every Muslim can be a vehicle for disseminating the values and practices of Islam.[55] For the Tablighis, Muslims ought to spend a portion of their time spreading the word of Islam, wherever they may be.

The Tablighi movement permeates mainstream Muslim life by using mosques as bases for their activities.[56] They try to spread their particular brand of Islam among Muslims and even use the *hajj* (pilgrimage) season for converting Muslims to their ideas. Tablighis prefer face-to-face encounters and relationships for communicating their message. Being influenced by traditional Islam, Tablighis have confined themselves largely to ritualistic elements of Islam. This has meant that they have been largely apolitical. Due to their emphasis on purity, personal contact, and a return to the practices of the Prophet, the Tablighis have been successful in attracting adherents to their movement.

Many Muslims of the diaspora do not have access to the traditional Islamic sciences offered in Muslim schools of learning or *madrasa*. By preaching to the Muslim laity in mosques, work places, and universities, the Tablighis fill a particular void. The effectiveness of the Tablighis essentially stems from their ability to provide an intensive religious training for individuals who have never attended the traditional places of Islamic learning. An increasing number of conversions in both Europe and the United States are due to the proselytizing activities of the Tablighis.[57]

An intrinsic part of the Tablighi message is a disdain for cultural accretions and an emphasis on the practices of the Prophet as interpreted by the Sunnis. For the Tablighis, this also means a repudiation of Shiʻism as a later heretical innovation. Hence, in their preaching in America, the Tablighis promote Sunnism while, at the same time, refute Shiʻi and Sufi beliefs and practices.

In contrast to the Tablighis, Hizb al-Tahrir is a more politically active movement. It was established in Jerusalem in 1952 under the leadership of Shaykh Taqiyuddin al-Nabahani. In his manifesto, al-Nabahani outlines three stages of implementing Islam in the modem nation-state. The first stage is identified as the "phase of informing people," during which the recruitment of believers to the objectives of the party takes place by educating them about Islamic goals. The second stage prepares members to interact with the nation and promote the adoption of the party's principles to set up an Islamic order as the entire nation's cause. In the final stage, the party would assume power and implement Islam comprehensively in all spheres of national life.[58]

To be sure, Hizb al-Tahrir insists that the Islamic community be transformed into a political entity in the form of a caliphate that will transcend geopolitical borders and rule over the whole *umma*. Muslims are to create an Islamic order if possible, even in the West.[59] Since it opposes all states that are not based on the *shariʻa*, Hizb al-Tahrir opposes any form of integration to the American sociopolitical order. It claims, for example, that registering to vote for a candidate in the United States is tantamount to registering to commit a religiously forbidden act. This is because participating in the American political process is tantamount to implementing man-made laws, which, in their understanding, is prohibited in the Qurʼan. During the 2000 elections, their motto was, register to vote, register to commit *haram*.[60] Thus, many Muslims eschewed participation in the American political system as they viewed the country as a secular state. Any involvement in it would violate the Islamic belief in the interfacing of church and state. Hizb al-Tahrir has actively disseminated its exclusivist ideology in American mosques and campuses where many Muslims have been captivated by charismatic speakers.[61]

The Egyptian-based movement, the Muslim Brotherhood *(al-Ikhwan al-Muslimun)* was founded by Hassan al-Banna (d. 1949) in 1928 during the period of British occupation. The movement was established to oppose Western colonial rule over Egyptian Muslim society and to promote Islamic values and moral codes. It also advocated a return to the fundamentals or sources of the religion, i.e., the Qurʼan and *hadith*. Members of the Muslim Brotherhood have come to study in the United States since the 1960s. Here, they joined other Muslim institutions like the Muslim Students Association (MSA) network and the Islamic Society of North America (ISNA). In the process, they filtered the ideology of the Brotherhood to these movements.

In contrast to other groups, members of the Muslim Brotherhood tend to encourage a more inclusive formation of relationships with the non-Muslim majority and active participation in the American political system. They also emphasize unity and spiritual purification to youth, college students, and young professionals. Members of the *Ikhwan* also encourage the proselytization of Islam *(da'wa)* and the sponsorship of prayer meetings, summer youth camps, and workshops.[62] The teachings of the Brotherhood are not as parochial or conservative as those of other extraneous groups. For example, the movement promotes the study and application of minority *fiqh* (jurisprudence) and encourages Muslim civic and political involvement in America. It has also sought to educate American Muslims on cultural and religious issues, indicating how to maintain faith in a secular milieu yet interact with the non-Muslim other.

The Dissemination of Fundamentalist Ideology in America

Fundamentalist ideology is often predicated on Qur'anic hermeneutics and *hadith* reports, which are often vulnerable to factional disputation and doctrinal prejudice. For many fundamentalist groups, loyalty to Islam necessarily entails intolerance toward those who fail to meet the criteria of pure faith, unsullied by the accretions and innovations that they believe have corrupted the authentic Islam of the Prophet and his companions. This pious restoration of faith means rejecting freedom of conscience and the removal of the cornerstone of religious tolerance. Such exclusivist claims by a group furnish its members a basis for intolerance and even aggression against those Muslims who do not share their convictions.

Fundamentalist movements have posited an exclusionary vision of the "other" and denied salvific space to those who do not share their outlook. The ideologies of the Wahhabis, Salafis, and Deobandis have been exported to America in the form of movements like the Tablighis, Salafis, Hizb al-Tahrir, and the Ikhwan. The ideas of these movements reflect the thoughts of fundamentalist thinkers like Abu 'Ala Mawdudi (d. 1979) and Sayyid Qutb (d. 1965), which in turn have influenced Muslim life in America and have, to varying degrees, been responsible for sectarian tensions in America.

The distinctive views of the various groups discussed above have been propagated in America in various forms. Friday sermons, lectures delivered by charismatic speakers, workshops, bookstores, tapes, CDs, the Internet, and print media have all become powerful tools in the dissemination of their thoughts. The fundamentalist message is also found on various websites. The Salafis have numerous websites in which they promulgate their ideology.[63]

The movements are far from monolithic and frequently exhibit tensions between them. Barelwi doctrine, for example, accepts the existence of *pirs,* or Muslim saints, whereas Deobandi doctrine rejects it. Because of this disagreement, the former consider the latter to be aligned with the Wahhabis.[64] Steve Johnson cites examples of clashes between these different movements. Salafi observers reported that at the 1987 Intensive Summer Arabic Program in Washington, D.C., sponsored by the Saudi Arabian Embassy and conducted by a large number of Salafi instructors, Salafi and Ikhwan students engaged in physical fights, resulting in several Ikhwan students completing the program early.[65]

The Salafis have also disagreed vehemently with the Tablighis. A *fatwa* from Sheikh Bin Baz in 1997 explicitly stated that the Tabligh was one of the seventy-two heretical sects of Islam. A Salafi website enumerates a list of deviant sects, which includes the Tablighi Jamaat and Deobandism.[66] Wahhabis and Salafis are also critical of the Tablighis' "innovations," especially as they lack a centralized religious leadership. They also criticize the Tablighis for their encouragement of lay persons to propagate Islam and their view that one does not need to be very learned to preach.[67]

These movements have ensured that sectarianism, often rooted in Middle Eastern or South Asian mosques or *madrasas,* is transmitted to Islamic bookstores and homes in cities like New York, Los Angeles, or Chicago. The United States has become a battleground for Muslim minds and voices as traditional sectarian divisions and strife have resurfaced, engendering further fragmentation of the Muslim community.

Polarization within the Muslim community has been further exacerbated by the influx of conservative immigrants. Immigration has resulted in the spread of a conservative spirit in many institutions, accentuating sectarian divisions and disputes between the Sunni and Shi'i schools of thought. Sunni and Shi'i immigrants have brought with them their own bitter experiences and prejudices. Hence, there is a tendency to replicate the invidious climate that prevailed abroad, making this country a battleground for sectarian differences. The concentration of Muslim populations in major American cities, and contact with the culture of the country of origin further accentuate sectarian conflicts.

There is another reason why the sectarian divide in the United States has amplified. Before the 1970s, most major cities had only one mosque, and Muslims of all denominations were forced to interact with each other. This allowed them to collectively shape the conscience of the American Muslim community. Since the 1980s, the Muslim community has increased exponentially. Increased migration led to the establishment of mosques along sectarian lines, and gradually the Sunnis and Shi'is became affiliated with their own sectarian and ethnic groups as both groups built their own centers of worship. In the process, the Muslim community in America allowed itself the luxuries of self-segregation and differentiation.

As we have seen, in many cities the Shi'i community has several centers of worship divided along ethnic lines. Few Shi'is and Sunnis worship or eat together as they once did. Some Shi'is have complained of experiencing discrimination in Sunni mosques. A survey conducted by Qunoot Foundation, a nonprofit organization based in Washington, D.C., reported that 47 percent of American Shi'is said they experienced overt or subtle forms of discrimination when attending Sunni-dominated mosques.[68] Even when there is no direct hostility, there is limited interaction between the two communities.

It should be noted that all the movements discussed above, the Tablighis, Salafis, Hizb al-Tahrir, and Wahhabis are Sunni in character. Activities of the only major Shi'i fundamentalist movement, the Hizbollah, have been largely confined within Lebanon. There are no Shi'i movements in America that propagate Islam from abroad because Shi'is are governed by a religious structure that demands imitation (*taqlid)* of the highest religious authority, the *marji' al-taqlid*. It is the *maraji'* (pl. of *marji'*) who shape and provide guidelines for Shi'i integration into the American sociopolitical order (see chap. 4 in this study).

Due to the hierarchical nature of Shi'i religious leadership, the interpretation of texts is not open to the laity. Stated differently, there is no "obvious" meaning of a text on the basis of which individuals may guide themselves. The meaning of the text—and also, very significantly, the meaning of a central concern of Islam, the law—are not easily accessible, and the lay Shi'i must refer these to a few learned scholars. As a result of this feature of Shi'ism, it misses the populism that is so important to the spirit and functioning of fundamentalism.

The Dissemination of Sectarian Literature

In recent times, Sunni–Shi'i conflicts have polarized the Muslim community in America. The affects of this bifurcation have been felt in various spheres of the American Muslim community, ranging from mosques to student bodies, the Internet, and even in American prisons. The attrition abroad has also led to a substantial rise in the publication and dissemination of sectarian literature in America. According to Steve John-son, organizations such as the Islamic Society of North America (ISNA) and MSA began to distribute anti-Shi'i literature such as *Up from Shiism, Khuttot al-Areedah,* and *The Devil's Deception of the Sheeah* in the 1980s. Salafi publications produced by al-Hijra in New Jersey, the Majliss of al-Haq Publication Society in Vancouver, and Salafi-oriented newsletters such as *al-Basheer* from Boulder, Colorado, and *as-Salaf as-Salih* and *Na-seeha,* produced by the Association of American Muslims in Blooming-ton, Indiana, are all critical of Shi'i beliefs.[69] For them, Shi'ism is the very antithesis of the essentialized Islam that they seek to promote. Nomani's book, *Iranian Revolution: Imam Khomeini and the Shiite Faith,* mentioned earlier, is easily accessible in English. Such literature has denounced Shi'i beliefs and practices and projected Shi'ism as an aberration from main-stream, normative Islam.

According to a flyer distributed by the Shi'i institution, Universal Mus-lim Association of America (UMAA), the World Assembly of Muslim Youth (WAMY), which was established in 1972 in Annandale, Virginia, is directly controlled by its central office in the Saudi capital, Riyadh. The flyer claims that WAMY has been deeply involved in preaching hatred against the Shi'is. UMAA's flyer states,

> For example, a booklet, *The Difference Between The Shiites And The Ma-jority of Muslim Scholars,* authored by Saeed Ismaeel, is distributed in English and Arabic by WAMY. It claims that a fictional Yemeni Jew, Ab-dullah ibn Saba, conspired with other Jews to create a division in Islam, and planted Jewish ideas which became Shi'i Islam. Ismaeel claims in his booklet, "the Jewish conspiracy represented by Abdullah ibn Sabaa, first influenced Muslims who were less knowledgeable about Islam and later on spread to the rest of the Muslim community." The author concludes his booklet by saying "the cornerstone of the Shia faith, as well as its di-mensions and evidence, are false and baseless."

UMAA's flyer continues by stating that in line with Wahhabi ideology, which promotes hatred against the majority of Muslims and all non-Mus-lims, WAMY publications assert that most of the world's Muslims are not Muslims at all, but rather unbelievers condemned to die if they do not embrace Wahhabi Islam.

Such vitriolic attacks have infuriated the Shi'is. They have responded by publishing and distributing their own genres of sectarian literature. In the 1990s, publications such as the Canadian-based *Crescent International* and *Islamic Forum*, as well as the Maryland-based *New Trend* and other books distributed through the Iranian Interest of the Algerian Embassy have affirmed Shi'i beliefs and views of current events. The Shi'is have also translated and circulated the works of Muhammad al-Tijani al-Samawi, a Sunni convert to Shi'ism, whose first work *Then I Was Guided*, has had a major impact in refuting Sunni beliefs and in converting Sunnis to Shi'i Islam.

The Sectarian Works of Muhammad al-Tijani al-Samawi

Born in Tunisia, Tijani was well versed in the Qur'an and religious sciences from his childhood. His position in the Sunni world was enhanced by his erudition and meetings with the teachers of Azhar in Cairo. His first book, *Then I Was Guided*, is a moving account of an inner struggle that led to his conversion. When he was traveling from Cairo to Alexander by ship his preconceived notions about Shi'ism began to be challenged. His subsequent meetings with Ayatullah al-Khu'i and Ayatullah Muhammad Baqir Sadr (d. 1980) in Najaf, Iraq, left Tijani perplexed and bewildered. He began to question his beliefs and developed an inclination toward Shi'ism. He thus started researching Shi'i beliefs and practices. In his four main books, *Then I Was Guided, Ask Those Who Know, To Be with the Truthful Ones*, and *Shi'as Are the Real Sunnis*, Tijani utilizes Sunni *hadith* literature extensively to argue against and challenge long-held Sunni axioms.

Tijani traces the provenance of Shi'i–Sunni disputes to the Prophet's time, exalting the virtues of early Shi'i heroes and chastising the companions for acts like fleeing battles and changing the *sunna* of the Prophet. He proceeds to emasculate Sunni arguments by questioning the integrity of Muhammad's companions. In this way he attacks one of the basic tenets of the Sunni Islam, namely, the belief in the moral probity of all companions.

In *Ask Those Who Know*, Tijani also takes to task the Sunnis' most influential literary source, the *Sahih* of al-Bukhari. He criticizes many traditions in al-Bukhari's work, claiming that they demean the status of the Prophet. He claims that Bukhari cites traditions that show that the Prophet duped and deceived, that the Prophet inflicted vile penalties and mutilated, and that he loved intercourse. Tijani also accuses al-Bukhari of citing traditions indicating that the Prophet forgot in his prayers and that he made an oath and then broke it. He further accuses al-Bukhari of forging and interpolating traditions to preserve and increase the status of 'Umar al-Khattab (d. 644).[70]

Having criticized and questioned Sunni archetypal models, Tijani replaces them with Shi'i ones. He contrasts the behavior of the disobedient companions with those who were completely loyal to the Prophet. Tijani thus turns the Shi'i–Sunni dispute on its head. The Shi'is, he claims, are the true Sunnis. They are the orthodox, the mainstream group from which others have deviated. This is seen in the title of his fourth book, *al-Shi'a hum ahl al-sunna* (*The Shi'is Are the [True] Sunnis*). By making the Shi'is the true Sunnis, he makes the Sunnis the true *Rafidis* (rejecters of the Prophetic *sunna*), which, according to Tijani, was preserved only by the household of the Prophet.

The Shi'is have also translated and circulated Muhammad Sharaf al-Din al-Musawi's *Muraja'at*, (translated as *The Right Path*) and *Masa'il Fiqhiyya* (*Questions of Jurisprudence*). In contrast to al-Tijani, al-Musawi is more scholarly and respectful in his approach. He seeks to prove the verity of Shi'i beliefs and practices by citing Sunni sources. Like Tijani, al-Musawi's works have been used extensively by the Shi'is in their anti-Sunni polemical discourses.

Through their polemical works, both Sunni and Shi'i scholars articulate and delineate a normative basis through which "orthodox" views and beliefs could be distilled and differentiated from those espoused by their opponents. The inherent motive for these disputations is to characterize the origins of the community as divinely sanctioned. In the negotiative process in which the polemicists are engaged, the questions of succession and authority after the Prophet's death have become a battle of rhetorical devices, often employing Qur'anic hermeneutics and traditions from the Prophet to vindicate their respective points. Polemical literature also helps conceive salvation along strictly sectarian lines and establishes the basis for each school's self-definition and its differentiation from the other.

The dissemination of this genre of literature in America further entrenches parameters of separation and differentiation, constructing, in the process, boundaries of identity and exclusion that divide American Muslim communities. The plenitude of polemical literature in Islam is certainly not new. In the past, both Sunnis and Shi'is have criticized, refuted, ridiculed, and even mocked each other. However, the fact that such literature is freely available in Islamic bookstores and mosques means that sectarian tensions are felt in American streets.

Sectarian Conflict in American Streets

The American invasion of Iraq in 2003 and subsequent sectarian clashes in Iraq further escalated sectarian tensions not only on the streets and mosques in Iraq but also in America, especially after the bombing of the golden dome in Samarra in February 2006. It is in Samarra that the tenth and eleventh Shiʻi Imams, ʻAli al-Hadi (d. 868) and al-Hasan al-ʻAskari (d. 870) are buried. Shiʻi traditions also report that the twelfth Imam, whom the Shiʻis believe is the messiah, went into occultation there in 874 CE.

As we read in chapter 2, Shiʻis in America mark the martyrdom of Husayn in the month of Muharram by holding processions in some major cities. The processions are often accompanied by acts of self-flagellation and rhythmic chest beating. For several years, Shiʻis have marched through the streets of Manhattan during this month to commemorate the event. During the procession in February 2006, Shiʻi mourners in the streets were met by protesters claiming to be from a Brooklyn-based group calling itself the Islamic Thinkers Society. The group denounced the Muharram ritual and passed out fliers condemning Shiʻis as heretics and unbelievers. Shiʻi sources also claim that they were subjected to verbal assaults. Insults were also directed at one of the highest Shiʻi authorities, Ayatullah al-Sayyid ʻAli Seestani and other *maraji*. This event was significant in that it marked the spread of sectarian conflict to American cities and streets.

After this event, the Shiʻi institution, Universal Muslim Association of America (UMAA), issued a press release stating, "We categorically reject their (Wahhabi) ideology of hate and violence, which is diametrically opposed to the values of Islam—which promote justice, human rights, and compassion of all humanity."[71] The incident was widely reported and condemned in Shiʻi circles. Shiʻi mosques all over America were quick to excoriate the incident, construing it as further attempts at inflaming sectarian tensions. Indeed, some Sunni institutions also condemned the incident.

Sectarian violence in Iraq and the ensuing Shiʻi ascendancy after the American invasion have further strained Sunni–Shiʻi tensions in America. Sectarian tensions in the United States were evident again after Saddam Hussein's execution in December 2006. The grisly video of Hussein's execution with his Shiʻi executioners mocking him was shown widely on American television stations and on the Internet. In the aftermath, three mosques and some Shiʻi businesses in Dearborn were vandalized.

Although no one was arrested, most in Dearborn's Iraqi Shiʻi community blamed Sunni Muslims for the attacks.

The Shiʻis have also contributed to the sectarian conflict in America. Especially in South Asian *Husayniyyas*, many *khutaba'* who speak during the month of Muharram regularly deride and revile the companions and ʻAʼisha, one of the wives of the Prophet. For South Asian Shiʻis, this has been a regular practice in their *majalis* from back home. In one North American city, a group of Shiʻis meet regularly in private sessions to praise and extol the virtues of the Prophet and his family, and to curse the companions of the Prophet. Such actions, even though they are conducted within the confines of the centers of worship, are bound to escalate the sectarian divide.

Sectarian Conflict on the Internet

The rise of the Internet as a communicative tool, the availability of Middle Eastern channels of satellite television, and the proliferation of sectarian literature have all changed the face of Islam in America. The availability of a wide variety of sources of information has led to the spread of prejudices against fellow Muslims and a focus on the differences between Shiʻis and Sunnis. In the world of a dispersed Muslim population, the Internet has become an important tool for the dissemination of various beliefs, prejudices, networking, religious instruction and advice, as well for the creation of virtual communities of faith. The amount of information and distinct ideas about what constitutes "true Islam" has led to a transformation of how the Muslim world is perceived and comprehended.

Due to the availability of the Internet, religious scholarship or opinions are disseminated by means of a virtual space in which all people, rather than simply scholars, have access to a variety of ideas or interpretations of religious text. Anyone using the Internet is able to pick and choose what fits their concept of orthopraxy or orthodoxy. The Internet provides a space for communication among peoples living in different places to both disseminate ideas as well as organize like-minded individuals into collective entities. Since there is no censorship on the Internet, ideas about other sects that are inaccurate or grossly exaggerated are circulated or propagated with ease. Thus, it is very easy to spread sectarian prejudices and to impose a particular understanding of Islam.

The Internet also lends itself to a fluid interconnectivity between diasporic or migratory individual Muslims and communities, leaders, and organizations without national or geopolitical borders. This also means that voices with radical viewpoints are able to make themselves heard and thus solicit extreme ideas without censorship from hierarchical power structures. Stated differently, the Internet has provided a medium in which a plethora of voices may be heard, accessed, and proliferated.[72] Being connected on the Internet is taking the place of actual communities of believers, and ideas are being circulated by self-proclaimed religious authorities.

Imams, fundamentalist or otherwise, are finding larger and often global audiences by the ability to upload sermons and other religious discourses onto the Web. Furthermore, many authorities who preach sermons use Western languages that transcend ethnic or national boundaries to reach large audiences of Western-born Muslims.[73] In this way, the Internet can reach local viewers as well as the entirety of international readership.

The Shi'i–Sunni conflict is also being played out on the Internet. Both groups have used it to advance their respective views. One site maintained in the States (http://www.kr-hcy.com/) encourages hatred against the Shi'is and declares them as unbelievers (the full title of the group is *Haq Char Waar Media Services: Unzipping SHIAs and Qadyanis*). The site advocates hatred against Shi'is by telling Muslims "you must not socialize with them, or eat with them or marry them, either a Sunni man marrying a Shia woman or the opposite. You should not extend greetings to them. The curse of Allah be upon them." The website also offers hateful books and *fatwas* (religious edicts) against Shi'is.

Another anti-Shi'i site, http://www.ansar.org/english/index.htm, holds such topics as "The Myth of the twelfth Imam," "Allah was planning against the Shiah", "Is the Imam better than the Prophet?" Refutation to the hadith Ghadeer Khumm" and "al-Taqiah in Shi'a's creed," and the like.

The Shi'is have responded with their own website, aqaed.com and http://www.answering-ansar.org/index.php. Some of the titles reflect the polemics being played out on the Web. These include "The Devil's Deception of Nasibi Wahhabis," "*Tarawih*: a Parody of Prayers," "Private lives of the Nasibi Salaf," and "Sunni myth of love and adherence to the Ahlulbayt [as]." The site also addresses the Deobandis and responds to their accusations.

The Shi'is have not only defended their beliefs, they have also attacked the Wahhabis on the Internet. Sites such as http://home.bip.net/hyla/Wahabia.htm and http://al-islam.org/encyclopedia/chapter9/7.html are indicative of the polemical disputations being played out on the Internet.

Another Shiʻi website, al-baqee.org is used to protest a Saudi *fatwa* on the destruction of Shiʻi holy sites. Several Saudi *ʻulamaʼ* are named and cursed for having issued the decree. The website states,

> The Muslim community of America condemns the repeat-assault on the al-Askariyan shrines in Samara on June 13th 2007. The wounds inflicted by the first assault on February 22nd, 2006, when the golden dome of the shrine was demolished, have reopened. Nevertheless, a recent *fatwa* has been issued by the evil-minded muftis of Saudia and Kuwait, encouraging the so-called students of Islam to demolish the holy Muslim shrines in Iraq and Damascus.

Another Shiʻi site, al-islam.org, has digitized a wide range of Shiʻi texts, which are available on-line. Some of the sites are polemical and reflect the anti-Sunni works of Muhammad al-Tijani.[74]

While sectarian prejudices and pejorative remarks about the "Muslim other" are often rooted in the Middle East or South Asia, the Internet has made such rhetoric and feuds widely available to American audiences. Some imams often have recourse to such sites when they prepare the Friday sermons delivered on campuses or in American correctional facilities.

Shiʻi–Sunni Youth Interaction

Relations between Shiʻi and Sunni students on American campuses have indeed been influenced by sociopolitical events in the Middle East and other parts of the world. In this globalized world, radical students have used the campuses as recruiting grounds for their conservative ideologies.[75] Their influence has made the MSAs more conservative. Differences on campus are apparent not only between Sunni and Shiʻi students but, as Genieve Abdo has shown in her admirable work, more moderate Sunnis are often confronted by conservative students who are influenced by Wahhabi, Salafi, or Hizb al-Tahrir ideology.

These foreign-based movements believe that fellow Muslim students have gone astray. They insist on the headscarf for Muslim women, exclude Shiʻis and Sufis from participating in their events, and maintain that Muslims should not interact or dialogue with Jews and Christians.[76] Extremist ideas have proliferated and spread to the MSAs. Larry Poston, for example, notes that the MSA has published a wide range of literature reflecting the thoughts of fundamentalist ideologues like Sayyid Qutb and Mawdudi.[77]

The websites of students' associations provide a forum for Salafi propaganda, specifically in the West, and their websites are generated in universities, mainly in the United States, Britain, and Canada. For instance, the MSA at the University of Southern California has a page borrowed from the Department of Islamic Affairs of the Saudi Arabian embassy in Washington ("Understanding Islam and the Muslims," 2003). In 1999, the website of the MSA at the University of Houston carried a lengthy Q and A session with the Salafi Shaykh, al-Albani.[78]

The spread of radical ideas and sectarianism among some student bodies is epitomized by the example cited by Geneive Abdo. Farhan, a president of the MSA at the University of Michigan's Dearborn campus, revolutionized the association by making it more open, less conservative, and more inclusive: women without headscarves, Shi'is, and those with different opinions were all welcome. Farhan was vehemently opposed by many other students at the campus, especially by those who were affiliated to the Salafis and Hizb al-Tahrir. He was also attacked and beaten for his stance.[79]

Clashes have been reported between Muslim students—the Salafis and Wahhabis on the one hand, and more moderate voices on the other. Such frictions have sometimes led to the creation of parallel Muslim student bodies on campus. There were, for example, two Muslim student bodies at the University of Miami in the 1990s, both of them Sunni. The Wahhabis' rigid ideology and vitriolic attacks against the Shi'is have further segmented the Muslim student body. Many Shi'i students complain of enduring religious discrimination, of being barred from participating in MSA activities, and of Sunni imams reviling and mocking Shi'is in Friday sermons. Abbas Barzegar, a graduate student at the University of Colorado, reports of being told of an African American mosque in Texas on whose front door was posted a sign that read "No Shi'a Allowed."[80] In Denver, some Salafis dissuaded Sunnis from consuming lamb sacrificed at *eid aladha* (commemorating Abraham's intended sacrifice of Ishmael) if it had been slaughtered by a Shi'i.[81]

Although Muslims on campus have transcended ethnic differences, the historical Sunni–Shi'i divide continues to perpetuate rather than abate in American universities. Shi'i students complain that they are frequently alienated on university campuses because of their Shi'i affiliations. The meta-minority complex—a minority within a minority—means that Shi'i youth have had to contend not only with being Muslims in America but also with being Shiʻis in Sunni organizations. Even in Dearborn, where the Shiʻis are a majority, Shiʻi students have had to deal with the issue on college campuses. Shiʻi students have to defend both Islam (from non-Muslims) and Shiʻism from fellow Muslims. In the words of ʻAbbas Kanji, a Shiʻi youth in Chicago, "The liberal and non-practicing Sunnis do not really care about us being Shiʻi. However, the devout Sunnis ask lots of questions that we are not trained by our parents and *madaris* to answer. Hence, some Shiʻis just get put off by getting involved with MSAs because they do not need to deal with someone questioning their faith."[82]

For some Shiʻi students, their experience is different from their Sunni counterparts because of whom their role models are. Having the family rather than companions of the Prophet as role models and looking to them as paragons of social justice and equality gives the Shiʻis a strong basis for community activism. In essence, Shiʻi youth are constantly conjuring images of their role models as soldiers for justice and resistance to persecution, and this colors their activism both on and off campus. According to one Shiʻi youth, "We were born and raised in the era of post-revolution Iran and the Shiʻi resistance in Lebanon, these factors have had a major impact on many Shiʻi activists."

The unity that marked the MSA in the first fifteen years of its life was shattered with the onset of the Iranian Revolution. The coming to power of Ayatullah Khumayni, his expressed intent to export the revolution, and the subsequent Wahhabi refutations against and hostility to Shiʻism led to conflicts and confrontations between Sunnis and Shiʻis on many campuses.

It was against this background that the MSA split in two; most of its Sunni members regrouped under the MSA, while a much smaller number of Shiʻi students formed a new organization called the Muslim Student Association Persian-Speaking Group (MSA-PSG). The institution, which was founded by Mostafa Chamran in the 1970s, holds annual conventions.[83] The MSA-PSG has not been able to organize itself or conduct activities in the way that the MSA has done on campuses throughout America. In addition, the MSA-PSG is not established on most campuses; neither has it reached out to non-Persian Shiʻis on campus. The majority of the Shiʻis do not identify themselves with the MSA-PSG especially as it is reportedly affiliated to the regime in Iran.

Shiʻi students are disadvantaged as there is no Shiʻi equivalent of the MSA or ISNA. Within the Sunni community, these institutions have been instrumental in fostering national and international ties among Muslims of all national origins and ethnicities. At the MSA, a multicultural Islam is created as students encounter fellow Muslims outside their ethnic groups. These socially mobile youth are comfortable in any setting as long as it is ethnically diverse. ISNA, for example, helps individuals from different ethnic groups to meet at its conferences and encourages its members to associate with other ethnically defined Muslims. Such bodies have also acted as support groups for Sunni youth as they connect thousands of Muslims across America. For Shiʻi students, the absence of such institutions within the Shiʻi community and marginalization from Sunni student bodies means that many Shiʻi students feel alienated from the Muslim student community. The Shiʻi struggle, both against Sunnis and the non-Muslim world, has deeply affected Shiʻi youth in a way that makes them unique.

There are many instances of acrimonious relationships between Sunni and Shiʻi students. In February 2007, the *International Herald Tribune* ran a story highlighting the strenuous relationship on many campuses between Sunni and Shiʻi students. For example, in the late 1990s at UC Berkeley, the MSA prohibited Shiʻis from leading Friday prayers. Mohammed Husain, a former student and a Shiʻi, said that was only part of the problem. Some Sunni members also questioned whether Shiʻis were proper Muslims, and they contended that Shiʻis did not believe in the Qurʼan or the singular importance of the Prophet Muhammad.[84] It was only during his final year at Berkeley, 2004/5, that the group let Shiʻis occasionally lead prayers.

According to Zeinab Chami, a Shiʻi student at the University of Michigan, the Sunni-dominated MSA pushed through two clauses in the MSA's constitution that Shiʻi students objected to: the first being that the constitution is described as being derived from the Qurʼan, the *sunna*, and the Sunni schools of law (thus neglecting the Jaʻfari school of law). Second, the MSA also decided to add an article at the end of the constitution that stipulates that prayer must be led in the manner prescribed by one of the four major schools of Islamic jurisprudence: Hanafi, Hanbali, Maliki, or Shafiʻi. The language of this clause not only bans Shiʻis from leading prayers but also suggests that Jaʻfari is not an accepted school of Islamic law.

The MSA executive board refused to amend the constitution and essentially gave Shiʻis the option of starting a new organization. The Shiʻis started the Thaqalayn Muslim Association (TMA).[85] Although there was a great deal of tension initially, relations over time have improved. Chami adds, "I think the MSA was a bit uncomfortable with how successful the TMA has been. But *alhamdulillah*, they put on events together, and there is now even a Shi'i brother on the MSA board." As far as involvement in the MSA is concerned, Chami states,

> When everything in an organization runs a bit differently than your be-
> liefs, then it becomes difficult because Islam is the one thing we cannot
> compromise. I could never imagine myself passing out MSA pamphlets
> to people on campus that contained *hadith* in which I do not believe. I
> could never imagine representing Islam in any frame but the intellectual
> and philosophical frame the Imams set for us. I would have a real inner-
> conflict if there were no Shi'is near me and the MSA was my only Islamic
> outlet. Though I personally respect MSA and my Sunni brethren, we be-
> lieve differently, and there is no denying that.
>
> The unique thing about TMA is that we can have events that bring our
> perspective to the table. We can hold events for '*Ashura*' and *Arba'in* (mark-
> ing the fortieth day after the martyrdom of Husayn), and have lectures cel-
> ebrating our Imams and their principles. Though it is unfortunate that we
> had to split, it is a kind of a blessing because now there is a completely Shi'i
> vehicle on campus, and we are free to operate from that viewpoint.[86]

Shi'i students at other universities have also claimed that they face constant prejudice. At Johns Hopkins University in Baltimore, Salmah Y. Rizvi, a junior who stocked a reading room with Islamic texts, said the MSA told her to remove the books because too many of them were by Shi'i authors.[87] Abbas Kazimi, a graduate student at Harvard and a devout Shi'i of Pakistani descent, has seen the divide affect friendships. A few years ago, when he was living in Houston, Kazimi said a Sunni friend advised him not to attend congregational Friday prayers at a local mosque when the friend noticed Kazimi prayed in the traditional Shi'i manner, with his hands by his sides rather than folded on his stomach. According to Kazimi, the animosity has created a climate of intimidation in which many Shi'is are now uncomfortable praying in Sunni mosques, even in America. "There is a constant paranoia in your mind that people are looking whether your hands are down, and that you have a small rock or leaf in front of you," he said.[88]

Azmat Khan, a twenty-one-year-old senior and political science major at Rutgers University, said that she, like other Shi'is on campus, was sometimes asked whether she was a real Muslim. "To some extent, the minute you identify yourself as a Shiite, it ousts you," Khan said. "You feel marginalized."[89] On some campuses, Sunni students have told other students not to enroll in Islamic courses that are taught by Shi'i instructors.

The fragmentation of the Muslim student body and the altercations between Shi'is and Sunnis on many campuses has led to Shi'is establishing parallel student groups in some universities. In the 1990s, for example, Shi'i students at the University of Toronto, founded their own *ahl al-bayt* organization, holding services on campuses separately from Sunnis. Shi'is at all three campuses of the University of Toronto have now established the Thaqalayn Muslim Association.

In some university settings, the student body has felt the need to ease tensions between Sunni and Shi'i students. At UC Berkeley, some of the divisiveness has recently ended. A Shi'i is even on the student association's board. Trying to ease tensions, the president of the MSA at the Ann Arbor campus of the University of Michigan invited a prominent Shi'i cleric to speak as she did not want Shi'i students to feel alienated.[90] Not all campuses have been affected by such disputes. Some campuses like Georgetown University and Cornell University are considered to be oases of tolerance. At the University of Denver, Shi'is occupy prominent positions in the MSA and fully participate in all its activities.

Sectarian differences have also surfaced at the institutional level. A pamphlet issued by the Shi'i based Universal Muslim Association of America in 2004 underscores Wahhabi-Shi'i tensions across America.[91] The pamphlet states:

> CAIR, ISNA, ICNA, MSA and other such organizations simply function as the outposts for this very large Wahhabi empire. UMAA as the sole national organization of American Shi'a Muslims continues to promote its agenda of humanity and Islam in America. However, this organization is faced with a much more dangerous and well-financed global Wahhabi establishment which threatens the very survival of the Shi'is and other non-Wahhabi Muslims at every corner of life. Shi'as and other non-Wahhabi Muslims have nothing to fear from the Christians, Jews and followers of other non-Muslim faiths. The enemy, whether it is Al Qaeda or Taliban, it is within Islam. This enemy is the cause of all the deaths and destruction and by investing billions of petrodollars they have littered the landscape with an intolerant and exclusionary Wahhabi doctrine. Shi'as and other non-Wahhabi Muslims must build coalitions and collaborate to defend and uphold the exalted stature of Islam.[92]

UMAA also accuses CAIR of being a Wahhabi-sponsored institution:

> CAIR has also engaged in a deceptive effort to assert that the majority of American Muslims (i.e. 70 percent) favor Salafism, a polite term for Wahhabism, in their mosques. This claim confirms the charge made by critics of the Wahhabis that some 70 percent of American mosques are under Wahhabi influence. CAIR has also engaged in extensive campaigns of personal defamation and intimidation targeting dissenters against extremist control over Islam in America. Although its Islam is Wahhabi, CAIR pretends to represent all Muslims in their relations with America as if practicing religious diplomacy. . . . Also, CAIR never criticizes the regimes of Jordan, Egypt and the Gulf States for their malicious and non-stop campaign of terror towards the Shia Muslims. Nor does CAIR in their numerous communiqués ever utter a word against Abu Musab Alzarqawi (an avowed enemy of the Shias), Ansar Al Sunna or Sipahe Sahaba for their systematic genocide of Shias in Iraq, Afghanistan and Pakistan.[93]

In essence, UMAA has challenged CAIR's claims to speak on behalf of all Muslims. As is evident from the above excerpt, CAIR is accused of being indifferent to the plight of Shi'is, both in America and abroad. Such vehement criticisms of CAIR by a major Shi'i institution indicate that sectarian tensions are not confined to campuses, mosques, and correctional facilities. On the contrary, such tensions are present between major Shi'i and Sunni institutions.

Sunni Shi'is Tensions in Correctional Facilities

An increasing number of African Americans in prisons are converting to Shi'ism. For various reasons, tensions between these African American Sunnis and Shi'is are felt most acutely in correctional facilities. A major challenge reported almost unanimously by Shi'i inmates is that they encounter widespread discrimination and pressure to renounce their faith. Inmates complain that Shi'i books, which are kept in prison libraries, have been removed by Sunni inmates. The acrimony between the two groups has often led to physical confrontation within the correctional facilities and to some inmates being placed in isolation. Some have even reported attempts to kill Shi'i inmates. Between November 2001 and February 2002, four Shi'is were reportedly attacked by Sunni inmates at the Great Meadow Correctional Facilities in upstate New York.

The following are excerpts from letters I received from some Shi'i in-mates. They are indicative of the sectarian tensions within the prison system.

Karim A. R. Talib   CAMP HILL

I had to "uncover" (*taqiyya*) in this prison. As soon as I did, I was handed a booklet printed by Saudi Arabia, "Shee'ah and the Muslims." I refute every page in the book.

A Shi'i inmate at ORLEANS

Here they fight against the *ahlul bayt*. The Islamic chaplain ig-nites this discourse. He begins with tapes by Bilal Philips bash-ing us Shi'as. When I first arrived here he expressed to me that the masjid is Ahlul Sunni and praying on stones is not permit-ted in the masjid.

A Shi'i inmate at ELMIRA writes:

I should note, that at the time I converted to Shia Islam, I was the wazir of Shunta for the Muslim community at Green Haven Correctional Facility. I was immediately relieved of my duties and suspended from all masjid activities. I was not even per-mitted to attend services on Fridays. An even greater problem arose when I informed my [practicing Sunni] family of my conversion to Shia. My wife left me and neither my sisters or brother in laws will speak to me.

There have been physical battles as well such as the time I was attacked by two Sunni Muslims.

Frankie Ali Cancel at FISHKILL

We were holding a few Shia study groups here, but when the Wahhabi influenced chaplain found out he told us that we could use a room next to the masjid; however, only us Shias could attend it and we cannot have other people or brothers attend. When a lot of Sunni brothers began to show interest in our study group, we were barred from utilizing the masjid or any other room for studying purposes. According to him and his underlings the only Islam that will be discussed and taught here is the form of Islam that they teach. We were told to ei-ther study what they teach or don't study at all. . . .I was going only for Ju'mah services, but after a few anti-Shia *khutbas* I was deeply offended. . . . Those *khutbas* were what made me file such complaints.

An Internet site has interviewed a number of former and current Shi'i inmates, and has documented the challenges they encounter both inside and outside the prison system.

Among the comments recorded include the following:

"Sunnis claim they have the right to kill us (Shi'is) because we are misrepresenting Islam."

"[They] hide our books as they don't want their followers to read them."

"Sunnis are not allowed to speak to homosexuals or Shi'is."

"A religious change paper has to be registered for all Shi'is. It is as if Shi'ism was a different religion. Why don't Sunnis have to fill a religious change paper?"[94]

A major complaint by Shi'i inmates is that Muslim chaplains are often influenced by Wahhabi ideology. Within the prison facilities, Wahhabi-influenced chaplains denigrate Shi'ism in their sermons, calling it a Jewish-inspired heretical movement. According to Shi'i inmates, some of the Wahhabi imams reportedly encourage the persecution of Black Shi'is.[95]

Shaheed 'Abd al-Rahman, another Shi'i inmate states, "I have been in prison for twenty years and for fifteen years as a Shia Muslim. It is hard to create a picture for you to see the hell I had to endure so that I may practice my faith. Even now, the Wahhabi chaplains and prison officials are trying to keep me quiet and prevent me from making my brothers and sisters aware of what's going on with me."[96] 'Abd al-Rahman complains he has been repeatedly beaten both by Sunni inmates and prison officials for advocating his cause. Prison officials punished him for filing grievance concerning the rights of Shi'i inmates.

'Abd al-Rahman states that he was asked to keep away from Shi'i inmates when he first went to Attica Correctional Facility. This made him more curious about Shi'ism. Later, he announced to everyone that he had become a Shi'i. Subsequently, he filed a civil rights complaint under the First and Fourteenth Amendment of the U.S. Constitution arguing that the Department of Correctional Facilities (DOCS) has established Sunni Islam as the official doctrine of Islam and denied Shi'i Muslims a chance to practice their faith.[97]

Frankie Cancel, who was an inmate at Fishkill Correctional Facility in New York State, complained that the Sunni chaplain in the facility did not permit the study of or recognize differences between sects of Islam and routinely labeled Shi'is as infidels, hypocrites, and satanic worshipers to shame them into converting to Sunni Islam.[98] Due to their conversion, Shi'i inmates lose the brotherhood and fraternity that other Muslim inmates enjoy, especially as they do not and sometimes cannot partake in the religious services offered by the Muslim chaplain.

Shi'i inmates also complain that anti-Shi'i material is widely disseminated in the correctional facilities. Anti-Shi'i literature such as *Khutut al-Areedha* and *Up from Shiism* has been widely distributed in America.[99] Another Shi'i inmate, Anthony Cook, complained that in 1999 at the Great Meadow prison, the chaplain distributed literature that condemned Shi'is as charlatans, reeking with the stench of chicken-heartedness, insincerity, greed, cowardice, and equivocation. Cook was later placed in protective custody after warnings that his life was in danger from other Muslims.[100]

Allegations of harassment and discrimination are further corroborated from the letters I received from Shi'i inmates. Most of them complained that they suffered some form of discrimination; many were either verbally or physically assaulted by Sunni inmates. Others also complained that only Sunni books are kept in the prison libraries. Many Muslim chaplains in New York's prisons were recruited by Warith Deen 'Umar who, under Saudi patronage, introduced Saudi ideology in the prisons. An article published in the February 5, 2003, issue of the *Wall Street Journal* states that 'Umar, who studied in Saudi Arabia at the government's expense, sees the 9/11 hijackers as martyrs. 'Umar who followed Louis Farrakhan at one point, has been preaching Wahhabism in prisons for more than twenty years.[101]

According to an article that appeared in the *New York Sun* in November 2007, the state's 7,987 Muslim inmates have been increasingly identifying as either Sunni or Shi'i, a phenomenon that prison chaplains elsewhere report is most pronounced in New York. The article further maintains that

Shiite inmates, who make up less than 4% of the Muslims incarcerated in the state, have long reported religious persecution by the Sunni-dominated Muslim chaplaincy employed by the state. The Sunni-Shiite divide has played a role in at least one stabbing between inmates in 2004, e-mails by prison officials show. Shiite inmates have long demanded their own chaplains and a separate place to pray on Fridays, apart from other Muslim inmates. A little-noticed federal court ruling improves the prospects that Shiite inmates will see their demands met. A recent ruling by the 2nd U.S. Circuit Court of Appeals opens the way for a trial in which jurors will weigh the demands of Shiite inmates seeking a separate Friday prayer service against the staffing and logistical concerns of prison officials. The court ruling overturns a court decision by a federal judge in Syracuse, Paul Magnuson, who ruled last year that Shiite Muslims could either pray individually from their cells or join the general Muslim service, which Shiite inmates say is Sunni-dominated. The 2nd Circuit's decision asks Judge Magnuson to look closer at whether joint prayer with Sunnis impinges on Shiite beliefs and at the prison system's capacity to accommodate separate prayer services.[102]

The letters I quoted are a small representation of the complaints received in my correspondence with Shiʻi inmates. Most of the inmates state that their lives are threatened more by Sunni than by non-Muslim inmates. Paradoxically, when African American Sunnis have demonstrated that they have not received the same treatment as other religious groups in prison, the courts have, generally speaking, upheld and protected their constitutional claims to religious freedom.[103] However, these inmates have denied Shiʻis the identical rights that they claim for themselves, i.e., to practice Islam according to their tenets. In many instances, Shiʻi inmates have been discriminated against in the same facilities where Sunnis demanded their rights. At Green Haven Correctional Facility (also in New York State), for example, inmate Brown charged that prison officials discriminated against him and his coreligionists by prohibiting religious services, spiritual advice, and administration from recognized clergy of the Islamic faith.[104] Paradoxically, Shiʻis have experienced discrimination at the same facility.

There are few correctional facilities that offer classes catering to the needs of the Shiʻis. Increasingly, these inmates now demand lectures that reflect their own faith and the right to perform rituals according to Shiʻi law. Despite voicing their complaints, they are not allowed to observe Shiʻi practices and holidays (like ʻ*Ashura*ʼ and Ghadir) in the prisons. In fact, they complain that the U.S. Department of Correctional Facilities is engaged in institutionalized discrimination against Shiʻis. Such tensions are not confined between Sunni and Shi'i inmates. They are also evident between Sunni Muslims and members of the Nation of Islam.[105]

It is important to bear in mind that the demands by Shi'i inmates for separate classes and recognition of their distinct needs is rooted in the fundamental differences between Shi'i law and the Sunni *madhahib* (schools of law). In many instances, Shi'i law is more strict. In the case of dietary laws, for example, Shi'i law demands that the animal be slaughtered in accordance with strictly prescribed rules: the animal be made to face Mecca, the *basmala* be recited,[106] and certain veins be slit. Some Sunni schools, on the other hand, state that if the *basmala* is recited before eating, the meat can be consumed regardless of how the animal was slaughtered. Shi'i law also differs from Sunni law regarding the timings for breaking the fast, the times of morning and evening prayers, and whether the afternoon and evening prayers can be combined. Such legal differences mean that Shi'i requirements will often differ from those demanded by Sunni inmates.

The Case of Frankie Cancel

In 1999, Frankie Cancel, a Hispanic convert to Shi'ism, complained that the Sunni chaplain at Fishkill correctional facility did not permit the study of or recognize sectarian differences and routinely denigrated and insulted the Shi'is.[107] He filed a grievance with prison officials alleging that the only Islamic services provided within the facility were those that were affiliated to Sunnism. Cancel filed an Article 78 proceeding challenging the denial of his grievance. He claimed that there were significant differences between Shi'i Muslims and the sect that official DOCS chaplains are associated with, the Sunni Muslims.

Cancel alleged that the Shi'is at his correctional facility were not allowed to have religious study groups or classes in which their beliefs and methods of prayer are taught, nor were they able to observe religious holidays because their holidays were not recognized by Muslim chaplains. Cancel also submitted an affidavit from the Education Assistant to an imam familiar with Shi'i practices. He argued that DOCS' refusal to accommodate the Shi'is violated its own Directive 4202. This directive provides, in part, that

> It is the intent of the Department to extend to inmates as much spiritual
> assistance as possible as well as to provide as many opportunities as fea-
> sible for the practice of their chosen faiths consistent with the safe and

secure operations of the Department's correctional facilities. If a chaplain or an outside religious volunteer is not available to serve the spiritual needs of a group of inmates of a known religious faith, the facility Superintendent, in consultation with the Director of Ministerial and Family Services, may authorize the inmates to participate in a religious education class or study group.

Cancel further alleged that Sunni faith and practices were inconsistent with his own, and that the Sunni imam did not permit the recognition of different Islamic sects. Cancel requested that a Shi'i clergy or registered volunteers be allowed to enter the prison and lead separate Shi'i services and discussion groups.

DOCS denied the grievance on the basis that it was "advised by the Department's imam (himself a Sunni) that all Muslim religious groups fall under Islam," and that "[a]ll practice the same faith and should not be separated, as the grievant suggests." Cancel filed a petition requesting the relief contained in his grievance. The Supreme Court granted the petition, and DOCS appealed to the Second Department. In affirming the decision of the Supreme Court, the Second Department made specific reference to Correction Law 610, that all prisoners in New York State "have the right to the free exercise of religion without discrimination or preference" and that regulations "shall recognize the right of the inmates to the free exercise of their religious belief, and to worship God according to the dictates of their consciences."

Reviewing the proof submitted by the parties, the Court concluded that the differences between Shi'i and Sunni practices warranted the relief requested. It opined that

> the differences between the historical and doctrinal beliefs, as well as the religious practices, of the two groups are significant. The nature of these differences mandates the conclusion that DOCS' determination that the spiritual needs of the inmates of the Shi'i Muslim faith can be met in religious services led by chaplains of the Sunni Muslim faith is arbitrary and capricious. (DOCS') determination is contrary to the objectives of DOCS Directive 4202 and the 1st Amendment right of religious liberty upon which it is based.

The Court also took note that Cancel's petition was denied based on the opinion of the imam, the very individual alleged to be guilty of religious discrimination. This did not provide a rational basis for the denial of the grievance. Furthermore, the Court found it "readily apparent" that the petitioner's spiritual needs had not been met, given the significant doctrinal differences between the two Muslim sects, and the denial of the grievance was therefore arbitrary and capricious, and in violation of Correction Law 610. However, the Court did make an express point that an inmate's religious freedom within a correctional facility was not absolute, and must be balanced against the facility's penological interests.[108]

In essence, DOCS was ordered to accommodate the religious practices of Shi'i inmates in Fishkill. As a result of the Cancel case, DOCS has tried to increase Shi'i inmate access to its sanctioned religious services and classes. It has also issued specific guidelines to accommodate the needs of Shi'i inmates in a Protocol for Shi'i Muslims Programs and Practices dated October 26, 2001. Article II of the document states,

> The Department will endeavor to consult with ecclesiastical authorities on Shi'ite Islam in the community at large (including but not limited to, individual Shi'ite Muslim scholars and clergy and Shi'ite Muslim organizations) for purposes of obtaining advice and guidance in the Department's efforts to reasonably accommodate the religious needs of its Shi'ite Muslim inmates. . . . The Department also expects to obtain guidance and recommendations from these outside ecclesiastical authorities with respect to the hiring of employee Shi'ite Muslim Chaplains.

Article IV of the same document states,

> Shi'ite Muslim Chaplains, whether they be employees or outside volunteers shall be entitled to officiate at the weekly Juma services in the same manner as any other Muslim chaplain or outside volunteer Chaplains. In any facility in which Shi'ite Muslim inmates are present in the general population, the Muslim Chaplain of that facility shall ensure that the Muslim Majlis shall have at least one Shi'ite Muslim member.

By 2002, DOCS had made some effort to give Shi'is equal opportunity and access to services and chaplains. However, a prominent Shi'i institute in New York, al-Khoei Foundation, expressed major reservations with DOCS' claims to have accommodated the needs of Shi'i inmates. A statement in its September 2001 publication, *al-Huda*, reads,

At the meeting of April 19 2001, with New York State Department of Correction's (DOCS) representative (cited in *Al-Huda* of Rabiul Awwal 1422 p.11), the question of appointment of Shi'a chaplain with full rights, authorities and respect as any other Muslim Chaplain was raised and stressed by The Center as the first step toward meeting the needs of the Shi'a inmates.[109]

The article stresses that among the forty-nine Muslim chaplains, not one was Shi'i. Al-Khoei Foundation insisted that it did not want mere volunteers who had no authority, were not paid by DOCS, and who had very limited roles.[110] The Cancel case was to have major ramifications in the prison system. Encouraged by the outcome of his petition, other Shi'i inmates sought to have Shi'ism recognized as an independent school of thought.

Since they are a minority and have, in the past, been depicted as the dissenters, it is the Shi'is in America who have felt the sectarian tensions most. Whether in correctional facilities, in mosques, or on campuses, they have been derided because of their faith and practices and have often been excluded from active participation in Sunni institutions.

Sunni–Shi'i Concordance in America

Leaders of Sunni and Shi'i communities have been alarmed at the escalating tensions. Some have voiced concerns that such tensions could escalate to sectarian violence on American streets. Many Muslims have realized that they need to defy the divisive policies of fundamentalist groups and to work toward religious reconciliation so as to establish harmonious relationships, which Islam mandates. Leaders from both groups have sought to bring the communities together and to unite the American Muslim community. After the golden dome in Samarra was bombed on February 22, 2006, some Sunni imams condemned the attacks and even volunteered to have fundraisers to rebuild the Samarra shrine. After Shi'i mosques and businesses were vandalized, Sunni and Shi'i leaders worked to repair their ties. The Council on American-Islamic Relations (CAIR) invited Sunni and Shi'i 'ulama' to meet in the presence of the media. Both groups condemned the bombing and the escalating violence.

Muslims in some American cities have held intrafaith dialogue to dispel some of the misunderstanding many members of the community have about each other. Sunni–Shi'i conferences have been held in which members of both communities are invited to participate. Although he is a Shi'i, imam Mustafa al-Qazwini of Los Angeles interacts regularly with Sunni imams. Al-Qazwini is a member of the *shura* council, which is composed of imams from both Sunni and Shi'i mosques, and he sometimes invites Sunni imams to speak at Shi'i events in his mosque in Orange County, California.[111] In March 2008, his center, the Islamic Educational Center of Orange County, held its third annual Shia–Sunni symposium. In Detroit, Shi'i and Sunni imams meet every month to discuss issues that impact American Muslims.[112]

In 2006, Sunni institutions like MPAC and CAIR condemned attacks against Shi'is participating in '*Ashura*' commemorations in Iraq and Pakistan, which killed nearly two hundred people. Such statements have mollified Shi'is who looked forward to Sunni condemnation against sectarian violence.

The need to bring the two communities closer has been felt in different parts of the Muslim world. In June 2008, Saudi Arabia's King Abdullah urged Muslims to speak with one voice in preparation for an interfaith dialogue with the Jewish and Christian worlds. The king entered the conference hall alongside ex-Iranian president Ali Akbar Hashemi Rafsanjani, who sat beside him on the stage. In his address, the king stated that extremism was a challenge to Islam that targeted the "magnanimity, fairness, and lofty aims" of the religion. Rafsanjani said that Saudi Arabia "presented a great message to all humanity in the world" and appealed for Shia–Sunni dialogue and mutual support.[113]

The Fatwa *of Ayatullah Fadlallah*

Shi'i religious leaders in America and abroad have been concerned at the possible ramifications of sectarian conflict. Messages of reconciliation have come from the Shi'i *maraji'* too. Recognizing one of the major points of tension, in 2006 Ayatullah Fadlallah issued a *fatwa* prohibiting Shi'is from insulting the Prophets' companions or abusing them under any circumstance. The Ayatullah was proscribing a well-known Shi'i practice, one that has been responsible for inciting sectarian tensions, since abusing the companions has remained one of the most sensitive issues that has caused major conflicts between Sunnis and Shi'is. By issuing this *fatwa*, Fadlallah was making significant progress in preventing strife on the one hand and unifying the Muslims on the other.[114] Religious leaders in both communities in the United States also sensed the need for reconciliation.

For example, in 2007 in Southern California, leaders launched a nation-wide movement to promote unity among different branches of the faith and to help prevent acts of violence here. In a ceremony that was later repeated in Detroit and at the ISNA conference in Chicago in 2007, Sunni and Shi'i religious scholars in Southern California signed a "code of honor" that offers strategies for overcoming and avoiding divisions within the community.

The local reconciliation effort, which began with a February 2006 meeting at the Muslim Public Affairs Council's office in Los Angeles, was prompted by spiraling violence in Iraq and several incidents of vandalism in Michigan. The code of conduct urges Muslims to be tolerant of one another's prayer traditions and also to respect the manner of worship of the majority in a given mosque.

Among the provisions of the code are:
- No group or individual should use, spread or tolerate the rhetoric of *takfir*[115] regarding anyone who believes in the oneness and supremacy of God, the role of Muhammad as divine messenger and the authenticity of the Koran, the Muslim holy book.
- Muslims should respect one another and the people, places and events that any Muslim group or individual reveres, even when they disagree about the relative importance of such people and events.
- Objective, scholarly study groups should be formed to examine Muslim history, creed and law, to further knowledge and aid reconciliation. If problems arise, a joint body of Muslim scholars from both Shiite and Sunni traditions should be consulted.
- Finally, Muslims in the United States should work to emphasize their commonality.[116]

The code also opposes the circulation of literature that incites sectarian hatred, and declares the intention to have balanced and objective discussions to encourage dialogue between Sunni and Shi'i scholars and to promote understanding.[117]

Although the code marks a milestone in that it acknowledges and accepts Shi'is as an integral part of the American Muslim community, its significance remains symbolic as it is not religiously binding (it is not a *fatwa*) and has not been endorsed by most Islamic centers in America. Few imams have mentioned it in their sermons. Surprisingly, neither Sunni nor Shi'i *'ulama'* abroad have endorsed it. The articles mentioned in the code are in the form of general recommendations and do not suggest any remedial action to counteract the vitriolic sectarian attacks I described above. It would not be an exaggeration to state that most Muslims in America have not even heard of the code of honor.

Since 2005, there have been many instances of Sunni and Shi'i calls for unity among Muslims, which have come from imams, Muslim teachers, mosque administrators, and journalists. In an article published by a national Muslim newsletter *The Muslim Observer*, imam al-Hajj Abdullah Bey El-Amin states:

> It makes no sense to interact with peoples of other faiths while refusing to acknowledge a fellow Muslim who happens to adhere to a different "school of thought." This insane behavior is on both sides of the fence. Shias are just as full-headed as Sunnis.
>
> In Detroit, much progress has been made in Sunni-Shia cooperation. Years ago we hosted what we believe was the first Sunni-Shia symposium of its kind. Many scholars from both "camps" participated and showed the world the true feelings most Muslims hold about this issue. It was hosted by a Sunni council and held at a Shia mosque.[118]

A Minority within a Minority

Scholars of Islam tend to pursue a binary analysis of Muslims in America, seeing the conflict only between non-Muslims and Muslims. However, such a trajectory misses the point completely. It ignores the nuances that exist within the Muslim community and the pressure Shi'is have felt to conform to both American and Sunni norms. Bruce Lawrence correctly points out that there is more to minority than prejudgment about race and class differences; it is a word that denotes lesser in numbers but it also entails lesser in terms of access, power, and privilege in the public sphere.[119]

When most Shi'is began migrating here in the 1980s, sectarian tension had just begun. Immigrant Shi'is resorted to building institutes that would provide basic services to community members, but they also sought to protect their youth from Western influences and Wahhabi ideology. There were no national Shi'i organizations or outreach institutions. Up to that time, relations between the Sunnis and Shi'is in America had been very amicable, with little or no sign of the sectarian division that was soon to plague the American Muslim community. Since Shi'is had fully participated in Sunni institutions like the Federation of Islamic Association (FIA) and MSA, they did not feel the need to establish their own, independent organizations. Until the early 1980s, it was the Islamic rather than the sectarian identity that had been promoted by both groups.

At the same time, the burgeoning Sunni community was beginning to build a number of mosques and other institutes. Various Muslim bodies were established in the 1980s, almost all of them by the Sunni community. By the late 1980s, the MSA had helped create branches on college campuses throughout the United States. In 1981, the MSA founded the Islamic Society of North America (ISNA). Soon, other immigrant organizations, such as the Islamic Circle of North America (ICNA) and the Islamic Association of North America (IANA) were established.

In 1988 the Muslim Public Affairs Council (MPAC) was founded by the multiethnic Islamic center of South California in Los Angeles. This political lobby has made important contributions in the last few years. In 1989, the American Muslim Alliance (AMA) was established in Northern California by a political scientist of Pakistani origin. On the East Coast, the American Muslim Council (AMC) was founded in 1990 in Washington, D.C. The AMC has established relations with various branches of the government. At the national level, the Council on American-Islamic Relations (CAIR), which was established in June 1994, has challenged the misrepresentation and defamation of Islam and Muslims in the workplace. Since 1996, CAIR has issued an annual report documenting incidents of anti-Muslim discrimination and violence.[120]

Although they claim to represent the American Muslim community, most of these institutions exclude Shiʻis from participating on their boards and do not condemn the anti-Shiʻi literature sold in Islamic bookstores or the sectarian sermons delivered in some mosques and correctional facilities. The increasing anti-Shiʻi literature and sectarian prejudices that were imported during this period meant that Sunni organizations were transitioning from being inclusivist to becoming exclusivist institutes. Shiʻis, who until recently were considered brothers in faith, were now denounced by some groups as heretics. They were gradually excluded from leadership positions in Sunni institutes and emerging MSA chapters on campuses.

With the increasing dissemination of fundamentalist ideology, the influx of foreign-based movements and immigrant communities, the Muslim community began to fragment along sectarian lines in the 1980s. Gradually, the bifurcation of the Muslim community was felt in mosques, on campuses, in prisons, and later on, over the Internet. To be sure, it was not only the Shiʻis that the fundamentalists targeted. Based on their bipolar understanding of Islamic revelation, any person who did not conform to their worldview was not considered a proper Muslim. The Sufis, Ahmadis, Nation of Islam, and all other indigenous African American movements would be included in this category.

Since they were a minority within the Muslim minority, Shiʻis had fewer resources, institutions, and, most importantly, access to power and influence in the public sphere. Henceforth, it was the Sunnis who defined and represented Islam in America. At the time when Sunnis claimed to speak on behalf of all American Muslims, the Wahhabis, an increasingly influential voice within the American Muslim community, were declaring Shiʻis to be infidels. Henceforth, Shiʻis were excluded from participating in many Sunni institutions.

The tendency to see American Islam through Sunni lens is evident in academic circles too. Most scholars who have studied Islam in America have done so from the majority, Sunni perspective. In the preface to Vernon Schubel's work *Religious Performance in Contemporary Islam*, the series editor Fred Denny echoes similar sentiments. Denny states,

> Islamic studies in the West and in the greater part of the Islamic world itself have long shared a bias that Sunni Islam is the normative tradition, whereas Shiʻism is at best heterodoxy and at worst heresy. In fact Shiʻism is earlier than Sunnism in its main and enduring emphases, which center in allegiance to ʻAli and through him the Prophet Muhammad and Allah. Sunni Islam developed over a long period, drawing from politically dominant, centrist tendencies and movements within the Umayyad and Abbasid caliphates. But the winners get to write the history books. So, the eventual Sunni hegemony over much of the Dar al-Islam by the second and third centuries after the Hijra read its own prefoundations as having been normative all along. This myth of the silent center has given Sunnis a sense of being heirs to a providential dispensation in ruling most Muslim domains, even where, as in Iraq and Lebanon, Shiʻites comprise a major part of the population.[121]

The tendency of scholars of Islam to look at issues in the Islamic world from the majority Sunni perspective is also evident in Omid Safi's *Progressive Muslims*. The book, authored by a number of Muslim scholars, aimed to bring about changes in the community in order to "implement the vision of justice and goodness and beauty that is rooted in the Qurʼan."[122]

Published after the attacks of September 11, 2001, *Progressive Muslims* tackles a number of topics that are germane to the global Muslim community, including Islamic fundamentalism, pluralism in the Islamic tradition, gender related issues, and homosexuality in the Islamic tradition. Yet, there is not a single chapter that deals with Shi'ism or an acknowledgement of the sectarian dilemma with Sunnis.

If the concern of the authors is to expose human rights violations in Muslim countries and to embrace a different vision of Islam than that offered by the Wahhabi and neo-Wahhabi groups, then one might think that a chapter on the Shi'i vision would be of great relevance, especially in a post-9/11 world.[123] Arguably, Shi'i scholars in Iran have done most to exercise *ijtihad* and to bring about reformation in the modern era. Shi'i scholars like Muhaqqiq Damad, Taskhiri, and Shabistari have claimed that while the Qur'an is a fixed text, the interpretive applications of its revelations can vary with the changing realities of history. Thus, these jurists have reinterpreted and restated Islamic law, invoking various hermeneutical principles to respond to the needs of the times. They have also maintained that Muslim scholars must articulate a theory of human rights that will incorporate notions of dignity, freedom of conscience, rights of minorities, and gender equality based on the notion of universal moral values as articulated by the Qur'an.[124]

Sunni domination and representation of American Islam is visible in other domains. When the State Department or the media want to talk to Muslims, in most cases it is to the Sunni institutions and mosques that they turn. Likewise, Sunni centers tend to have more access to the media than Shi'is do. When the press reports that American Muslims offer special night prayers in Ramadhan (called *tarawih*), the average non-Muslim reader or viewer naturally assumes that Shi'is offer these prayers too. In fact, Shi'is do not offer the *tarawih* since they maintain it was a *bid'a* introduced by 'Umar, the second caliph. When a newscast reports that a Muslim can divorce his wife by reciting the "triple divorce" statement, it is referring to a distinctly Sunni practice, one that Shi'is reject.

This has been the Shi'i dilemma of minority-ness in America. Not only have the Sunnis represented Muslims, Sunni practices have been assumed to be normative, embracing all Muslims, whether Shi'is accept them or not. It is the Sunnis who speak on behalf of the Muslim community. Not only have the Shi'is been subsumed, they have been presumed to speak the language of the majority Sunnis. Shi'i voices have been drowned by Sunni ones. During the course of the twentieth century, Shi'is have learned that being a minority means, at least in the American context, being the invisible other within the other.

Conclusion

Shi'i categorization as the "other" in America is, of course, correct. Yet it is only partially correct because they are the other within the other. Shi'is have the challenge of not only negotiating American culture but also of safeguarding their beliefs and praxis against Sunni (primarily Wahhabi-Salafi) attacks. On the one hand, there is pressure to assimilate and acculturate in a pluralistic socioreligious ambience. Yet there is concurrent pressure exerted by the majority Sunni community who question the very validity of Shi'i beliefs and practices. In fact, in this country Shi'is tend to be more fearful of the attacks from fellow Muslims than from the cultural impingement of non-Muslims. Arguably, the first challenge is the most potent one since it threatens to destroy the very fabric of Shi'i beliefs and practices.

In the early part of the twentieth century, Shi'is and Sunnis were far more connected and integrated than they are now. The two groups are now not only disconnected but, in some cases, exhibit much hostility and animosity toward each other. Sunnis and Shi'is complain of continuous discrimination in post–9/11 America, yet they continue to discriminate and denigrate each other. These conflicts are not confined to one realm; rather, they are apparent in all spheres of American society. They are seen in the mosques, between institutions, on campuses, on the Internet, in correctional facilities, and even at work places.

Shi'is and Sunnis in America are in the same struggle yet they do not share it. Each group continues to define itself against rather than with each other; they emphasize theological disconnectedness rather than their common grounds. This is reflected in their discourses, the literature disseminated and sermons delivered in the centers, in the MSAs, the correctional facilities, and in their refusal to come together to resolve issues affecting the American Muslim community. Both groups need to accept the American experience as a primary challenge in shaping their common Islamic identity. Instead, more often than not, it is their separate sectarian identity that shapes their world views in America as each group insists on perpetuating its historical prejudices against the other.

4

Shi'i Leadership and America

An important aspect of American Shi'ism is how members of the community have drawn upon their religious leaders, who are based in the Middle East, to shape and guide their religious and sociopolitical lives in America. The Shi'i leadership is predicated on a highly stratified hierarchical system called the *marji' al-taqlid,* or *marji'iyya.* The term refers to the most learned juridical authority in the Shi'i community whose rulings on Islamic law are followed by those who acknowledge him as their source of reference or *marji'.* The followers base their religious practices in accordance with his judicial opinions. The *marji'* is required to demonstrate mastery in various disciplines of Islamic religious sciences and must be of upright conduct. He is also responsible for reinterpreting the relevance of Islamic laws to the modern era, and is imbued with the authority to issue religious edicts, thereby empowering him to influence the religious and social lives of his followers all over the world.

The process of following the juridical edicts of the most learned jurist (*a'lam*) is called *taqlid* (literally imitation or emulation).[1] In Shi'i jurisprudence, *taqlid* denotes a commitment to accept and act in accordance with the rulings of the *shari'a* as deduced by a qualified and pious jurist. *Taqlid* also suggests that ordinary Shi'is adopt the rulings of a jurist without having to investigate the reasons that led the jurist to make his decisions. Stated differently, *taqlid* generates confidence in the believers that their religious practices, which are based on the juridical pronouncements of the *maraji'* (pl. of *marji'*), approximate the will of God.

The concept of *marji' al-taqlid* is a corollary to the rational necessity to consult those who are experts in matters pertaining to juridical ordinances. In Shi'ism, acting upon the religious pronouncements of a *marji'* is an obligation imposed on all adherents of the faith. Hence, matters pertaining to religious practices are defined and regulated by the *maraji'* who become a source of reference on all religious issues.[2] The importance of following a *marji'* is underscored by Ayatullah Seestani, who is recognized by many Shi'is as the most learned jurist of our time. In the chapter on *taqlid*, he states in his juridical treatise, "In matters of religious laws, apart from the ones clearly defined, or ones which are indisputable, a person must:

- Either be a *mujtahid* (jurist) himself, capable of inferring and deducing from the religious sources and evidence;
- or if he is not a *mujtahid* himself, he should follow one, i.e., he should act according to the verdicts (*fatawa*) of the *mujtahid*;
- or if he is neither a *mujtahid* nor a follower (*muqallid*), he should act on such precaution which should assure him that he has fulfilled his religious obligation. For example, if some *mujtahids* consider an act to be *haram* (prohibited), while others say that it is not, he should not perform that act. Similarly, if some *mujtahids* consider an act to be obligatory (*wajib*) while others consider it to be recommended (*mustahab*), he should perform it. Therefore, it is obligatory upon those persons who are neither *mujtahids*, nor able to act on precautionary measures (*ihtiyat*), to follow a *mujtahid*."[3]

According to Seestani, religious acts performed without following a *mujtahid* could be rendered void: if a person performs his acts without the *taqlid* of a *mujtahid* and later follows a *mujtahid*, his former actions will be valid [only] if that *mujtahid* declares them to be valid, otherwise, they will be treated as void.[4] In effect, according to Seestani, it is the *mujtahid* who can determine whether a person's acts are valid or not if she or he has not followed a *marji'* before. Historically, the first scholar to explicitly rule that the practice of a Shi'i layperson was invalid if that person did not follow a *mujtahid* or observed prudence was Ayatullah Muhammad Kazim Yazdi (d. 1919). He stated that *taqlid* was obligatory on all Muslims and that the acts of one who did not observe it were invalid.[5]

The institution of the *marji'iyya* has created a sense of loyalty between the *marji'* and one who accepts to follow him, the *muqallid*. This sense of loyalty to the *marji'* is rationalized through a juridical prescription of an ordinary believer to declare her or his intention to follow the *mujtahid* through *taqlid*. The requirement to follow the well-defined and structured religious leadership of the *maraji'* (the religious authority located in the Middle East), dictates the demeanor of the followers in America. The *taqlid* factor has required American Shi'is to be allied with the *maraji'* rather than to any foreign government. It has also acted as a catalyst for unity in the Shi'i community in America by fostering ties among different Shi'is who have often been divided by cultural, ethnic, and linguistic considerations.

There are quite a few *maraji'* who are considered as sources of reference. These include figures like Ayatullahs 'Ali Seestani, Hussein Waheed Khorasani, Lutfallah Safi Gulpaygani, Taqi Behjat, Nasir Makarim Shirazi, Khamene'i, and Mohammed Hussein Fadlallah.

The Influence of the Maraji' *in America*

The obligation to follow the religious dictates of the *marji'* has meant that the interpretations and pronouncements of the *maraji'*, formulated in the Muslim lands, are seen as both normative and binding on their followers. Such a structured system of religious leadership and imitation of the most learned is lacking in Sunni Islam where there is no recognized clergyhood that can claim sole monopoly of the interpretation of religious texts. Due to the pervasive influence of the *maraji'*, there is no Shi'i equivalent of a Fiqh Council or group of religious scholars that could interpret legal issues in the American context independently of scholars in the Middle East. Within the Sunni community in America, the Fiqh Council of North America was established in 1988 to create a larger and more authoritative body of Muslim scholars to confront the many legal issues facing Muslims in North America.[6] The Fiqh Council further seeks to extract juridical rulings from the revealed texts and rational sources by employing principles and methodologies of *usul al-fiqh* (the science of inferring juridical rulings from textual and rational sources). The council is even empowered to depart from rulings stated by classical jurists. The presence of a council that could derive laws directly from the revealed sources or through reasoning is not possible in American Shi'ism since such an institution would be viewed as a usurpation of the religious authority vested in the eminent religious scholars.

Authority, when it is strictly defined and hierarchical as it is in Shi'ism, reduces the chances of digression and the scope of divergent hermeneutics. For most devout Shi'is, the *maraji'*'s pronouncements are final and beyond critique. Religious matters not covered in the juridical literature composed by the *maraji'* are referred to their offices. There are very few Shi'i scholars in America who are qualified to state a juridical opinion independent of, let alone one that is opposed to, the edicts of the *maraji'*. Due to this factor, the Shi'i outlook in America is shaped by the *maraji'*'s pronouncements, which are often formulated in the religious circles in Iraq and Iran.

The *maraji'* have consolidated their position within the community especially as, in recent times, access to the *maraji'* has become easier. The offices of the *maraji'*, which are located in America and abroad, have access to the Internet. Hence, many Shi'is email their questions to a *marji'*'s office. The *maraji'*'s offices have also established their own Internet sites that contain their latest rulings.[7]

In addition, the *maraji'* are now more accessible to their followers by appointing representatives who can handle matters on their behalf. Shaykh Fadhil Sahlani of al-Khoei Foundation in New York, for example, is a representative of Ayatullah Seestani in all religious matters. He is authorized to approve and execute divorce petitions from wives, handle financial affairs, and all other issues that impact the Shi'i community in America.

The *maraji'* also recognize the need to foster closer ties with their followers in the West. Besides establishing religious centers and Internet sites, they are trying to be more accessible to their followers in America by sending emissaries to visit them. Ayatullah Seestani, for example, regularly sends his agent, al-Sayyid Murtaza Kashmiri, to the West to monitor the progress of and report on the needs of the community. Other Shi'i *'ulama'* in America are in continuous contact with the offices of the various *maraji'*. Shaykh Hisham Husainy of Detroit was, for some time, the representative of Ayatullah Muhammad Baqir al-Hakim. Similarly, imam Mustafa al-Qazwini in California was the representative of Ayatullah Ruhani. The Imam 'Ali Center in New York caters to the needs of those who follow Ayatullah Khamene'i. The Imam Mahdi Association of Marjaeya (IMAM) under the leadership of Sayyid Muhammad Baqir Kashmiri, is currently the liaison office of Ayatullah Seestani in America.

The appointment by the *maraji'* of financial and religious deputies to act as their representatives has enabled community members to provide facilities for religious education for the Shi'i community in America and has generated the confidence to engage in major projects such as the construction of mosques, Islamic centers, and institutions considered necessary for the continued religious and spiritual well-being of the community. For example, in 1989, Ayatullah al-Khu'i offered several million dollars to the Islamic Center of America, the Jami', to build an Islamic school in Detroit. The school was to be under the jurisdiction of the New York based al-Khoei Foundation. The offer was declined by the Jami' because the board members wanted complete control over the school.[8]

The Khumus *Factor in America*

A corollary to the institutions of *marjiʻiyya* and *taqlid* is the Shiʻi practice of giving religious dues to the *marjiʻ* or one who is authorized to collect on his behalf. During their times, the Shiʻi Imams would often receive gifts, alms, charitable donations, and endowments. To facilitate the collection of these dues from their distant followers, they authorized special agents (*wukalaʼ*) to handle the dues on their behalf. Among the various dues is the *khumus*, a religious tax, according to Shiʻi jurists, that is levied on income and other forms of wealth. Half of the *khumus* is to be distributed to the needy from the descendants of the Prophet, whereas the other half is to be spent for the welfare of the community.[9] Besides the *khumus*, the system of collecting religious dues on behalf of the Imams include the *zakat* and other voluntary donations and endowments.

The institution of the *marjiʻ al-taqlid* and the *khumus* revenue that is generated have made it possible for the community to organize its affairs independent of the control of Muslim governments in the Middle East or elsewhere. Thus, the political or religious interference that characterize some Sunni institutions, which are funded by countries like Saudi Arabia, Egypt, Kuwait, or Libya, do not exist for most American Shiʻi communities.

Within the Shiʻi community, *khumus* can also be utilized to pay for the salaries of scholars and teachers who serve the community. The scholars are thus able to exert autonomy from the congregations they serve in their capacity as religious guides.

American Shiʻi Institutions and the Marajiʻ

Shiʻi religious centers in America tend to affiliate themselves to different *marajiʻ*. Khoja, Pakistani, and Iraqi centers generally follow the rulings of Ayatullah Seestani whereas many Iranian centers do the *taqlid* of Ayatullah Khameneʼi. Lebanese Shiʻis tend to follow either Ayatullah Fadlallah or Seestani.

The institutionalization of different centers under the leadership of the agents of the *marajiʻ* has sometimes resulted in competition for the loyalty and *khumus* money of their followers. For instance, the earliest Shiʻi center in New York was founded by a prominent *marjiʻ* of the time, Ayatullah al-Khuʼi (see chap. 2). Besides providing basic religious services, it also has a daily Islamic school where both religious and secular subjects are taught. After the death of Ayatullah al-Khu'i in 1992, al-Khoei Foundation chose to ally itself with Ayatullah Seestani, who was regarded by many as the most learned (*a'lam*) after al-Khu'i.

Located quite close to al-Khoei Foundation is the Imam 'Ali Center, which runs a parallel daily Islamic school and offers services similar to those provided by al-Khoei Foundation. The Imam 'Ali Center caters mainly for the Iranian community. Al-Husseini *Madrasa*, run by the Khoja community, is also located in the vicinity. Although ethnically different, these institutions duplicate the services rendered to the Shi'i community. Similarly, in Dearborn, Michigan, more than seven Shi'i religious institutions render similar services to the local community. An identical situation exists in Houston, where two Shi'i centers are located close to each other.

Differences within the American Shi'i community are often precipitated by representatives of the *maraji'*. A representative (*wakil*) of a *marji'* may be authorized to perform different kinds of functions. A *wakil* who has received comprehensive deputyship (*al-wakil al-mutlaq*) has no limits imposed on the extent of his authority and can perform various kinds of functions, including appointing other deputies on the *marji'*'s behalf. The authority of most other kinds of representatives is more restricted.

A *marji'*'s representative in America conveys and explains his *fatawa*, promotes a *marji'*'s candidacy, distributes his books, and, according to imam Mustafa al-Qazwini, might even solicit people to change their *taqlid* to follow the representative's *marji'*.[10] He also collects *khumus* money on behalf of the *marji'* and might be authorized to handle cases of divorce and other social and religious matters. Such a system of deputyship has often led to competition for *khumus* dues as a representative seeks to increase a *marji'*'s sphere of influence and the number of his followers in America.

Although *taqlid* has united different ethnic groups under the leadership of a particular *marji'*, institutions that are affiliated to different *maraji'* have often precipitated differences and even acrimony between Shi'i centers. As I shall discuss, tensions between centers become apparent at the celebration of the *eid* holiday when, depending on their affiliations, centers often commemorate the beginning or end of Ramadhan on different days.

A comparison between the experience of Shi'i institutions with that of Sunni centers in America indicates that the latter are influenced by foreign-based movements, which try to permeate the lives of ordinary Muslim. As we read in chapter three, many Sunni mosques have been suffused by South Asian and Middle East movements such as Tablighi Jamaat, Jamaat Islami of Pakistan, and Ikhwan al-Muslimin. American Sunnism is also characterized by the infusion of various Salafi and Wahhabi ideologies. The Shi'i experience is quite different: instead of the influence of extraneous movements and their ideologies, it is the religious leaders residing abroad who exert much influence by appointing representatives to establish centers and to guide their followers.

Besides establishing religious institutions and community centers for their followers, the *maraji'* are concerned with furnishing their followers with guidance, especially in matters that pertain to legal ordinances. They have tried to meet the needs of their followers by responding to their questions and issuing juridical edicts appropriate for the current milieu. The *maraji'* have responded to the challenges of living in contemporary times in different ways, ranging from the reinterpretation and reformulation of erstwhile juridical pronouncements to issuing new laws based on the needs of those living in the West. It is essential, therefore, to examine the juridical tracts of the *maraji'* and their influence on American Shi'ism.

Muslim Minorities in Non-Muslim Lands

To comprehend the role of the *maraji'* in America, it is necessary to understand the applicability of traditional Islamic jurisprudence in areas where Muslims live in a minority context. Islamic jurisprudence was formulated when Muslims lived in areas where they constituted the majority population. In the eighth and ninth centuries, Muslim jurists attempted to construct a legal edifice by developing and elaborating a system of *shari'a* law binding on all Muslims. The early legal cases in the Islamic juridical corpus were arrived at through a sense of realism in assessing the relative social and political milieu and its ramifications for the Muslim community. The laws were stated in general terms with a view to revising or correcting ethical-legal judgments in the face of specific contingencies. Jurists also understood the need to modify the generality and rigor of the legal contents of the Qur'an and the *sunna* to cope with the novel circumstances created by the hegemonic gains of the first two centuries of the political history of Islam.

The jurists interpreted and developed Islamic law, invoking various hermeneutical principles like *maslaha* (derivation and application of a juridical ruling that is in the public interest), *qiyas* (analogy), *istihsan* (preference of a ruling which a jurist deems most appropriate under the circumstances), and other innovative interpretive principles to respond to the needs of the times and to go beyond the rulings stated in the revealed texts, i.e., the Qur'an and *sunna*. Gradually, the jurists constructed a program for private and public living centered on the *shari'a*.

As the Islamic empire expanded and Muslims had to live under non-Muslim rule, classical Muslim jurists came up with various solutions as to how Muslims could live in a minority context. The medieval jurists divided the world into the abode of Islam (*dar al-Islam*) and the abode of war (*dar al-harb*). These two phrases highlight the normative foundation of Muslim religious convictions about forming a transcultural community of believers who must ultimately subdue and dominate nonbelievers. The territory of Islam signified a political entity that acknowledged and upheld Islamic values and laws. As it purportedly upheld the *shari'a*, this abode was seen as the territory of peace and justice. The ascendancy of Islam and the promulgation of the *shari'a* in this abode was protected by a Muslim government.[11] The enforcement of *shari'a* was important as it regulated and harmonized relations among its constituent elements. *Dar al-harb*, on the other hand, was seen as the land of infidels, the epitome of heedlessness and ignorance that posed a threat to the Islamic order. The absence of the *shari'a* in the abode of war was presumed to epitomize injustice and to foster lawlessness and insecurity. *Dar al-harb* denoted a territory in which Islam could not be practiced and Muslims lived under the threats of conflict, oppression, expulsion, or death.[12]

It is important to note that the dichotomization of the world into two spheres was a juristic innovation. The Qur'an does not suggest a perpetual state of war between *dar al-Islam* and *dar al-harb*, as do the jurists. In fact, these two realms do not appear in the Qur'an. Rather than reflecting the Qur'anic pronouncement on relations with the other, the legal bifurcation of the world into *dar al-Islam* and *dar al-harb* is indicative of the historical realities that the 'Abbasid jurists had to contend with.[13]

Like Sunni jurists, Shi'i scholars constructed their theological and legal discourses in light of historical realities confronting them. Shi'i jurists differed from their Sunni counterparts in that they distinguished between *dar al-iman* (the abode of true faith) and *dar al-Islam*. Thus, they distinguished between an abode ruled by Sunni rulers and that which falls under the sovereignty of an infallible Imam. For example, the famous Shi'i theologian and jurist, Shaykh Mufid (d. 1022) states that when a place is imbibed with [the conditions of] faith, then it is to be called *dar al-iman*.

When a state is governed by the *shariʻa* but not based on the teachings (*qawl*) of the Imams from the family of the Prophet, then it is to be considered as part of *dar al-Islam* but not *dar al-iman*. For al-Mufid, it is only when a state is ruled by both the *shariʻa* and bases its practices on the teachings of the Imams that it is both *dar al-Islam* and *dar al-iman*. Al-Mufid further states that this is the view held by a number of Shiʻis who have transmitted traditions from the family of the Prophet.[14]

In the absence of *dar al-iman*, Muslims may continue to reside in corrupt territories as long as they can freely practice their religion there.[15] Shiʻi jurists also asserted that it was not necessary to reside in or migrate to *dar al-Islam*. Like the Sunni jurists, the thirteenth-century Shiʻi jurist al-Muhaqqiq al-Hilli (b. 1277) declares that migration to *dar al-Islam* is obligatory only upon those unable to practice Islam in *dar al-harb*.[16]

Some traditions preserved in Shiʻi *hadith* literature encourage Shiʻis to migrate to non-Muslim lands. Jaʻfar al-Sadiq, the sixth Shiʻi Imam, is reported to have stated that Muslims can better serve Islam in a non-Muslim country.[17] According to him, lands in which justice and knowledge are to be found are better than lands that are formally associated with Islam.[18] In all probability, such statements from the Imams reflect the political vicissitudes that the Shiʻis endured under Sunni rule. They were often persecuted by fellow Muslims and, at times, were treated better by non-Muslims than by fellow Muslims.

Many of the previous juridical decisions were formulated on the assumption that Muslims were the dominant group and non-Muslims were minorities living in a Muslim country. Such formulations have become irrelevant in the modern context. Modern Shiʻi jurists have gone beyond the traditional demarcation of *dar al-harb* and *dar al-Islam* in their juridical discourse. They have introduced new rulings to respond to the present sociopolitical realities where up to one-third of the Muslim community has voluntarily migrated to non-Muslim countries.

In the new literature emerging from the Shiʻi seminaries in Qum and Najaf and in the discussions of contemporary Shiʻi jurists, the old bifurcation of the world into *dar al-Islam* and *dar al-harb* is completely omitted. Whether Muslims should migrate to non-Muslim countries or not is not discussed. On the contrary, the discussion is now focused on how, rather than if, a Muslim can live in the West. Living in the West has also forced many jurists, both Shiʻi and Sunni, to reconsider the applicability of traditional Islamic jurisprudence. Many scholars within the religious seminaries argue that the discourse has to change to reflect the new global realities. Instead of delineating the boundaries of *dar al-Islam* and *dar al-harb*, and discussing whether Muslims should migrate from the latter to the former, Ayatullah Shabistari, for example, argues that

> Today, an important part, or perhaps most, of the problems we must deal with are "novel matters" *(mustahdathat)*. Whereas once the question to be answered was whether the pledge of allegiance *(bay'a)* of "those who loose and bind" was a legitimate basis of authority, the novel matters we need to take into account today are popular elections and revolutions. Instead of asking if it is permissible for the ruler to fix the value of currency, we should study how economic planning and free enterprise can be reconciled. In the past, jurists were concerned with defining the boundaries of the domain of Islam and the "domain of war" *(dar al-Islam, dar al-harb)*, but today we must ask ourselves if it is permitted to violate the sovereignty of any people or nation. . . . We must search the Qur'an and *sunna* for solutions to contemporary problems such as these. This is what is meant by the universality of Islam, otherwise, Islam belongs to the Hijaz.[19]

Fiqh for Minorities

Settlement in the West has necessitated a paradigm shift in the Islamic legal discourse. Muslim jurists have been forced to restate their rulings, from the *fiqh* of conflict to that of coexistence with the non-Muslim other. It has to be remembered that Islamic law initially developed in a context in which Islam was the dominant political culture. Muslims were not only the majority, they were also the rulers.

Discussion of the legal status of minorities focused primarily on Jews, Christians, and polytheists, not on Muslims living in non-Muslim lands. Whereas Sunni *fiqh* was written from a majority perspective, Shi'i jurisprudence reflects their minority status under Sunni governance. On many issues, Shi'i jurists advised their followers to adopt or appropriate elements of Sunni law when their lives or property were at stake. These statements are reflected by terms such as *taqiyya* (dissimulation) and *mukhalif* (one who opposes [the truth]) that appear frequently in their legal treatises to refer to cases where Shi'is had to interact with the Sunni majority.[20]

Living in the West has challenged jurists to revise some of the classical formulations. The new situation necessitates a revision of the *fiqh* of majority and a formulation of a new *fiqh* of minority.[21] For the Shi'is, the new situation requires an elaboration of how to live under a non-Muslim as opposed to a Sunni rule where they are now more free to express themselves and do not have to dissimulate or hide their identity.

Fiqh for minorities is a specific discipline that takes into account the relationship between the religious ruling, the conditions of the community, and the location where it exists. This type of *fiqh* does not mean a complete reformulation of traditional Islamic jurisprudence; rather, it refers to the revision of certain points of law to accommodate the needs of Muslim minorities living among non-Muslim majorities with special needs that may not be appropriate for other communities.[22] To cater to Muslim minorities, a jurist needs to relate the general or universal laws of Islamic jurisprudence to the specific circumstances and conditions of a specific community.

Fiqh for minorities is not a mere reproduction of old *fatawa* (juridical rulings) in contemporary language. The operative rule of this genre of *fiqh* is "changes of *al-ahkam* (rulings) are permissible with the times." The tools that are discussed and elucidated in *usul al-fiqh* present a significant amount of flexibility in proposing novel ways of interpreting traditional sources. Principles within Islamic jurisprudence are invoked to facilitate social and political exigencies. These include duress (*ikrah*), necessity (*darura*), and public welfare (*maslaha*). When facing new situations that cannot be located in the revelatory sources and do not have legal precedents, jurists can formulate rulings that will best protect the interests of the community while remaining faithful to the Islamic frame of reference. These interests are called *masalih mursala*.[23]

By deploying such principles, jurists gave themselves flexibility in circumventing rules in any given circumstance, even those that may have explicitly stated prohibitions. The *fiqh* of *darura* can be invoked in cases of imminent danger to the life or physical welfare of the community or to the lifting of dietary restrictions when a person's health is jeopardized. In the past, the *fiqh* of *darura* was employed by Sunni jurists during times of crises such as the Mongol invasion or the coming of the Crusades in Muslim lands. Most of the rulings were on an ad hoc basis and did not reflect a fully refined juridical system. Thus, the laws articulated in these periods fell under the category of legal exception by virtue of necessity.

Jurists have resorted to similar tools in seeking solutions to the challenges confronting American Muslims. Most jurists have opined, for example, that it is permissible to shake hands with a member of the opposite gender only if a piece of cloth is placed between them or under an unusually critical situation, one that will cause extreme difficulty (*al-haraj al-shadid*) if one refuses to shake hands.²⁴ Ayatullah Tabrizi goes even further. He states that shaking hands with the opposite gender is not allowed even under extreme circumstances since not touching the opposite gender is among the distinctive markers and an identity of Islam, something that must to be preserved whenever possible.²⁵

For the *maraji*, the presence of their followers in the West has put pressure on them to search for ways in which they can respond to the needs of the Shi'i community beyond their traditionally recognized function of managing religious donations (such as *khumus*, *sadaqa* [voluntary alms]) and of providing guidance limited to the religious realm. The multifarious challenges faced by Shi'i communities around the globe, especially those in the West, have forced the *maraji* to deduce rulings from the Islamic sources in order to respond to the widening gap between the religious and secular existence in a non-Muslim milieu.

Many questions have been posed to Shi'i jurists regarding rulings for those residing in a minority context. The *maraji* have articulated and, at times, applied hermeneutical devices in the elucidation of the legal precepts reported from the Imams. The *maraji* have also composed literature oriented specifically to the conditions of Muslims in the West.

The Reevaluation of Islamic Jurisprudence in Contemporary Times

Within the academic circles in Iran, there have been important voices calling for a radical rethinking of the religious tradition. Many of these have emerged after the 1979 Iranian revolution. Such formulations have come from religious intellectuals like 'Abdolkarim Soroush, but importantly others emanate from within the religious seminaries itself.²⁶ Scholars like Ayatullah Sane'i, Ayatullah Jannati, Ayatullah Mohagheg Damad, Hujjatul Islam Muhsin Sa'idzadeh, and Mohsen Kadivar have called for a reevaluation of traditional juridical pronouncements on many issues. In my discussions with some *maraji*, I detected a distinct silent revolution within in the seminaries in Qum. The views of the *maraji* are, on many important issues, polarized.

According to the contemporary jurist Ayatullah Mohagheg Damad, since civil rules are variable, Islamic laws must change accordingly. Thus, in our own times, Islamic legal rulings must be reinterpreted based on the principle of harm and benefits and other principles established in *usul al-fiqh*. Stated differently, there is a need to enact laws that are conducive to the welfare of the community even though such laws are not found in earlier texts. In view of such principles, Islamic sacred sources have to be read in different ways. Damad argues, for example, that based on the principle of *la darar wa la dirar* (there is neither harm nor injury), the political and social needs of an Islamic state can override the interests of individuals.[27]

Jurists in Iran have proposed a wide range of revision in classical formulations based on such principles. Scholars like Mohsen Kadivar have argued for freedom of religious thought and belief. He states that there is no Qur'anic basis for the killing of apostates and the imposition of religion on infidels.[28] Ayatullah Bojnourdi, a former member of the Supreme Judicial Council in Iran, advocates for a change in the Islamic penal code. He maintains that if the process for execution of penalty results in the denigration of Islam and causes people, especially the youth, to demean the religion, then the process should then be revised so that the image of Islam should not be tarnished.[29]

Other Iranian jurists have also come up with novel interpretations of traditional rulings. In 1999 a senior cleric, Ayatollah Yusuf Sane'i, said it was wrong not to allow women to become judges or to accept them as full witnesses in courts. Another jurist based in Qum, Ayatullah Jannati, stated that it is not necessary that a *marji' al-taqlid* be a man. It is permissible for a woman to hold a judicial position provided she is qualified to do so.

Such revisions of traditional *fiqh* suggest that many Shi'i jurists are attempting a reformulation of the laws stated in the classical juridical manuals. However, these pronouncements are made primarily within the Iranian context where reforms in the laws of apostasy, penal code, and women in the judiciary can be enacted. Many of the new *fatawa* discussed (punishment, female judges, labor relations, state intervention in cases of matrimonial disputes) assume the enactment of the *shari'a* in an Islamic state where Muslims are in the majority. Most of them are not applicable to Shi'is residing in America.

The Responsa and Mustahdathat *Literature*

The *maraji'* have responded to the needs of Shi'i communities that live as minorities in the West by recasting Islamic legal discourse on Muslim minorities and reconciling Islamic legal categories to the demands of the times. New situations and contingencies have prompted the experts in the field to delve into the sources and to appropriate methodological devices so as to deduce fresh juridical rulings in order to deal with novel problems and issues. In their writings, the *maraji'* have articulated the juridical and moral parameters within which the followers are to base their demeanor. At times, they have adjusted these parameters in light of specific circumstances, using principles like *darura*, *maslaha*, and *haraj*.

Indeed, the Shi'i legal tradition accords a prominent place to the faculty of reasoning in discerning and applying the purposes of God. The priority of reason in the Shi'i epistemological outlook is premised on the view, established in Shi'i rational theology, that reason is prior to both sources of revelation, the Qur'an and the *sunna*. For Shi'i scholars, it is reason that acknowledges the comprehensiveness of revelation and discovers all the principles needed to create a viable public order.

Armed with this potent weapon, the *maraji'* have sought to deduce legal opinions in response to the multifarious questions of their followers. Their *responsa* are evident in different genres of juridical literature. Some texts are predicated in the form of a dialogue between two parties; another genre reflect the *responsa* of the *maraji'* to the various questions posed to them. A third source is composed by the *maraji'* themselves, reflecting their legal opinions. These legal treatises (*al-Risala al-'amaliyya*) take the form of an enumeration of the *maraji'*'s rulings on various issues.

With the increased migration of Shi'i communities to the West, Shi'i scholars have sensed the need to make Islamic jurisprudence more perspicuous to the lay readers, especially those residing in the West. The title of 'Abdul Hadi al-Hakim's book, *Jurisprudence Made Easy* makes this agenda evident. Al-Hakim stresses in his preface that jurisprudence must be in a language that is "down to earth" so that the subject can be more accessible to the lay readers.[30] In addition, the rulings in the book accord with the *fatawa* of Ayatullah Seestani. A novel feature of this work shows up in the form of questions and answers between a fictitious father and his son who has just attained puberty. The first chapter is devoted to a dialogue on *taqlid*; the second chapter is titled "Dialogue on *Najis* (ritually impure) Things."

Shi'is living in the West have posed a wide range of questions to the *maraji'* ranging from the permissibility of taking mortgages to praying in areas where the sun does not rise in winter. They have also asked sensitive issues such as examining and touching the reproductive organs of the opposite gender, looking at photographs of naked persons for studying physiology and anatomy, taking the pulse and other vital signs of patients of the opposite gender, and the like. The *maraji'* in the Shi'i theological centers of Qum and Najaf have responded by composing a distinct genre of juridical texts called the *mustahdathat* (lit., new matters or occurrences). The literature is a collection of the *maraji"s responsa* to questions posed by their followers, and directed especially toward those living in the West.

The growing need to address the concerns of the Shi'i community in the West is further illustrated by the title of another recently published book, *Fiqh lil Mughtaribin* (Jurisprudence for those residing in the West) translated as *A Code of Practice for Muslims in the West in Accordance with the Edicts of Ayatullah al-Udhma as-Sayyid 'Ali al-Husaini as-Seestani*. 'Abdul Hadi al-Hakim, who authored this work as well, reminds us that many of the topics covered in this text have not been treated in Seestani's juridical treatise, *A Manual of Islamic Laws*. Al-Hakim states in the preface that he has attempted to make laws accessible to the laity.[31] The emphasis on "new laws" further corroborates my observation that the *maraji'* have formulated new rulings in response to questions posed by their followers in the West. The concern to address issues confronting Shi'is in the West is also evident in the title of another work *Ahkam al-Mughtaribin* (Legal Rulings for those living in the West). The author, al-Sayyid Husayn al-Husayni, juxtaposes and contrasts the views of ten *maraji'* on important juridical questions.

In the new juridical response literature, *Fiqh Lil-Mughtaribin and al-Mustahdathat* (translated as *Current Legal Issues*), Ayatullah Seestani couches legal norms with a concern to uphold moral and ethical codes in the West. For Seestani, moral imperatives and injunctions apply to Muslims wherever they are. Thus, Muslims must faithfully discharge all their contractual obligations and they may not violate the property of non-Muslims. Like other Muslim jurists, he states that Muslims in the West must uphold Islamic law, serve the public and individual interest of Muslims, and fulfill the pledges or agreements made to a non-Muslim state. If Muslims enter or reside in a territory, they must abide by the laws of the land.[32] They may not cheat, lie, fiddle with gas meters (!),[33] or give false information to government agencies like immigration officials.[34] Seestani also states that a Muslim cannot obtain a passport illegally,[35] nor can he leave anything on the roads that may harm others.[36]

When asked whether it is permissible to deceive an insurance company in a non-Islamic country if one is confident that this will not lead to the

image of Islam and Muslims being tarnished, he states quite unequivocally that deception in any form is not permissible.[37] Seestani is clearly
concerned that Muslims uphold ethical principles, especially when residing in non-Muslim countries.

Most questions asked of Seestani refer to the elucidation of religious
edicts that are germane to Muslims all over the world, especially to those
living in the West. These include such questions as whether inhalers can be
used while fasting,[38] the permissibility of consuming products that contain
gelatin,[39] and if copyright laws are to be observed by Muslims.[40] Ayatullah
Khamene'i was even asked if it is permissible to place a hidden camera inside a grave so as to observe what happens to the body after burial.[41]

Seestani also seeks political and economic empowerment for his followers. He encourages them to participate in elections and run for office.[42] According to imam Mustafa al-Qazwini, during his meeting with
Seestani, the Ayatullah told him that anything that serves the interests of
Islam in America, including interfaith dialogue, should be promoted. Besides political engagement, he encourages interaction with non-Muslims
in all spheres of American life. Seestani states that Muslims can greet
non-Muslims on Christmas and other festive occasions. This is in stark
contrast to the views of some Sunni fundamentalist groups, which declare
greeting non-Muslims or any participation in Christian holidays to be
forbidden.[43] The Saudis prohibit any type of cooperation between Muslims, Jews, and Christians.[44]

Seestani was further asked whether it was permissible to rely on DNA
test results that indicate a child was born out of wedlock. Even though
there is no authoritative precedence in the normative texts, he says: "Who-
soever shall attain certainty through other means, be it through blood test
or any other means, should feel free to act upon it." Seestani cautions that
such a test is not a legitimate means to determining adultery and that the
Islamic penal code will not be applicable based solely on DNA results.[45]
Seestani was also asked about the genres of music that his followers are
permitted to listen to (*halal* music), offering prayers in a space craft, the
permissibility of having test-tube babies, and praying and fasting in places
that have extremely long days or nights.[46]

Another Ayatullah, Muhammad Hussein Fadlallah, is one of the most
controversial *maraji'*. His novel views can be discerned from his ruling
on women. He allows them to be *mujtahids* and for people to do their
taqlid.[47] Fadlallah's appeal to Muslims in the West also lies in the fact that
some of his views are in stark contrast to those held by the majority of

Shi'i scholars. The majority of the *'ulama'* consider polytheists, atheists, and idolaters to be ritually impure (*najas*). Thus, their food cannot be consumed. Fadlallah disagrees, saying that, intrinsically, no one is impure. The impurity, he argues, lies in matters of beliefs, not in essence.[48] Hence, he rules that Hindus and Buddhists are ritually pure and that their food may be consumed.

Fadlallah even allows couples to watch pornographic movies under certain circumstances. He was asked,

Q: Is it permissible for a frigid wife or husband to watch pornographic scenes?

A. If a husband or a wife, or both suffer frigidity in the absence of any means of treatment, whether natural—through mutual excitation—or through medication, and if the only treatment is watching pornographic scenes, then this will be permissible, only because this is the only means, keeping in mind that this should be done apart from any excess, just like taking the proper dosage of the medicine prescribed, provided that this passive situation may threaten their matrimonial life.[49]

Like Fadlallah, Ayatullah Sane'i is well known for his radical views regarding women. He states that since the social circumstances of women have changed, the framework of civil laws must change too. "Current laws are in line with the traditional society of the past, whereas these civil laws should be in line with contemporary realities and relations in our own society."[50]

In an interview with a Sunni newspaper, *al-Sharq al-Awsat*, Sane'i goes even further and states,

I said that women are capable of becoming the Wali al-Faqih [guardian jurist] and that they could lead the prayers while the men pray behind them. I wrote these statements in my scholarly thesis at the *hawza* (Islamic seminary) and all my disciples act in accordance with this. My book about women's jurisprudence is one of the *hawza*'s principal books. Today, I have colleagues among the Sunni scholars who are starting to become convinced that women could lead men in prayer and that they can hold the office of president.[51]

The hermeneutical constructs that are intrinsic to their interpretive and legislative enterprises means that the *maraji'* often disagree with each other and sometimes issue contrasting *fatawa* on the same topic. The following are examples of questions that are asked by their followers. The *maraji's responsa* are documented in the *mustahdathat* literature, and they epitomize some of the differences that have emerged from the seminaries. As we shall see, the ramifications of such divergent *fatawa* have had major repercussions for their followers.

Halal *Music*

Although the Qur'an contains no strictures against music, traditions from the Prophet and Imams caution against playing or listening to music and using musical instruments. As such, music, which can corrupt a person's moral and ethical values, has been frowned upon in religious texts. Many jurists draw a distinction between music that is allowed and that which is forbidden. Ayatullah Seestani was asked about the genres of music that is permissible to listen to:

> 546. Question: Many questions are asked concerning permissible and forbidden music. Is it correct to say that the music that arouses sexual, lustful urges and promotes unstable and degrading behavior is the forbidden one? And is it correct to say that the music that soothes the nerves or causes relaxation, the music that forms the background of a scene in a movie to increase the effect of the scene on the viewers, the music that is used for physical exercise during workouts, the music that dramatizes a particular scene by its tune, or the one that arouses the zeal [in soldiers] is the permissible one?
>
> Answer: Forbidden music is the music that is suitable for entertainment and amusement gatherings, even if it does not arouse sexual temptations. Permissible music is the music that is not suitable for such gatherings, even if it does not soothe the nerves like the martial music and that played at funerals.

> 547. Question: Just as many questions are asked about *halal* and *haram* music, many questions are asked about *halal* and *haram* songs. Is it correct to say that *haram* songs are those that arouse sexual, lustful urges and promote unstable and degrading behavior? Is it correct to say that songs that do not arouse lustful desires, but elevate the souls and thoughts to lofty levels like religious songs of praise dedicated to the Prophet Muhammad and the Imams or the songs that lift the spirits and morale [of the fighters] and the like are *halal* songs?

Answer: All songs *(al-ghina')* are *haram*. Based on the definition that we accept, *al-ghina'* is the entertaining expression by way of tunes that are common to those who provide entertainment and amusement. In this prohibition, we should include the recitation of the Holy Qur'an, supplications *(du'as)*, and songs of praise of Ahlul Bayt uttered to the accompaniment of those tunes [that are used by the entertainers]. The prohibition of reciting other non-entertaining expressions—like songs intended to lift the morale [of fighters]—is based on compulsory precaution. However, the tune that cannot be described as such is not *haram* by itself.[52]

Seestani rules that music that is suitable for entertainment and amusement gatherings is forbidden. The ruling leaves it to the conscience of the individual to decide whether a particular form of music is *halal* or *haram*. When questioned as to how to distinguish between *halal* and *haram* music, Seestani's predecessor, al-Khu'i, states that if local custom *('urf)* is divided in determining whether a particular form of music is *halal* or not, and it is not possible to ascertain its permissibility, then the music can be presumed to be *halal*. Al-Khu'i further adds that music is *haram* for those who are aroused by it but not for those who are not.[53]

Ayatullah Fadlallah's views on music are quite different. He states,

Our view is that music which does not fan the impulses; does not lead to entertainment which alters the normal state of the person and has nothing which may lead to lust must be seen permissible, by virtue of all this.

If what is called classical music falls within the parameters, it is permissible; likewise for symbolic or inspirational music, the kinds that raise spirits, calm the nerves, soothe the mentality, etc.

Perhaps the jurists who had ruled on prohibiting it were referring to the illicitness, wantonness and evil of the people of corruption.[54]

Fadlallah also states that it is well known that classical music stimulates intellectual thought and is more than simple amusement or delight. "If this, indeed, is the case, then one may rule on its permissibility."[55] Not only does Fadlallah's ruling differ from Seestani's, he elucidates the basis for his ruling, and indicates, albeit briefly, why he disagrees with erstwhile and contemporary jurists.[56]

Ayatullah al-Sanei is more equivocal in his stance on music. He states,

It is legally forbidden and sinful to perform, produce, provide the tools and instruments for making, or to listen to any music, song, sound, and frivolous discourse which causes man to go astray and deviate from the way of Allah and beatitude. It should be said that spreading and encouraging indecencies, mental and physical sins, or laziness which leads to burdening the society, drug and alcohol addiction, and all other sins are among the cases of deviation from the way of Allah, and one must avoid all the ways and means which lead to committing them; therefore, any music which leads to committing such sins is illegal, irrespective of what kind the music and the instruments are; however, any music which does not involve misleading people, and which is not performed along with other sins being committed, such as mixing men and women to do vulgar things, is considered legal and permissible.[57]

The pronouncements by Shi'i jurists regarding the permissibility of listening to music are quite ambiguous. There is no clear response as to what kind of music is permissible to listen to. Excerpts from their juridical pronouncements indicate that the *maraji'* do indeed differ among themselves on how to differentiate between *halal* and *haram* music. In many cases, as Khu'i's response shows, local custom can determine whether a particular type of music is deemed permissible to listen to or not.

Biomedical Ethics: Artificial Insemination

The principle of *ijtihad* that undergirds Shi'i jurisprudence means that there is a multiplicity of interpretive possibilities on any legal topic. Shi'i jurists have pronounced a wide range of opinions on biomedical issues such as organ donation, euthanasia, sperm donation, and IVF (In Vitro Fertilization). One of the most startling examples of variant edicts issued by the *maraji'* relates to embryo fertilization. While there is agreement among them as to whether fertilization can take place outside the womb, there is some difference on the question of fertilizing a wife with the sperm of a stranger. According to Seestani,

> Q136: The husband's sperm and the wife's egg are taken and fertilization is completed in a test tube, then the egg is returned to the wife's womb.
> A: This is also permissible as such.

Q137a: The sperm of the husband and the egg of another woman who is not his wife are taken for fertilization, then are transferred to the wife's womb.

A: This is also permissible as such.[58]

However, Seestani does not allow insemination of a woman with the sperm of any man other than her husband.[59] In his *Ajwibat al-Istifta'at*, under the heading "artificial conception" *(al-talqih al-Sina'i)*, Ayatollah Khamene'i responds to whether In Vitro Fertilization (IVF) using a husband's sperm and wife's egg is permissible.[60] He replies in the affirmative. Khamene'i is also asked about the case of a married woman who is unable to have children due to a lack of eggs. Given that this inability of a wife to provide her husband with children might lead to the breakup of her marriage, would it then be permissible for her to use the eggs of another woman, fertilized with her husband's sperm by IVF and then transferred to her womb? He replies: "There is no problem in the *sharia* in itself, except that the child born in this way is related to the sperm and egg producers, and its relation to the owner of the womb is problematic, and they [dual form: the husband and wife presumably] must take care to be cautious regarding the particular legal rulings of kinship relation [*nasab*]." That is, the child will be related to the egg donor and not the wife, the recipient, who will carry and bear it; the child will not then inherit from the latter, the "social mother" and, were it a boy, issues arise as to her veiling before him on puberty.[61]

Khamene'i is next asked, "if the husband is infertile, is it allowed to fertilize the wife with the sperm of a stranger, by placing the sperm in her womb?" In the Islamic context, artificial insemination by donor (AID) is a very controversial and sensitive procedure as the sperm is deemed to be a polluting substance. The insemination of another man's sperm could lead to a charge of adultery. Khamene'i's response is very different from those articulated by other *maraji'*. He states "There is no legal obstacle to fertilizing the woman with the sperm of a stranger in itself, but avoidance of forbidden concomitants like prohibited looking and touching and suchlike is enjoined. And in any case if a child is born in this way, it is not related to the husband, but to the producer of the sperm and the woman, the owner of the egg and the womb."[62]

Khamene'i's edict is a radical departure from the views stated by other jurists. Morgan Clarke cites email correspondence with the offices of Ayatollah Sane'i, who is seen by many as quite liberal in his rulings. Sane'i states that artificial insemination by donor is not permissible. He continues,

> Inserting and using the sperm of a foreigner in the woman's womb is absolutely *haram* and such works should be avoided and other ways which are legitimate and lawful should be tried to solve the problem of not having child like fertilization of the sperm of a man and the egg of the woman, of course in the outside (i.e., laboratory conditions) and then the produced fetus can be inserted in the woman's womb. In such a way the woman who owns the egg is considered as the mother, and the owner of the sperm is the father if he has not given up the matter. In other words, if the owner of the sperm has given up his sperm ownership, for example he has delivered his sperm to the sperm bank to be used by anyone, then he is not considered as the father. But if the owner of the sperm is recognized, then the matter of marriage should be not only cautioned but the ruling is that caution should be certainly considered.[63]

Khamene'i goes so far as to allow the use of sperm after death. He is asked: "If sperms were taken from the husband and after his death an egg from his wife were fertilized with it and then placed in her womb, then, firstly, is that deed legally permitted? And secondly, is the resulting child the child of the husband and legally related to him? And thirdly, does it inherit from him?"

Khamene'i replies that "There is no problem with the stated procedure in itself and the child is related to the wife, although he only finds it 'possible' that it is related to the husband, and is clear that it will not inherit from him."[64] Khamene'i also allows transgender surgery where a person has male external characteristics, but is female "psychologically," in order to "reveal" their "actual" sex; he also allows gender assignment surgery in the case of a "hermaphrodite" (*khuntha*).[65] Most *maraji'*, with the exception of Gulpaygani, allow gender change if a person feels that she or he is trapped in a body of the opposite gender.[66]

Euthanasia

In Islamic ethical discourse, there is a difference between those jurists who assert the *shar'i* criteria for designating the moment of death (when the heart stops beating and the soul leaves the body) and those who accept that brain death signifies death and allow lifesaving machines to be disconnected at that point.

Traditionally, Muslim jurists regarded the complete cessation of heartbeat as a sufficient criterion to declare a person legally dead. However, a further dimension has been added to this formulation of death in view of the modern medical technology that can intervene to prolong life through the life-support system in the case where all brain functions have ceased. This development has given rise to the question whether brain death can be recognized as a valid formulation of death without first defining the criteria of life in Islam. Can innate integration of vegetative functions without cognition in a brain-dead person be used as the necessary and sufficient condition of life? It must be remembered that the terms cerebral death and brain death are neologisms in Muslim societies, which continue to see death as the cessation of vital functions in a single organ system rather than a part of the organ.[67]

Ayatollah Tabrizi was asked about the definition of death in Islamic law and whether it is the cessation of brain function or the function of heart. His response is quite revealing of the early stages of debate on brain death in jurisprudence. He says that for that distinction one must refer to a physician who is, after all, an expert on the subject: "It is necessary to refer to the medical specialist in order to decide whether the first or the second conforms to the definition of death. Some experts are of the opinion that if the brain waves show the cessation for more than two and a half minutes, then death is definite and there is no way that life could return."[68]

Ayatullah Seestani was asked whether it is obligatory to save a person's life by giving CPR (cardiopulmonary resuscitation). For him, the answer is contingent on a person's faith. He states that if the patient is not a Muslim, there is no objection to not giving him life-saving assistance. However, if the patient is a Muslim, all means have to be exhausted to rescue her or his life.[69] Along the same lines, Seestani rules that if the patient is not a Muslim, life-supporting devices can be removed. However, if the patient is a Muslim, then it is not permissible to remove the device even if the patient's relatives ask that this be done.[70]

Fadlallah, on the other hand, does not distinguish between Muslim and non-Muslim life.

Q: By whom is mercy killing determined: the doctor, the religious authority or the patient himself?

A: If "mercy killing" means relieving a patient's unbearable pain, then it is impermissible, because putting an end to a man's life is illegal even if it is based on pity and sympathy. And if mercy killing means putting an end to a patient's life to comfort his parents on the basis that he is going to die in the coming few days, then it is also impermissible because we are not authorized to rob him of his life even if one hour of survival is possible. On the other hand, if mercy killing means brain death, when the patient is considered medically dead and when the possibility of the brain's re-functioning is less than one percent, then we can say that it is not a must to use the apparatus that elongates the body's life represented by the heart's movement. So, it is lawful to remove this device should the concerned doctor so decide. . . . This is based on the belief that the obligation of saving a patient's life doesn't include the life of cells, but the life of the human being. This type of life, that of the cells, can be compared to a similar type of life in a snake tail after the snake is killed.[71]

It is important to note that Seestani's definition of life differs from that of Fadlallah. When asked if a person who has been pronounced brain-dead be considered dead, Seestani's response is to appeal to the common understanding (*'urf*) of death. He states, "The criterion in applying the term *dead* in so far as the application of religious laws go is the common perception of the people, in the sense that they would call him "dead." And this is not proven in the situation mentioned in the question.[72] Fadlallah, on the other hand, maintains that a brain-dead person can no longer be considered a living being since only her/his cells are functioning. Tabrizi, as we have seen, defers the matter to medical specialists.

Seestani also differentiates between Muslim and non-Muslim life when the question of organ donation is raised. He states that donating organs is permissible only if the life of another Muslim depends on receiving the organ.[73] The distinction between saving Muslim and non-Muslim life is troubling for many Muslims. In all probability, the differentiation is anchored in classical texts on warfare where it was declared that if non-Muslims refuse to accept Islam or pay the *jizya*, male unbelievers may be killed. This implies that the guilt of refusing to adopt Islam deprives a non-Muslim of the right to life, and therefore, such a person deserves whatever harm may come to her/him.[74] The moral guilt of not accepting Islam means, in the case of medical ethics, that beneficence is optional with respect to non-Muslim lives, whereas it is obligatory with respect to the lives of Muslims. The implication is that Muslim lives are more important than non-Muslim lives.

Juridical pronouncements such as these from the *maraji'* reflect a departure from traditional Shi'i jurisprudence where these issues were not discussed. The *maraji'* have employed hermeneutical devices at their disposal to arrive at rulings that respond to the questions posed by their followers, many of whom live in the West. Not only have the Shi'i scholars formulated new juridical rulings, they have done so at the expense of differing with the views stated by many of their peers.

Differences between the Maraji' *and their Ramifications in America*

There is no *marji'* who can claim sole jurisdiction in the articulation and interpretation of Shi'ism. This means that there are multiple authorities or figures whom Shi'is can and do follow. As we have seen above, the views of Ayatullah Khamene'i on AID differ radically from those pronounced by other *maraji'*. The *fatawa* of the *maraji'* appear on their websites and the literature emanating from the seminaries in Qum and Najaf. Since the websites are easily accessible, the ramifications of the polarized *fatawa* of the *maraji'* are felt among their followers in America.

Differences between the *maraji'* often translate to disputes in the religious practices of members of the Shi'i community in America. In fact, the imported *fatawa* often create more problems and differences within the Shi'i community than they resolve. These problems manifest themselves in different forms. For example, the question of the direction of prayer from North America had polarized the Muslim community in the 1990s. Based on a *fatwa* issued by Ayatullah al-Khu'i, many Shi'is prayed facing toward the Southeast whereas the majority continued to pray toward the Northeast. Interestingly, Seestani rules that Muslims in North America should pray facing the Northeast, a radical break from his predecessor, al-Khu'i.[75] Faced with conflicting *fatawa*, a Shi'i center in New York deployed a portable *mihrab* (prayer niche) that could be moved based on whether the congregation was praying toward the Northeast or Southeast. (I witnessed two people praying next to each other, but in different directions.)

The *maraji'* have also issued contrasting *fatawa* regarding the beginning of the new Islamic month. Unlike the Sunni community, differences between American Shi'is center not only on whether the moon is sighted but also revolve around which *marji'* one is following. This is because the *maraji'* have issued divergent opinions on establishing whether one can follow the sighting of the moon in places that have a different horizon.

Ayatullah al-Khu'i's *fatwa* on the moon was straightforward and simple. If the moon is sighted anywhere in the world, one can act upon the report and observe the beginning of the new month as long as one shares even a part of the night with the place that has sighted the moon.[76] Seestani's ruling on the issue is very different. According to him, sighting the moon in one area of the world does not necessarily apply to other areas. In his opinion, if astronomical data indicates that the moon cannot be sighted on a certain night in a particular locality, that region cannot consider the next day as the first of the new Islamic month. He even rejects the testimony of witnesses who have claimed to have seen the moon in an area considered by the astronomers to be outside the visibility curve. This is explained in his *Fiqh Lil'Mughtaribin*:

118. Question: During certain months, it is declared that the sighting has been proven according to some religious scholars in some Eastern countries. This is based on the testimony of those who have sighted the new moon. Such declarations are usually coupled with the following facts:

1. The witnesses who sighted the moon and who number around thirty, for example, are scattered in various cities such as 2 in Isfahan, 3 in Qum, 2 in Yazd, 4 in Kuwait, 5 in Bahrain, 2 in Ahsa', and 6 in Syria, etc.

2. The sky was clear in a number of cities in the West, and the believers went out in the attempt to sight the moon; and there was nothing preventing the sighting.

3. The observatories in England announced that it was impossible to sight the new moon that evening in England except by using a telescope; and that its sighting with the naked eye would be possible only in the following night. So, what is the ruling in such a case? Please guide us, may Allah reward you.

Answer: The criterion is the satisfaction of the individual himself [1] about the actual sighting [of the new moon] or [2] the proof of sighting without any counter claim. In the case mentioned above, satisfaction is not normally achieved concerning the appearance of the new moon on the horizon in such a way that it could have been sighted by the naked eye. On the contrary, one is satisfied that it was not sighted and that the testimony [of sightings in the Eastern cities] is based on illusion and error in sight. And Allah knows the best.[77]

For Seestani, to establish the beginning of the Islamic month, the sighting of the new moon must be observable with the naked eye (disregarding any local visible obstructions). If the sighting is reported in a certain locality, then the first of the month is also established in all the other localities that share the same horizon. He further states that if the moon is sighted in the East, those countries that are located in the West can accept the sighting as long as they share the same latitude. Thus, for example, if the moon is sighted in Kenya, Brazil can accept that sighting but Toronto, located farther north, cannot.

Ayatullah Fadlallah differs from both al-Khu'i and Seestani. For him, the physical sighting of the new moon is not essential to establish the beginning of the new Islamic month. He maintains that astronomical data provided by observatories regarding the birth and possibility of observing the new moon are sufficient proofs in establishing the beginning of the new month.[78] Thus, a few days before the beginning and end of the month of Ramadhan, his office sends out emails advising his followers when to start and end their fasts.

The ramifications of such divergent rulings are felt all over the Shi'i world, not only between different communities but also within the same family. Based on the rulings of different horizons between Ayatullah al-Khu'i and Seestani, if a husband follows al-Khu'i and the wife follows the rulings of Seestani, then, if the moon is sighted in Africa, the husband living in North America would be feasting while the wife, although living with him in the same house, would be fasting.

The extent of the confusion that the divergent ruling on the sighting of the moon has created in America can be discerned from the following email I received in December 2007. The email is from the Young Muslim Association (YMA) of The Islamic Center of America in Dearborn. The notice starts in a somewhat sarcastic tone,

With the influx of Islamic Jurisprudence and the heightened enlightenment of individuals, Muslims have been blessed with having multiple followings. Our blessed and most knowledgeable leaders have differing opinions which all fall within Islamic bounds. It is therefore the YMA's most humble opportunity to give our community a double dosage of blessings. The Islamic Center of America will be holding two separate Eid Prayers lead by Sheikh Mohammad Dboukh. The first will be on Thursday December 20th, beginning at 9:00 am and 10:00 am. The second will follow on Friday, December 21st at 9:00 am. Please refer to your particular following (*taqlid*) for more details.[79]

Similarly, take the case of a couple that follow different *maraji'*. Suppose a woman marries a Hindu convert to Islam. According to Ayatullah Seestani, she cannot consume her in-laws' food (as they have remained Hindus) and when she shakes their hands, she must wash them if they are wet. The husband, who follows Ayatullah Fadlallah, can consume his parents' food and shake their hands even if they are wet. Effectively, the wife can visit her in-laws but she cannot consume the food that they have prepared.

Another instance where the disparate *fatawa* of the *maraji'* can have major repercussions for a Shi'i pertains to marriage: If a Sunni girl who follows the Hanbali, Maliki, or Shafi'i schools chooses to follow the specific Hanafi ruling that the permission of her guardian is not necessary when a virgin girl wishes to get married, is a Shi'i boy allowed to marry her without her guardian's permission based on the ruling in the Hanafi school? According to Ayatullah al-Khu'i, she cannot follow the Hanafi ruling in this case unless she adopts the Hanafi school of law (*madhhab*) in all her acts. However, Ayatullah al-Tabrizi differs from him, stating that she can follow Abu Hanifa's ruling in this instance even though she is not a Hanafi.[80] In this case, whether the Shi'i boy can marry the Sunni girl without the consent of her guardian will effectively depend on the *marji'* he follows rather than on the Sunni school of law she follows.

The Institutionalization of the Marji'iyya

When the *marji'iyya* was instituted in the nineteenth century, the *maraji'* centralized the Shi'i religious hierarchy and played multifaceted roles, especially as their activities were interwoven with their functions as politically conscientious figures. In addition to giving legal opinions on religious matters and administering learning centers and endowment foundations, the *maraji'* came to be considered as the final authority in several important areas. They were instrumental in determining heterodox and innovative ideas, checking against the incursion of foreign values, preserving the economic interests of the Shi'i community, as well as serving as intermediaries between the people and the government by balancing monarchical absolutism and the defense of Shi'i interests and land.[81] They were also seen by the people as protectors of the poor against the rulers and as leaders of the masses.[82]

Social and political integration have always been considered important for Shi'i religious leaders since their authority is, in part, contingent on recognition from the public. Historically, the Shi'i *'ulama'* could and often did intervene in the sociopolitical affairs of the community. They played major roles in the nineteenth-century protests against concessions made to non-Iranian nationals. The *'ulama'*s involvement in the Tobacco Revolt in 1891 and the Constitutional crisis in Iran (1905) demonstrated that their sphere of influence extended well beyond the religious and administrative domains. Ayatullah Mirza Hasan Shirazi's tobacco *fatwa* not only overruled the decision of the sovereign king (Nasir al-Din Shah) to grant concession to a British company but also demonstrated that the *marji'iyya* could curtail the powers of the monarch in Iran. Similarly, Shi'i *'ulama'* in Iraq joined the country's revolt against British rule in 1920 and, in 1922, issued rulings urging their followers to boycott local elections.[83]

For most of its history, the *marji'iyya* has functioned within a particular religious and social universe where the Shi'is constituted the majority population. Accordingly, the *maraji'* responded to the particular challenges that confronted their followers. The challenge for the *maraji'* now is to make this establishment effective for Shi'is living in a minority context where, so far, religion has become the only binding force between the lay Shi'is and the religious elite.

The *maraji'* have to formulate a coherent legal discourse in dealing with issues facing their followers in America. Muslim existence here is neither casual nor transient. Invoking principles like *maslaha, darura, ikrah,* and *haraj* in America imply a lack of a cohesive plan of engagement with the outside world. The fact that Shi'is ask whether it is permissible to interact with the outside world and be politically engaged in a non-Muslim country shows a lack of a cohesive and integrated system of jurisprudence.

It is important for the Shi'is that their legal system in America should not be predicated on situations of crisis or emergency. Such a system of legal rulings would lead to the issuance of piecemeal *fatawa*, which would be nullified on a regular basis as circumstances change.[84] Laws that are based on principles of adaptations to necessity or permissibility to perform certain acts under special dispensation (*rukhsa*) suggest temporary measures and residence. Such principles engender minority consciousness and can isolate communities especially as they suggest that Shi'is can perform certain acts only under extreme or extenuating circumstances. These temporary measures do not resolve issues on a long-term basis. Basing their demeanor on temporary principles also means that Shi'is can live but not flourish, participate, or be fully engaged in America.[85]

For the Shi'is, the new rulings issued in the seminaries establish parameters within which they can shape their lives in America. It is essential that the jurists review and revise the law in keeping with the dictates of changing circumstances. Living in a minority context on a permanent basis will require the jurists legislate and issue *fatawa* that can respond, on the one hand, to the demands of living in a secular society and yet be faithful to Islamic normative jurisprudence on the other.

Most of the *maraji's'* writings are confined to the field of jurisprudence and pertain to such issues as wearing silk ties, consuming gelatin, shaking hands with the opposite gender, buying lottery tickets, and economic issues such as insurance, forms of investments, and the like. Legal prescriptions are often conjoined with statements exhorting unity within the community and admonitions to follow the guidelines provided by Islamic revelatory sources, the Qur'an and *sunna*. A study of the *mustahdathat* and other genres of contemporary juridical literature confirms that a feature of normative Islamic ethical and juridical discourse is the underlying commitment to casuistry—that is, the examination of specific cases rather than the exposition or elaboration of abstract rules or principles. Again, most of the *responsa* are on an ad hoc and piecemeal basis. Whether in their compositions or statements on the Internet, the *maraji's* pronouncements present Islam as a legal code of dos and don'ts, often ignoring the particular American context in which these laws are to be applied.

Although the *maraji''s* writings and juridical edicts are important in the religious lives of ordinary American Shi'is, the lack of detailed and specific rules governing Muslim political, social, and civic engagement in their writings means they do not impinge on their followers' daily lives in America. The legal discourse of the *maraji'* has to respond to the emergence of new epistemological, social, and political realities of their followers living in non-Muslim countries. Many within the Shi'i community are seeking not more legal treatises but a more comprehensive discourse, one that will impact their daily lives.

While it is true in general that in America religious norms have no binding force in the social and political spheres, the *maraji'* have to go beyond general moral maxims and articulation of religious norms that pertain to the dos and don'ts. To be relevant to the lives of ordinary Shi'is, the *maraji'* need to articulate an integrated worldview that can relate and respond to the socio-political and economic needs of the community. There is little direction in the *responsa* or *fatawa* from the *maraji'* or any other genre of literature on specifically American issues such as methods and extent of political engagement, civic duties, forms of interfaith dialogue, how to bring the Shi'i community together, and so forth.

The *maraji'* have also not tackled the youth-related issues discussed in chapter 2 of this study. These include the challenges of negative peer pressure, creating a postethnic American Muslim community, promoting marriages within the Shi'i community or, as we shall see in the next chapter, the requirements of African American Shi'is. According to imam Mustafa al-Qazwini, the limited scope of contemporary legal discourse can be explained by the fact that Shi'i law has yet to evolve to reflect the realities of the time. He states that twenty years ago, the questions currently discussed in the *mustahdathat* literature would not have been raised. Immigration to the West and the challenges that Shi'is encountered forced the *maraji'* to respond to the needs of their followers. It is possible, he argues, that an integrated or wholistic approach to Shi'i law will develop as the *maraji'* become aware that they have become irrelevant to the lives of most American Shi'is.[86]

The deficiencies within and parochial vision of the *marji'iyya* were highlighted by Muhammad al-Baqir al-Sadr (d. 1980), the brilliant Shi'i jurist-cum-philosopher. Writing in the 1970s, he complained of inconsistencies in the institution coupled with its failure to clearly articulate goals. For al-Sadr, the *maraji'* made decisions concerning the welfare of the whole community in consultation with relatives and close associates whom they depended upon.[87] He did not see the informal relationship between a *marji'* and his representatives as being effective in facilitating the needs of the community.

Al-Sadr proposed the establishment of a consultative body that would propose policies and suggestions and participate in the decision-making process with the *maraji'*. Committees and boards within this body would replace the current arbitrary and haphazard decision-making process.[88] The consultative process would protect the *marji'iyya* from adopting policies that might be influenced by personal predilections and preferences. As al-Sadr states, "The (institutional) administration would then replace the *hashiya* (*marja*'s personal entourage), which is but an arbitrary irrational apparatus composed of individuals gathered by coincidence . . . to meet immediate needs with a fragmented mentality of no clear and specified objectives."[89]

The structural organization that al-Sadr proposes would provide expertise and long-term planning for attaining the goals set by the previous *marji'*. Such a central administration and council of the *marji'iyya* would also ensure the perpetuation of the policies enforced by a *marji'* beyond his lifetime.

Similar complaints regarding the ineffectiveness of the *marji'iyya* have been voiced by Murtaza Mutahhari.[90] Ayatullah Fadlallah complains that the *maraji'* have remained aloof and are not in touch with the needs of modern times. The *marji'*, Fadlallah states, should not be confined to his quarters in Najaf or Qum. Rather, he should visit Muslim communities throughout the world and have a say in their daily lives. Fadlallah is concerned not only to reform the structure of the *marji'iyya* but also to expand its degree of its influence. To be effective, its influence must be extended to cover all major issues in both the Muslim and non-Muslim worlds.[91]

The vision of Shi'i thinkers like al-Sadr, Mutahhari, and Fadlallah are especially germane to the sociopolitical universe of American Shi'is. Unfortunately, almost thirty years after his death, al-Sadr's suggestions have been largely ignored by the *marji'iyya*. Excessive reliance by the *maraji'* on their representatives and relatives and a lack of an articulated vision for the community has made this institution redundant in the lives of many Shi'is.

Interfacing Islamic and American Laws

To be fully engaged in the American political and social order, Shi'i jurists need to articulate rules of Islamic law that interface with American customary law. Rather than essentializing and modifying certain aspects of Islamic law based on the legal order articulated in classical texts, American customary law (*'urf*) must be recognized as a valid source of prescription, especially where Islamic law allows recourse to local custom. Unless there is an explicit legal prohibition, Shi'is need to use American law for self-empowerment and to gain access to the highest political and civic positions. Equally, local customary law should be seen as a valid legal basis to formulate newer rulings.

Usage of local custom as a source of legal prescription is predicated on the principle that where there is no explicit prohibition, there is no need to observe precaution. It is assumed that all reasonable beings accept and behave according to common norms and values. This being the case, a particular principle can be established by arguing that the pattern of behavior is common to all rational beings, whether they lived in the times of the Imams or not, and that no objection had been raised by the Lawgiver. The agreement by intelligent beings on a particular form of behavior is sufficient proof to deduce that the lawgiver (*shari'*) has endorsed the act.[92]

For example, Ayatullah Khamene'i was asked whether it was permissible to apply *kohl* (eyeliner) to the eye during the Islamic months of Muharram and Safar for purposes other than adornment. His response was that if *kohl* is not considered to be an adornment by the common people, then there is no objection in its application. However, if it is construed by the masses as a form of beautification, then it should not be applied, especially if it appears to demean the importance of these occasions.[93]

Jurists often appeal to local customs in the derivation of different kinds of juridical rulings. As we have seen, when asked if a person who has been pronounced brain-dead be considered dead, Seestani's response is to appeal to the common understanding of death. Similarly, al-Khu'i states that local custom can determine whether a particular type of music is deemed permissible to listen to or not.

It should be remembered that in the past, *'urf* has been accepted as a valid principle for extrapolating a particular ruling based on the principle of *maslaha*. Since it was originally within the parameters of the theory of jurisprudence that *'urf* was allowed to operate, many notions and maxims taken from its corpus were deployed in the course of a legal argument.

It would be unreasonable to expect the *maraji'*, who reside in the Middle East, to be fully aware of the challenges their followers encounter or to propose appropriate solutions especially as Shi'is are scattered in different parts of the world. It would be equally unfair to expect them to provide a comprehensive vision on their own. They rely on their representatives and offices to apprise them of such details. Seestani's representative occasionally visits America but has limited grasp of the situation here. The offices of the *maraji'*, such as al-Khoei Foundation and IMAM, have established Islamic schools and places to commemorate religious events and other educational infrastructures but have not been able to formulate a coherent worldview that would impact the lives of the *maraji's* followers in America. Neither have these offices created a forum to bring the Shi'i community together to engage the challenges that the younger generation of Shi'is face or to provide the sociopolitical directives that I have outlined.

It is important that the *maraji'* consult not only their representatives but also local *'ulama'*, university-trained scholars and intellectuals, socially active Muslims, and those organizations and institutions that are fully conversant with the American political and civic culture so that their followers can better employ the system to attain political and economic empowerment. It is only by establishing consultative boards along the lines suggested by Muhammad Baqir al-Sadr that the *marji'iyya* can become an effective institution in the American milieu. As I discuss in the next chapter, in the absence of guidelines from religious leaders, private individuals and institutions have sought civic and political empowerment in different states. These are isolated, regional efforts and have had limited impact on the community.

So far, due to the limited scope of their influence, the *maraji'* have become a reference point for ordinary Shi'is on issues that pertain to juridical ordinances only. *'Ulama'* who have addressed contemporary American issues in their sermons may not have the erudition or qualifications that the *maraji'* have, but their comprehension of local conditions and relations with the Shi'i community have enabled them to exercise more influence and authority in the lives of many Shi'is than the *maraji'* do. These *'ulama'* have become more relevant in the lives ordinary American Shi'is. According to imam Mustafa al-Qazwini, some Shi'is have requested him to be their *marji'* because they can relate more easily to him than to Seestani.

That the institution of the *marji'iyya* has become irrelevant for many American Shi'is is confirmed by Linda Walbridge in her study of the Lebanese Shi'is in Dearborn. She states,

> Through formal interviews and less formal conversations, I found certain trends arising. It is apparent that the issue of the *marji'* did not loom large in the lives of the Lebanese Shi'a before the Iranian revolution, and for many it still does not. Several people I spoke with, some of whom considered themselves very religious, did not recognize the term *marji'* and needed to have it explained. . . . One highly educated man from Baalbek who is around forty years of age said that he had never known anyone who followed a *marji'*. In fact, he had not become aware of this concept until he lived in Dearborn. As I interviewed a young college student from the Bekaa, his sister, who was visiting from Saudi Arabia, interjected that it was only in the past year that she had learned that the people were supposed to follow a *marji'*.[94]

In another case, Walbridge asked a Lebanese resident in Dearborn on the role of the *marjiʻiyya* in America. He responded rather sarcastically, "What role?"[95]

The ʻUlamaʼ *and the* Marajiʻ

In private circles and conversations, many Shiʻi *ʻulamaʼ* are critical of the roles that the *marajiʻ* play in the lives of ordinary Shiʻis, believing that the *marajiʻ* have had little or no impact on the lives of American Shiʻis. Some scholars are openly vocal. Muhammad Ilahi, the imam at the Islamic House of Wisdom in Dearborn, states that the *marajiʻ* do not view America as a priority because they seem to have more pressing issues and challenges in their own countries. Ilahi adds that instead of contributing to the financial needs of Islamic centers, the *marajiʻ* expect a portion of the *khumus* contribution to be sent to the Middle East. This has created a financial burden for many centers.

Imam Ilahi would like to see the *marajiʻ* pay closer attention to the requirements of their followers in America and to prepare scholars who can meet those needs. According to Ilahi, there is a dire need to prepare a new curriculum in the seminaries that will cater to the needs of Muslims in the West. In the long run, Ilahi continues, there is a need to establish a full-fledged seminary in the West to train scholars who are more versed with local culture and better equipped to serve communities here.[96]

Most scholars believe the *marajiʻ* need to play more active roles in the lives of the American Shiʻi community members. Echoing complaints that many *ʻulamaʼ* have voiced, Shaykh Fyzee of Bayt al-ʻIlm in Chicago bemoans the lack of communication between the *marajiʻ* and the American Shiʻis. He states that most *marajiʻ* are concerned with the affairs of their own hometowns or country and are not fully conversant with the various challenges the community is confronted with in America.

Another scholar who prefers to remain anonymous (imam X) is very critical of the role of the *marajiʻ* in America. He states that there is little connection between the *marajiʻ* and the two million Shiʻis in the United States. In fact, imam X states that the *marajiʻ* are almost absent in the lives of many Shiʻis. Their representatives visit this country only to collect religious taxes. Due to the *marjiʻ* factor, imam X feels that the American Shiʻi community has become more fragmented. That this scholar has asked not to be identified is indicative of the stigmatism attached to any criticism of the *marajiʻ* within the community.

Reflecting a somewhat different view, Shaykh Fadhil Sahlani of al-Khoei Foundation in New York states that the *maraji'* are aware of the needs of the community due to the information they receive from their representatives, institutions, and visitors who visit them in the holy cities. Sahlani also adds that the *maraji'*'s capacity to act is often restricted due to political conditions in their countries of residence. Due to these circumstances, they may not be able to play as prominent a role as they might wish.[97]

The issue of the *maraji'* and their impact in the States was discussed at an imam's council conference in New Jersey in 2004. Many scholars complained that the *marji'iyya* was not responding to the various needs of the community and that the institution has actually divided not only the community but also the *'ulama'*. Shaykh Haeri in Washington, D.C. hints at a possible reason for the division between the *'ulama'*. He states that some scholars divide and differentiate themselves based on the *marji'* they follow. Paradoxically, the institutions of *marji'iyya* and *taqlid* have engendered more division than unity within the scholarly community. Haeri further adds that while many Shi'i *'ulama'* sit with Sunnis or non-Muslims to discourse, there is hardly any dialogue between the Shi'i scholars themselves.

Other scholars at the conference complained that the *maraji'* do not provide sufficient financial support for community projects nor do they provide guidance to confront the challenges confronting the younger generation within the community. The views of the scholars concerning the *marji'iyya* demonstrate the tensions that have arisen within the leadership of the American Shi'i community. Many Shi'i scholars believe that the *marji'iyya* has distanced and disconnected itself from the lives of their American followers. Concerns over the role of the *marji'iyya* and the lack of communication with the Shi'i community have been addressed, to some degree, by the establishment of the Imam Mahdi Association of Marjaeya (IMAM).

Established in 2004, IMAM acts as a liaison office of Ayatullah Seestani. IMAM aims to be a religious organization that acts as a source of communication between all members of the Shi'i community in North America and the *marji'iyya*. IMAM's vision is to encourage, equip, and develop all Shi'i Muslims in North America with the proper education and learning for the application of their faith, reflecting the Shi'i Muslim teachings and raising the status of the followers within their respective communities. IMAM has also tried to cater for the socioreligious needs of the Shi'i community. Thus, where necessary, it intervenes to deal with matters such as marriage, divorce, wills, inheritance, along with other social issues within the community, like helping the indigent. IMAM has also established an Islamic Institute for Higher Education. The intellectual and religious department of IMAM is dedicated primarily to the preparation of leaders for the congregations served by IMAM. Presently, IMAM is the only national religious organization that functions under the auspices of a *marji'* and provides various services to the Shi'i community across America.[98]

The Council of Shi'i 'Ulama' in North America

Apart from the *maraji'*, authority in the American Shi'i community is also wielded by the religious scholars, the *'ulama'*. Most Shi'i *'ulama'* have migrated to America since the 1980s and originate from the Middle East or South Asia. Dearborn, with its large concentration of Lebanese and Iraqi Shi'is, has the largest number of scholars in any American city.

Presently, the Shi'i community in North America comprises of about one hundred and fifty religious scholars. The majority of these scholars are affiliated with Shi'i centers and perform basic religious functions like leading prayers, delivering sermons, performing funerals, and marriages. Most Shi'i *'ulama'* with whom I spoke complained that there is little communication among them in America.

Imam X says there are two types of *'ulama'*. The traditional *'ulama'* see their tasks as that of delivering sermons, holding ritualized commemorative gatherings in Muharram and Ramadhan, and other routine activities. Neither the *'ulama'* nor their speeches are connected to the daily lives of the people. Imam X is even more scathing in his remarks when he states that some of these traditional *'ulama'* bring their village mentalities from their home countries to this country. There are, however, other *'ulama'* who are more open to political participation and dialogue and who want to engage with rather than isolate themselves from Americans. Imam X adds that these *'ulama'* mobilize Muslims so as to actively contribute to the American milieu, but unfortunately, they are few in numbers. Most of the *'ulama'* with whom I spoke in the United States complained of divisions among the scholars and the need to establish a nationwide body that will bring the scholars together.

In an effort to unite the diverse ethnic groups that make up the American Shi'i community, an indigenous Council of Shi'i *'Ulama'* was formed

in 1993. Composed of scholars in North America, the council meets annually to discuss issues germane to the community. Among the stated aims
of the council is to support the American Shi'i community by strengthening unity and cooperation between the Shi'i *'ulama'*.[99] In addition,
the council seeks to deal with issues that require the collective efforts of
'ulama' and to defend Islam in general and the *madhhab* (school of law)
of the *ahl al-bayt* in particular.

Although it has been in existence since 1993, the council has failed to
formulate any definitive direction for the Shi'i community, nor has it been
able to bridge the chasm that has divided different ethnic groups within
the community. A comment heard from many council members is that
the *'ulama'* are too preoccupied with their own centers to be concerned
with the Council of *'Ulama'*.

At a conference of *'ulama'* in 2004, the attendees agreed that the Council of *'Ulama'* had so far been largely ineffective. Eleven years after its inception, most Shi'is were not even aware of the existence of the Council
of Shi'a *'Ulama'* or of its objectives and mandates. Since 2004, the council
has become more active and is closely affiliated to IMAM, meeting annually to discuss issues that impact the American Shi'i community.[100] However, the council has so far failed to bring the scholars together or unite
the community. Many Shi'i *'ulama'* are skeptical of the goals and future
direction of the council. They do not officially affiliate with it or attend its
meetings. Some of the South Asian *'ulama'* have formed a separate body
distinct from the North American Council. The North American Council of *'Ulama'* also suffers from a dearth of financial and administrative
resources. There is thus a distinct lacuna in the leadership, which could
direct the social, economic, and political activities of the Shi'i community
in America.

Few *'ulama'* in the West are conversant with issues relating to the local community or fully instructed enough in the Islamic tradition to articulate a proper solution to the challenges faced by community members.
Community leaders who have been raised in the American environment
understand the problems of adjustment that Muslim immigrants face.
However, they have little grounding in the sources of Islamic tradition
that can provide solutions to these challenges. On the other hand, religious leaders imported from Iran, Iraq, and South Asia are thoroughly
versed in the religious tradition but often have little understanding of the
problems encountered by Shi'is in the American context. Many of these
scholars are not able to converse in English, and the contents of their

sermons are deemed by many to be irrelevant to the challenges of living in contemporary America.

This situation has made it extremely difficult for members of the Shiʿi community to keep the younger generation interested in their faith. Thus far, the solutions offered by community leaders have been temporary, failing to affect the resolution necessary for the future religious loyalty and spiritual well-being of the members. The lack of religious leaders who are both locally trained and fully instructed in Islamic tradition has been identified by many Shiʿis as the most urgent concern facing the future survival of the community in the secular American environment.

The Shiʿi community is becoming aware of the need for Islamically trained but indigenous American religious leadership. The need to train local scholars has arisen because the ambit of activities that imams have to perform in America has increased considerably. Besides offering basic religious services, imams are also required to provide pastoral care, counsel members of their congregation, visit the sick and needy, adjudicate disputes between members of the mosque, participate in interfaith dialogue, and promote a positive understanding of Islam.

Recognition of the problems of imported imams has led some community members to train indigenous imams. The Khoja-based institution, the World Federation of Khoja Shia Ithna-asheri Muslim Communities (KSIMC), for example, is embarking on an ambitious project to train religious scholars, educating them in the traditional sciences and courses that are offered in universities. The intent is to better serve Shiʿi communities in the West and to reach out to the younger generation. Others have sought to create local scholars by introducing online religious classes. However, these attempts are often premised on utilizing the curriculum and methodology taught in the traditional Shiʿi seminaries in Iraq, Iran, and Syria.

Conclusion

In the pluralistic international order in which Muslim and non-Muslim nations share equal membership, classical juridical rulings have remained a sacred point of reference. Shiʿi jurists have had to rethink and reinterpret aspects of Islamic law in order to respond to the challenges of living in a minority context. Some jurists have argued that the juridical decisions in the past were interwoven to the political, cultural, or historical circumstances in the eighth century. Thus, they have reinterpreted and restated

Islamic law, invoking various hermeneutical principles to respond to the needs of the times and to go beyond the rulings stated in the revealed texts.

Globalization and improved modes of communications have led the *maraji'* to increase their influence in America. Due to the Internet and easier access to the offices of the *maraji'*, the religious leadership is now able to permeate the lives of American Shi'is more effectively. Traditional legal scholarship has accommodated matters that are important in present-day America.

The new literature emerging from Shi'i seminaries demonstrates the workings of the *maraji'* in dealing with questions that arise among Muslims, especially those living in the West. In most cases, the *maraji'* respond to the questions of their followers on an ad hoc basis. The casuistic methodology pursued by the jurists is inconsistent with the universal character of the solutions they propose by assuming a temporary rather than permanent residence in the United States. The *maraji'* have yet to propose solutions that relate to both the personal and public lives of their followers in the West. Unless this is done, the institution will not be able to permeate the lives of many Shi'is.

5

Shi'i Outreach Activities in America

As the number of Shi'i immigrants increased, they envisioned the need to establish institutions that could reach out to non-Muslims and challenge the negative portrayal of Islam in the media. Until the 1980s, most of the outreach work had been undertaken by members of the Sunni community. For the Shi'is, the need to proselytize and depict a positive image of Islam in general and Shi'ism in particular became more acute after the Iranian revolution in 1979 and the ensuing hostage crisis because many, if not most, Americans had associated Shi'ism with militancy and terrorism.

The emergence of Hizbollah after the Israeli invasion of Lebanon in 1982 and the subsequent capture of American hostages in Beirut further exacerbated the situation for American Shi'is who had to counteract the negative publicity that Shi'ism received in the media. In addition, the Gulf War created an awareness of the presence of the Shi'is in various Arab countries. It is within this context that we can understand Shi'i outreach activities and engagement in *da'wa* (proselytization) projects in America.

A study of Shi'i proselytization also necessitates a discussion of the interaction between the Shi'i community and indigenous African Americans. The chapter therefore discusses a topic that has been largely ignored by scholars of Islam in America, the African America Shi'is in America. So far, there has been virtually no mention of this group in any academic study of American Islam. My observations on the African American Shi'is will, in part, be based on correspondence with some twenty inmates at various correctional facilities.

Shi'i outreach activities were also impacted by the horrific events of September 11, 2001, when Muslims of all persuasions were targeted and profiled. This chapter also examines how the events of 9/11 impacted the Shi'i community and discusses how the Shi'i community responded to the denigration and demonization of Islam after 9/11.

Da'wa *Activities by the Shi'i Community*

"When [you travel to] the land of non-Muslims, talk [to others] about us."[1] This advice was reportedly given by the sixth Shi'i Imam, Ja'far al-Sadiq, to his followers in the eighth century. Based on this and other traditions, some Shi'is maintain that it is a collective obligation on the community (*al-wajib al-kifa'i*) to propagate Shi'ism whenever and wherever they are able to do so.[2] It is within the context of the tradition (*hadith*) that we can discuss Shi'i institutes and their *da'wa* activities in America.

Shi'i outreach activities in America began on a small scale in the 1970s, when members of the Shi'i community migrated to the American shores. In the late 1970s, foreign organizations such as the World Organization for Islamic Services in Iran sent books for distribution to Yasin al-Jibouri's Islamic Societies of Georgia, which was established in 1973. The Bilal Muslim Mission in Africa also sent many books to America. By July 1977, about 5,770 books and booklets had been mailed out.[3] With increased immigration to America in the 1980s, some Shi'i centers and private individuals engaged in outreach activities. Private sources like Ansariyan Publications based in Qum, Iran, sent Shi'i literature to American prisons. In the early 1990s, the Canadian based Islamic Research and Education Center started a correspondence course to teach Shi'ism to potential or actual converts. This outreach endeavor continued until the late 1990s.

It is important to consider that as most Shi'i centers have been established since the 1980s, few of these centers or mosques have reached out to non-Muslims or engaged in interfaith dialogue in a substantive way. Instead, these centers have used their limited financial resources to establish and consolidate their religious institutions and engage in communal activities rather than proselytize or help improve the image of Islam outside the community. One question in my survey related to the types of *da'wa* activities undertaken by the centers. Most centers did not respond to the question. Table 2 shows that only 6 percent of the centers thought that responding to the needs of the converts was an important future challenge.

Most Shi'i institutes in America lack the financial support that is afforded, for example, to the Saudi-backed Muslim World League (MWL). Lack of diplomatic relations between America and Iran, the only Shi'i country, has meant that the latter has not been able not provide the institutional infrastructure or financial support necessary to furnish Shi'i outreach work in America. Shi'i proselytization activities have been limited to a few poorly funded organizations that are not properly structured for extensive *da'wa*. It is correct to state that Shi'i centers of worship are introverted rather than outward-directed. The activities of most centers are directed at providing such basic religious services as facilitating prayers, conducting marriages and funerals, and counseling members of the community. The focus on preservation rather than extension of boundaries is corroborated by letters that I received from Shi'i inmates. These indicate that most converts from the African American community convert to Shi'ism as a result of their own efforts and research, or because a friend approached them rather than from proselytization by the Shi'i community.

Other factors also challenge the Shi'i community's capacity to reach out to non-Muslims. The arrival of newer migrants has impinged on the American Shi'i community as it experiences Islam mainly through the phenomenon of "imported Islam." As we have seen, newer immigrants tend to revive traditional norms and impose a conservative and extraneous expression of Islam. The immigrants' major concern is to preserve the traditional understanding of Islam instead of reaching out to potential converts or engaging in dialogue with non-Muslims. Recently arrived immigrants tend to coalesce around their own ethnic enclaves and feel threatened by "the other," especially if they have not engaged in dialogue with other faith groups or other forms of outreach activities in their countries of origins.

For many immigrants, isolation from mainstream American culture is seen as being loyal to Islam. It is as if loyalty to or engagement in America was tantamount to being unfaithful to Islam. Since most Shi'i centers were established after the 1980s, few, if any institutions have reached out to non-Muslims to correct the popular stereotypes against Islam. In the survey I conducted, almost 38 percent of the centers did not reply to the question of any outreach work undertaken (Table 8).

The Iranian Influence in America

Since Iran is the only Shi'i country in the world, it is necessary to comprehend the Iranian influence in promoting American Shi'ism. Due to Iran's strained relations with America, Iranian-backed activities are not overt. While the ambit of its activities is not as extensive as the Saudi-backed Muslim World League, Iran has managed to spread its ideology and promulgate Shi'ism in less conspicuous ways: through the influx of Iranian

Shi'i immigrants, through the Internet, and via the importation of foreign literature. Iranian centers in America invite speakers from Iran especially in the months of Ramadhan and Muharram. Although they do not represent the Iranian government, these speakers are able to propagate Shi'ism within the Iranian community here. In addition, Iranian channels are now widely available on satellite television. In August 2007, an Iranian channel (Press TV) began to broadcast on satellite television in English, targeting a Western audience. This, together with access to the Internet, allows the dissemination of official Iranian ideology in America. While quite effective, these modes of communication are accessed primarily by devout Shi'is.

Unofficial Iranian groups have also been active in the States. The Ansariyan Publication of Qum has published a large number of Shi'i books that it sends to converts in American prisons. These books are also sold in Shi'i bookstores and on the Internet. Iranian sponsored magazines and journals such as *Mahjuba, Islamic Echo,* and *Tawhid* are widely circulated. In addition, the writings of Iranian intellectuals like Murtaza Mutahhari, 'Ali Shari'ati, and Abdul Karim Soroush have been translated and extensively publicized in America. The writings of both Shari'ati and Soroush have been read by Shi'is and non-Shi'is alike, and these authors have influenced the thinking of many American Shi'is.

As I discuss below, many African American Shi'is have been influenced by the Iranian revolution. Having studied in the seminary in Qum, some of them teach in American institutions while others preach in mosques or proselytize. Some have become community activists in America.

Shi'i Institutes in America

To understand the role of institutions in promoting Shi'ism, it is important to differentiate between those Shi'i institutes that cater primarily to the needs of the faithful within the Shi'i community and those that focus on outreach programs oriented toward a non-Muslim audience. Here, I briefly discuss some of the main "external" and "internal" institutes.

Most Shi'i outreach activities began in the 1990s when Shi'i immigrants became aware of the success that the Sunnis had in converting Americans, both white and black, to Islam. In contrast to Shi'i proselytism, Sunni *da'wa* in America is characterized, as we have seen, by the presence of numerous movements, most of which originate in the Middle East or South Asia. These movements have imposed their distinct ideologies and views here. Besides the extraneous movements, indigenous African American movements like the Nation of Islam, the Moorish Science Temple, Ansaru Allah, the Five Percenters and others have also proselytized in American prisons. The movement of the late Warith al-Din Muhammad, now called the American Muslim Society, has been a powerful advocate for Islam in America. Financial support from the Saudi government has emboldened his movement, which has been the primary voice of African American Sunni Muslims in America.[4]

Since the majority of the Muslims in America are Sunnis, most Muslim institutions were founded by them. These include institutes like the Federation of Islamic Associations in the United States (FIA),[5] the Muslim Student Association (MSA), the Islamic Society of North America (ISNA), the Islamic Circle of North America (ICNA), the Islamic Association of North America (IANA), the Muslim Public Affairs Council (MPAC), the American Muslim Alliance (AMA), the American Muslim Council (AMC), and the Council on American-Islamic Relations (CAIR).[6]

By convening seminars, publishing articles in magazines and Islamic newsletters, delivering lectures at various conventions and workshops, these institutions have altered the way Muslims think about the United States and about themselves. Gradually, they have transformed Muslim political and civil consciousness in this country to the ways Muslims could interact with Americans and yet maintain their own distinctive identity. The vision is now on repositioning Islam as an important element of American national interest.[7]

In the 1980s Shi'is became aware that Sunni organizations had influenced how Islam in America was presented and perceived. Increased tensions between America and Iran and Israel and Hizbollah made the need for Shi'i self-representation in American public space more imperative. Furthermore, due to the enhanced Sunni–Shi'i tensions in the 1980s, the Shi'is quickly realized that they could not depend on Sunni institutions to represent them or speak on their behalf. As more Shi'i immigrants settled here, they came to view the United States as a fertile place for promoting a better image of Islam and for seeking converts. Hence, the 1980s saw the establishment of Shi'i institutions that reached out to the non-Muslim community.

An early Shi'i institute was the Tahrike Tarsile Qur'an (TTQ). Established in New York in 1978, TTQ has the specific aim of publishing copies of the Qur'an, which are distributed to different parts of the world, including in American prisons. TTQ's founder, Aunali Khalfan, started the organization from his personal premises on a very modest scale. So far, TTQ has published thirty editions of the Qur'an, most of which have been sent to non-Muslims throughout the world.

Khalfan notes that there has been a dramatic increase in the demand for the Qur'an since 9/11. He states that before the events of September 11, 2001, TTQ published 80,000 copies per year. Now, it publishes 250,000 copies every year.[8] The increased demand for copies of the Qur'an reflects the growing interest in Islam among Americans after 9/11. Since its activities are confined to the publication and distribution of Islamic literature, TTQ sends literature but not proselytes to American prisons. Neither does it engage in interfaith dialogue.

Established in 1987, the Qur'an Account Inc. (QAI) was initially called the Islamic School System. QAI was founded in Washington D.C. by Dr. Hashim, a retired pediatrician from Iraq. Its primary focus has been to educate inmates in correctional facilities about Islam. Since the institute's inception, Dr. Hashim has converted more than 6,300 people to Islam. The institute sends copies of the Qur'an and other books to various prisons, and has published the quarterly *Bulletin of Affiliation* for twenty-three years. Inmates, non-Muslims, and even Muslims themselves request copies of the Qur'an and other genres of Islamic literature. Dr. Hashim corresponds with both Shi'i and Sunni inmates, and like other proselytes, he complains that most Shi'i centers ignore the needs of converts. He is also frustrated by the fact that there is little or no communication between Shi'i institutes that proselytize.[9]

An important Shi'i institute is al-Khoei foundation in New York, which caters to both the Shi'i and non-Shi'i communities in America. In 1997, the foundation became the fourth Muslim organization—and the only Shi'i Muslim organization—to hold General Consultative Status in the United Nations, where it currently promotes work on human and minority rights. The foundation's public relations officer teaches classes for imams to work on their communication skills. This is a part of a collaborative effort with Sunni organizations on a Good Practice Guide for Mosques and imams.[10] Al-Khoei Foundation also corresponds with Shi'i inmates, interacts with DOCs to ameliorate the conditions of African American Shi'is in correctional facilities, and addresses their needs in New York.

Al-Khoei Foundation has an established daily Islamic school whose director, Shaykh Fadhil Sahlani, is a representative of Ayatullah Seestani designated to handle all matters, religious or otherwise. The foundation also has a state-of-the-art Islamic center where commemorative events are held regularly.

The Islamic Information Center (IIC) is a grassroots organization founded in 2003 to negate stereotypical images about Islam and the Muslim community. According to Mawlana Rafiq Naqavi, the founder of the IIC, after the September 11 attacks, many in the community sensed the need to disseminate correct information about Islam. IIC is also engaged in interfaith dialogue and publishes articles and interviews on Islam. It publishes a bimonthly newsletter addressing issues that pertain to Islam and the Muslim world. Through educational and interfaith programs, IIC seeks to promote understanding and trust among people of all faiths and cultures.

Several Canadian-based Shi'i institutions also proselytize in the States. The Islamic Humanitarian Services (IHS) operates from Kitchener/Waterloo, in Ontario. The organization has published various books and engages in *da'wa* work in correctional facilities in America. IHS has also translated some important Shi'i works to English and has been involved in various humanitarian projects abroad.

Established in the mid-1990s in New York, the Bilal Muslim Mission of Americas now operates from Orlando, Florida. Initially, most of its outreach activities focused on Trinidad. BMMA tried to correct misconceptions about and promote a better understanding of Shi'ism especially during the month of Muharram when the Hosay processions were held. BMMA responds to letters from inmates in various correctional facilities in the United States and sends them books on Islam.

A different form of outreach is satellite television. Salaam TV broadcasts from Los Angeles in both Farsi and English. So far, its programming has consisted of a series of English lectures, supplications, and programs in Farsi that appeal to devout Shi'is. The programs are neither captivating nor intellectually engaging and have not touched upon the substantive issues that impact the American Shi'i community, especially the needs of the younger generation. More importantly, since most of its English programs are in the form of interviews and lectures delivered in Islamic centers by Shi'i imams, Salaam TV has not been able to reach out to a Western audience. Salaam also suffers from a dearth of financial resources that are required to sustain a wide range of programming. Due to these factors, Salaam TV has not been able to exploit the tremendous potential at its disposal and has, so far, not been able to reach the non-Muslim community.

Universal Muslim Association of America (UMAA)

The most important Shi'i national institution is the Universal Muslim Association of America (UMAA). According to an UMAA booklet, after the ISNA convention in 2002, members within the Shi'i community approached both ISNA and CAIR seeking Shi'i representation in the organizations. They were rebuffed, and it was against this background that UMAA was formed in 2002 in Maryland. Leaders of the organization felt that the Shi'i community needed an organization that could represent, speak on behalf of, and unite the Shi'is.

UMAA proclaimed its distinct identity as a Shi'i Muslim national organization and was the first multiethnic Shi'i national movement in America. Its first convention was held over the Memorial Day weekend in 2003. Initially, the movement was endorsed by some prominent Shi'i scholars, both abroad and in America. UMAA's stated agenda is extensive, seeking to provide a forum to foster unity among Muslims, encouraging Muslims to fulfill civic and political responsibilities, dispelling misgivings about Islam and Muslims, and helping Americans better understand Islam in the light of the Qur'an and the teachings of the Prophet and his family. UMAA also seeks to promote an accurate portrayal of Islam and encourage both inter- and intrafaith dialogue. It provides a forum to foster an effective grassroots participation by Muslims in the United States and to network with other organizations.[11]

UMAA aims to facilitate discussion on social, political, and economic issues affecting the Muslim community. It seeks to encourage Muslims to vote and participate in the political process, coordinate with the media and educate it on issues relating to Islam, and to provide a common platform and forum for Muslim youth. UMAA also endeavors to train Shi'i imams to serve the community in America.

Like al-Khoei, UMAA wants to cater to both the Shi'i and non-Shi'i communities. Since its inception, UMAA has tried to bring together and unite different Shi'i ethnic and cultural groups under its umbrella, which has often led to clashes and criticisms. In particular, UMMA has been criticized for being too liberal in its outlook. UMAA was also chastised by many Shi'is for having Paul Wolfowitz, the U.S. Deputy Secretary of Defense in the Bush administration, speak at its first convention in Washington, D.C.

Five years after its inception, UMAA has yet to achieve any of its lofty goals, including that of transcending ethnic differences within the Shi'i community. Most of the attendees at its annual conference are from the South Asian community; thus, its sphere of influence has been circumscribed. Despite several attempts, UMAA has, so far, struggled to attract Lebanese, Iranians, Khojas, Iraqis, or Afghani Shi'is to its meetings. Most Shi'is do not identify themselves with and are openly critical of UMAA; they claim that the institution has little to offer apart from annual conventions and occasional press releases. Without the support of the Shi'i leadership and community, UMAA has so far failed to match the success of its Sunni counterpart, ISNA. Internal wrangling and the fact that its leadership is dominated by members of the South Asian community have further undermined the credibility of UMAA.

Internal Shi'i Institutes

Besides the institutes outlined in the previous section, there are many "internal" Shi'i organizations that cater primarily to the American Shi'i community. An early Shi'i institute was the Alawi Foundation based in New York. This Iranian-based nonprofit organization owns more than 50 percent of an office building in Midtown Manhattan. Since the Iranian revolution, the Alawi Foundation has helped establish Shi'i religious centers in major American cities like Houston, Washington, and New York. The foundation engages in charitable and philanthropic projects with an emphasis on education and civic concerns. It also provides financial assistance to nonprofit organizations involved in the teaching of Islamic culture and Persian language (Farsi). Currently, the Alawi Foundation is sponsoring a translation of the voluminous Qur'anic exegesis, *al-Mizan fi Tafsir al-Qur'an*, of 'Allama Tabataba'i. However, the foundation has had limited engagement with non-Muslims and has yet to develop the institutional infrastructure necessary to undertake extensive outreach programs in the United States.

The Muslim Congress was established in 2005. Its primary goal is to provide educational services that will directly benefit members of the Shi'i community. The Muslim Congress has established a state-of-the-art website, which serves as a focal point for all its activities, but the organization is in an embryonic stage.[12] It has promised to provide community services such as family counseling, matrimonial services, career/ business guidance, online discussion forums, and the like. Within Shi'i circles, it is seen as rivaling UMAA as it duplicates many of the goals of and services rendered by UMAA. The Muslim Congress is more clerical-based but, like UMAA, has yet to make a definitive impact on the Shi'i community in America.

The Organization for Islamic Learning (OIL) is different from the other institutions mentioned. This Canadian-based organization was formed in Toronto in 1999 and has a branch in the States. Its stated objective is to promote learning based on Islamic Revelation: the Qur'an and the *sunna* of the Prophet Muhammad and his family. It also seeks to promote religious and civic participation in society and interfaith tolerance. OIL seeks to present Islam in a way that is stimulating and thought provoking, in a manner that encourages learning, and in a format that fosters constructive discussion. OIL holds seminars and lectures, and frequently invites speakers who are deemed controversial by other Shi'i organizations.

OIL holds lectures primarily during the month of Muharram, but it also invites speakers at regular intervals during the year. In 2005, it tried to bridge the gap between universities and the community by holding university-style classes for members of the Toronto community. In addition, OIL has a number of thought-provoking articles on its website, many of which challenge the traditional or classical understanding of Islam.[13] OIL has been able to reach only a limited audience as many in the Shi'i community do not agree with its liberal stance and the speakers it invites.

The establishment of OIL and its educational activities in the form of seminars, retreats, classes, and lectures indicate that many members of the Shi'i community seek programs that differ from the mosque-based ritualized services like the *majalis* and *nawahi*. Many are also seeking programs and lectures that are more intellectually engaging. The genre of programs that OIL convenes also indicates a clear division within the Shi'i community. Due to its stimulating and often controversial topics, OIL has attracted audiences from both the Shi'i and Sunni communities.

In an attempt to unite the various ethnic Shi'i groups in North America, the North America Shi'a Ithna-asheri Communities (NASIMCO) was established by the Khoja community in Toronto in 1980. Twenty-four Canadian and American Shi'i communities consisting of about 20,000 people are currently members of NASIMCO. Most non-Khoja members have chosen not to join NASIMCO or participate in its activities.[14]

One of the few national Shi'i institutes was the Ahlul Bayt Assembly of America (ABAA). In the early 1990s, ABAA, located in Washington D.C., was founded to unite Shi'is in North America under the umbrella of the family of the Prophet.[15] Among ABAA's stated objectives are to safeguard and further the religious, moral, social, and educational interests of Muslims in the United States and to create, cultivate, and maintain goodwill and understanding among the followers of Islam and followers of other religions. ABAA held a national conference in November 1996, the proceedings of which were published by the institute. The proceedings outlined the activities of different Shiʻi organizations, which ranged from different genres of publications to other forms of educational and devotional activities.[16] ABAAʼs current functions are spasmodic and largely irrelevant to the lives of ordinary American Shiʻis, most of whom have not even heard of ABAA or its activities.

The Qunoot Foundation was founded in 2005 by three American Shiʻi Muslims in Washington D.C. Qunoot Foundationʼs primary focus is to create a platform for young Shiʻis to articulate their concerns on sociopolitical matters. The organization was formed after the 2004 American presidential election. At the time, young Shiʻi Muslims visited various Shiʻi centers in the States and urged people to register and vote. They realized that many community members had little or no exposure to policymaking decisions. More surprising was that political ambivalence was prevalent among many youth. Qunoot was then created to equip Shiʻi youth with the skills and knowledge to engage civic issues in America; it also organized conferences and workshops. The first conference, "Exploring the Layers of Our Identity," was put together in November 2005 as a forum to explore issues within the Shiʻi community and included topics such as gender relations and domestic violence, political participation, and Sunni–Shiʻi relations on college campuses.

Qunoot has reached out to the community by resorting to podcasts. Since few Shiʻi organizations had utilized the new technologies, Qunoot members sought to explore new mediums to reach out and disseminate information. The podcast series began in 2005 and was the first podcast to explore issues on Islam from a Shiʻi perspective. In the two years that Qunoot maintained the podcast, they received around fourteen thousand downloads, or about five hundred downloads per episode.[17]

The Academy of Islamic Learning (ALI) teaches a wide range of short-term courses on Shiʻi history, theology, jurisprudence, ethics, and other related subjects. Courses are geared toward adults and children, and are taught both onsite and online. ALIʼs primary goal is to provide religious instruction to lay Shiʻis whose main source of knowledge on Islam has been restricted to the *madaris* and *majalis*.

These Shiʻi institutions have been established in America since the 1980s. They are privately run, founded by individuals who have sensed the need to perform diverse activities both within and outside the Shiʻi community. However, there is no leadership within the Shiʻi community to unite these different institutions, and there is little or no discourse within these institutions on engaging the multitudinous challenges that confront the American Shiʻi community. Neither the *marjiʻiyya* nor the Council of Imams have grappled with issues such as political activism, civic engagement, the unity and future direction of the Shiʻi community, or an articulation of the terms of engagement with both the non-Muslim and Sunni communities. Institutions that discuss these issues do so on a regional basis, often with little or no co-ordination with other Shiʻi organizations, since most of their activities are based within local communities.

The various institutions mentioned are indigenous, created and maintained by ordinary Shiʻis, independent of the *marajiʻ* or *ʻulama*. Their character is distinctly grassroots. Since most Shiʻis do not derive any tangible benefits from organizations like BMMA, ABAA, NASIMCO, UMAA, or the Muslim Congress, it would not be an exaggeration to state that organizations that cater to local or regional communities have had more impact on local communities than national bodies. On the other hand, very few institutes have reached out to the African American community.

Islam and the African American Community

Scholars of Islam in America have amply documented the provenance and experience of the African American Muslim community. Much has also been written on American indigenous movements such as the Moorish Science Temple, Ansaru Allah, and the Nation of Islam. However, scholars have paid little attention to the African American Shiʻis (Black Shiʻis). For example, in his *American Jihad*, Steve Barboza profiles several African American Muslims. They range from members of the Nation of Islam and the Moorish Science Temple to members of the Sunni community. Yet, not a single Black Shiʻi is profiled, nor is the existence of African American Shiʻism acknowledged.

The potential of Islam as a viable source of empowerment was introduced to the black community through such groups as the Moorish Science Temple and the Nation of Islam. The dominant theme of African American Islam was to cure the black community of various social ills by enforcing Islamic tenets such as the prohibition of alcohol, drugs, and promiscuity. African American Muslims have also created an alternative community identity and an avenue for independent and creative community building.

It is important, initially, to understand the appeal of Islam to the African American community. Many of them convert to Islam as they see it as a religion of their forefathers. It is estimated that about 15 percent of the slaves brought from Africa were Muslims. Thus, Islam is seen by African Americans as the religion of their ancestors and, by converting to Islam, they affirm their African heritage and ancestral roots.

Others are attracted to Islam because of its emphasis on discipline and purity. That Islam prohibits alcohol, prostitution, drugs, and abortion is highly significant as it enables converts to reform themselves and abide by much stricter rules. For many black Americans, especially those who are incarcerated, Islam offers a counterdiscipline, which has caused some to be restructured to an extent they never thought possible.[18] Islam gives this structure to their lives so that a prisoner can, as it were, reside in another place within the same confining walls.[19]

Islam also appeals to non-Muslims due to its insistence on upright human conduct, ethics, dignity, and hard work. This is one main reason why many African Americans turned to the Moorish Science Temple (established in New Jersey in 1913 by Timothy Drew) and the Nation of Islam. The latter movement, which was led by Elijah Muhammad (d. 1975) in the early 1930s in Detroit, attracted converts because of the social benefits and services it offered to the black community. The movement also created employment opportunities, imparted a sense of dignity, and offered a solution to the moral crisis they were confronted with.

Converts were also granted protection and a new identity by the Nation of Islam. The emphasis on hope based on principles of dignity, hard work, and ethical living has characterized all of the indigenous African American Islamic groups. Members are called to a transformation of life in which they are challenged to reach their best potential. Despite its racist and heretical preaching, the Nation of Islam was able to convert many African Americans to its brand of Islam.

For some African Americans, Christianity is viewed as a white man's religion because, in their view, the deeply entrenched racism that pervaded white America in the nineteenth century had informed both the teaching and practice of Christianity. Many blacks feel that Christianity condoned slavery and ill-treatment. They found Islam's egalitarian principles to be an attractive and viable alternative to the racism and prejudice that seemed to have been inextricably bound to Christianity in the United

States. Since Islam is purportedly a color-blind religion and emphasizes equality and justice for all races, it is attractive to many African Americans.[20] Islam discourages asceticism and renunciation of this world and is anchored, instead, on a community's construction of an order based on egalitarianism, justice, and a concern for the moral and social well-being of its citizens, another attractive feature for many within the African American community.

The simplicity of the Islamic declaration of faith has also proven to be attractive to many converts. To become a Muslim, a person merely has to accept one God and the prophecy of the last Prophet, Muhammad. In contrast, Christianity contains beliefs that are considered by some to be problematic and difficult to comprehend, such as those of the doctrines of Trinity, the resurrection of Christ, and the belief in Jesus as the Word of God.

Some whites, Hispanics, Native Americans, and others have also embraced Islam, many of them because they want to marry a Muslim. American women converts say that among the reasons they are attracted to Islam are the support of a community (which they prefer as an alternative to Western individualism) and the ethical structure of Islam, which provides relief from what they see as the increasing immorality of American culture. Hispanic and Native American women claim to see in Islam those elements that resonate with their own individual cultures, such as respect for family and elders, appreciation of the rhythms of nature, and the integration of religious and spiritual beliefs with the whole of life.[21]

The letters I received from Shi'i inmates cited multiple reasons for their conversion to Islam. The most important factor was that they thought Muslims were smarter people. In all probability, this response reflects the organization, bonding, and discipline that hold Muslim inmates together within the prison system. Another reason cited for conversion was that there was a perceived need to be close to Allah. This suggests that inmates feel that there is a spiritual vacuum within the prison system and that conversion to Islam instills a sense of hope and renewed vigor.

The African American Shi'is

Historically, the African American community had established a strong relationship with Islam long before and independent of immigrant Muslims. In its early history, Black Islam in America was characterized by the presence of charismatic leaders like Timothy Drew (d. 1929) and Elijah Muhammad, both of whom led ideological and resistant movements against white Christian America. The presence of such charismatic figures and the appropriation of Islamic symbols made Islam an attractive proposition for many African Americans. Conversion to these pseudo-Islamic movements came to be seen by the black community as enlightenment and a return to the religion of their African forefathers.

The charismatic leaders of the African American movements appropriated elements of Sunni rather than Shi'i Islam in their teachings. This was, in all probability, because Shi'ism in the early 1920s and 1930s did not have a visible presence in the American public sphere. In fact, most black leaders were not aware of the nuances that differentiate Sunni from Shi'i Islam. Even when they abandoned their indigenous movements, those leaders turned their followers to Sunni rather than Shi'i Islam especially as some, like imam Warith al-Din Muhammad, were supported by Saudi Arabia.[22] Iran, which has the highest Shi'i population in the world, remained largely indifferent to the plight of African Americans, even though in the 1970s, Iran enjoyed close relations with the U.S. government. Even the Shi'i religious leaders based in the Middle East, the *maraji'*, remained indifferent to exploring the possibilities of reaching out to the black community. As we read in chapter 4, the *maraji'* were more concerned with catering to the needs of Shi'i communities in the Middle East than with proselytizing in the United States. Consequently Shi'ism remained, for many African Americans, an alien school of thought until the 1980s.

Up to the 1960s, Islam in America was defined and understood through the prism of indigenous Muslims, primarily the Nation of Islam and, before that, the Moorish Science Temple. Shi'ism, whether in the form of immigrants or African Americans, had no voice in American Islam. It was only in the aftermath of the Iranian revolution in 1979 that the African American community started looking at Shi'ism as a possible expression of normative Islam. It is estimated that by 1982, due to the influence of the Islamic revolution in Iran, more than one thousand African Americans had converted to Shi'ism in the Philadelphia area alone.[23]

'Isa Muhammad, the head of the Ansaru Allah, was the only known black leader to appropriate elements of Shi'i Islam in his teachings. He preached that 'Ali, the first Shi'i Imam, was a black man. He also affirmed his genealogy from the Prophet through Fatima and 'Ali. The title that he used for himself, the Mahdi, fits well with Shi'i messianic teachings.[24] However, 'Isa Muhammad neither accepted nor preached Shi'ism; he merely synthesized elements of Shi'ism that gave credence to his messianic preaching.

The emergence of "Black Shi'ism" in America in the 1980s was both slow and painful. Unlike black conversion to the Nation of Islam, there was no communal acceptance of Shi'ism. There were no Shi'i proselytes visiting members of the African American community, either inside or outside incarceration facilities, encouraging them to convert. Instead, most of those who accepted Shi'ism did so after initially accepting Sunni Islam.

When Black Shi'ism did emerge, it lacked charismatic figures who could provide an ideological basis for a dynamic movement. In fact, there was no movement to speak of at all. Black Shi'is could not afford to provide protection, social services, or employment opportunities to those who joined their ranks. Due to their rather tenuous position, the ideological basis of Black Shi'ism was tied to the interpretation provided by the immigrant Shi'i community.

Even after the Iranian revolution, transition to Shi'i Islam was deemed as an aberration and possibly even heresy by many in the black community. The Wahhabis, who by that time were actively promoting their ideology in America, had pronounced Shi'ism to be a heretical sect, and by converting to Shi'ism, African American Shi'is became alienated not only from their family and friends but also from the Black Muslim community, which felt betrayed by the Black Shi'is. For many African American Sunnis, Black Shi'ism represented cultural and religious heresy. In all probability, this explains the instances of discrimination and violence reported by Black Shi'is in correctional facilities and other spheres of American society.

As powerful and pervasive as Warith al-Din's movement was, it certainly did not embrace religious diversity. Black Shi'is were not welcome to his movement; in fact, within the prison system Black Shi'is complain that their precepts and praxis are attacked more by Sunnis than by non-Muslims. By embracing Shi'ism, black Shi'is moved from being a minority in America to becoming a minority within the African American and Black Muslim communities.

The transition from Black Nationalism to American Shi'ism signaled a radical shift in the worldview and religious experience of African American Muslims. The goals of self-determination and restoration of dignity to a community that had experienced economic deprivation and social oppression were transformed into that of religious empowerment and spiritual excellence. The focus was now on Shi'ism as transmitted by the household of the Prophet, and it was the religious rather than the social element of the Islamic vision was now stressed.

The Appeal of Shi'ism to the Black Community

Why do some African Americans find Shi'ism appealing? Because it was considered to be "the other," Islam gave many African Americans a new identity. But Shi'ism in particular had a special appeal for many in the black community. Since it has been a minority religion in much of the Islamic world, it bears a sense of what Charles Long has called "lithic consciousness"—a state of mind and being that in confronting reality invokes a *will in opposition*, a veritable cosmic *no*.[25] Deeply ingrained within Shi'ism are the concepts of resistance and opposition to tyranny, and fighting for a just cause.

As Sherman Jackson has reminded us, the "central and most enduring feature of Black Religion is its sustained and radical opposition to racial oppression." It is this spirit of resistance and opposition that could be perpetuated to its fullest extent in Shi'i rather than Sunni Islam, which had, on many occasions, accommodated itself to tyrannical rulers as it did not want to create *fitna* (schism). Many traditions were circulated to quell opposition to the ruling elite. An evil ruler, it was declared, was better than anarchy in the community. Obedience to the rulers was tantamount to obedience to God.[26]

The Shi'i paradigm of opposition to tyranny and injustice was further emboldened after the Iranian revolution. Khumayni's defiance of the United States and his characterization of it as the great Satan was a view that Black Shi'is could readily endorse. Indeed, many Blacks converted to Shi'ism after visiting or reading about Iran. Black Shi'is were impressed by the revolutionary fervor of the Iranian regime. More than any other factor, it was the Iranian revolution and its defiance of American hegemony in the Middle East that attracted many African Americans to Shi'ism.

Shi'i opposition against injustice was further affirmed by the formation of Hizbollah and its defiance of Israeli occupation of Lebanese and Palestinian lands. The movement appropriated Shi'i symbols and paradigmatic figures like 'Ali and Husayn in its opposition to Israel and America. American converts to Shi'ism like Jihad Saleh were impressed by the "Shi'i oppositional mode" as he describes it. Most Black Shi'is are not interested in theology, at least not initially. Rather, it is the culture of resistance and opposition to a hostile majority that is appealing to them, Jihad states. The Shi'i oppositional mode is further amplified by the Shi'i personification of the Imams as the victims of Sunni injustice. Such notions resonate strongly with the conflict between white and black America that many African Americans have had to contend with.

The Shi'i oppositional mode is also discerned by the fact that Shi'is have been labeled as *Rafidis*, the dissenters. Jihad Saleh stresses that most African Americans are not afraid of labels; in fact, they welcome them. The appellation is quite attractive for many blacks as it connotes the idea that Shi'is are opposed to mainstream Sunni injustice.[27]

Shi'ism also posited role models from whom Black Shi'is could derive inspiration in their quest for socioeconomic justice. Shi'i Imams, especially 'Ali and Husayn, have become role models due to their opposition to tyranny and injustice. Such notions resonate strongly with African Americans who have suffered from racism, unemployment, and discrimination. Shi'ism offered them not only the spirit but also the role models of protest and resistance to tyranny. Iran provided the contemporary paradigm of release from bondage and subjugation to white America. The special empathy that Iran harbors for the sufferings of the black community in the States was demonstrated when black hostages, who were held in the U.S. embassy siege in 1979, were released soon after their captivity.

In addition, the emphasis on *'adl* (justice) in Shi'i theology is a component that is attractive to many Black Shi'is. Historically, Shi'i theology was closely aligned with Mu'tazilism especially its emphasis on reason and justice, whereas the majority of contemporary Sunnis espouse the Ash'ari doctrine of predestination, a notion with which Black Shi'is cannot identify. For many Black Shi'is, the accentuation of *'adl* as an important component in Shi'i theology indicates the need to strive to establish a just social order, a notion exemplified by the revolution in Iran and the Hizbollah in Lebanon.

Another aspect that appeals to many African Americans is the Shi'i emphasis on messianism. Shi'i rejection of the golden period of the first three caliphs, its emphasis on the injustices committed by them against the family of the Prophet, and its accentuation on the establishment of a just sociopolitical order when the twelfth Imam (the Mahdi) appears is highly appealing. It especially resonates with a concept that African Americans were taught in their churches: the Second Coming of Christ. The binary opposition of an oppressed past and a golden future under the guidance of an eschatological messianic figure is a concept that many African Americans can readily identify with.

Another possible reason for the appeal of Shi'ism to Black Americans is that when Black Shi'ism appeared on the scene in the 1980s, Black

Sunnism had lost the spirit of resistance to and defiance of white America that it possessed during the times of Elijah Mohammed and Malcolm X, especially as Warith al-Din had reconciled his movement with white America. Under the influence of Khumayni's Iran, Shi'ism was just beginning its opposition to American hegemony in the Middle East.

Black and Immigrant Shi'i Interaction

After converting to Shi'ism, Black Shi'is encountered immigrant Shi'is who had their own agendas and priorities in America. Embracing Black Shi'is was not one of them. Rather than extending its religious boundaries, the majority of American Shi'is are more concerned to ensure that the younger generation within the community is not assimilated to American culture and is not influenced by Wahhabi and Salafi rhetoric against Shi'ism.

The experience of Black Shi'is is very different from their Sunni counterparts. In the case of the Black Sunnis, they preceded, by and large, the immigrant community and for a long time were the singular voice of Islam in America. It was only in the 1950s and 1960s, when more immigrants arrived here that African Americans lost their interpretive voice. Black Shi'is, on the other hand, did not experience an existence independent from immigrants nor did they enjoy the kind of communal conversion that Black Sunnis witnessed when transitioning from the Nation of Islam to traditional Sunnism. Therefore, the immigrant Shi'i community did not have a viable black community to contend with. Instead, it had to deal with earlier Shi'i settlers, many of whom had assimilated into mainstream American culture. Consequently, tensions within American Shi'ism arose between different immigrant communities rather than between the black and immigrant communities.

It is to be noted that Black Sunnis comprise almost half of the American Muslim (about 45 percent) population.[28] Other estimates claim that 42 percent of American Muslims are African American.[29] In contrast, the overwhelming majority of Shi'is are immigrants who have little or no interaction with the black community. Thus, Black Shi'is form a fringe minority in the Shi'i community. The African American community is the largest ethnic group among Sunni Muslims, whereas Black Shi'is are the smallest ethnic group among Shi'i Muslims. This observation means that there is no specific black movement or group that can help Black Shi'is resist absorption by or conformity to Shi'i immigrant groups. In the case of Black Sunnism, such groups have been significant in demarginalizing African American converts to Islam. Movements such as the Nation of Islam or the American Muslim Society of Warith al-Din are important in offsetting the otherness that comes with conversion. Black Shiʻis, on the other hand, are deprived of movements that might be able to embrace or empower them.

It is within this framework that we can comprehend the relationship between immigrant and Black Shiʻis. Shiʻism came to African Americans through the immigrant community rather than through pseudo-Islamic movements. The views, outlook, and perceptions of Black Shiʻis were informed by the cultural lens that immigrant Shiʻis brought to America, and it was through this interaction with the immigrant Shiʻis or literature written and imported by them that Shiʻism came to the black community.

Unlike Black Sunnis, Black Shiʻis could not claim to have an independent attachment to Shiʻism before the arrival of immigrant Shiʻism because there was no proto-Shiʻi movement to match the Moorish Science Temple or the Nation of Islam, both of which had preceded Shiʻi immigration. In addition, there were no charismatic leaders within the Black Shiʻi community who could nurture or forge an identity or movement independent of the immigrant community, thus making Black Shiʻism largely dependent on and vulnerable to immigrant Shiʻism.

Dependency on the immigrant community has been accentuated by the fact that Black Shiʻis did not possess the resources to build their own institutions or centers. To date, there are only a handful of Black Shiʻi mosques in America. The fact that they emerged only after the Iranian revolution when many Shiʻis had migrated here meant that Black Shiʻis largely capitulated to rather than challenged the immigrant expression of Shiʻi Islam.

There was an additional reason why the Black Shiʻi community became largely dependent on immigrant Shiʻis. Black Shiʻism is a relatively new phenomenon; indeed, the number of Black Shiʻis does not exceed a few thousand. Lack of resources, religious training, and a dearth of charismatic leadership have made the Black Shiʻis dependent on immigrant Shiʻis who have largely defined and imposed their own cultural understanding of Shiʻism in America. In addition, immigrant Shiʻism has always outpaced Black Shiʻism. Hence, it is the Shiʻi immigrants who have defined American Shiʻism, a fact that denied Black Shiʻis an interpretive voice in the community. In fact, it would not be an exaggeration to state that their Islamicity was tied to conformity to immigrant Shiʻism.

Depending on where they were, Black Shiʻis were attached either to Arab, South Asian, Khoja, or the Iranian expression of Shiʻism. Whether in matters related to Shiʻi law, the manifestation of rituals, or the expression of a particular culture, Black Shiʻis followed the interpretation of and articulation by immigrant Shiʻis. Consequently, American Shiʻism came to be identified with the immigrant as opposed to the Black Shiʻi community. This factor, together with the fact that many Black Shiʻis are linked to the underclass and underprivileged, makes them a minority within the minority Shiʻi community.

The Ethnic Factor and Black Shiʻism

Besides the lack of resources and an interpretive voice, the nascent Black Shiʻi community had to further contend with the problem of ethnicity within the American Shiʻi community. The ethnic factor intrinsic to American Shiʻism has made it more difficult for blacks to integrate into any of the ethnic mosques. Immigrants expect newcomers to the faith to absorb not only Shiʻi Islam but also their own national or cultural identities. Converts become cultural chameleons—they are expected to absorb not only a new belief system but also to adjust to different Shiʻi cultures and identities, which are often imposed on converts. Within the framework of converting to a religion composed of different ethnic groups, a convert has competing and sometimes opposing identities to fit into. This factor increases the considerable challenges that she or he faces after conversion.

Immigrant Shiʻis tend to experience their faith through a cultural prism (see chap. 2). Immigrants decide on how the mosques are to be run, what are acceptable dress codes, language, and political behavior. The increase in immigrant Shiʻis meant that all that was alien to immigrants was seen as alien to Shiʻism itself.[30] To compound the ethnic factor, Black Shiʻis are not represented in the mosque administration nor in planning the genre of programs or services offered there. They are not invited to speak nor voice their concerns and needs; they can attend but hardly participate in any mosque programs. Interaction between the different ethnic centers is limited, engagement with the African American community is spasmodic. It is only in the multiethnic centers where different ethnic groups come together that many blacks feel more comfortable to express themselves.

Having come from a Sunni or Christian background, Black Shiʻis find the rituals endemic to a particular ethnic community difficult to participate in. When they visit an Arab *Husayniyya* or a Khoja *Imambargah*, few blacks will participate in the flagellations or other rituals. Equally, most Black Shi'is would feel uncomfortable in celebrating the Persian New Year (*nawruz*) with Iranians or participating in the poetry sessions in South Asian centers. It would not be an exaggeration to state that within the context of an ethnically fractured American Shi'i community, immigrant and Black Shi'is tend to live in different worlds, with limited or no interaction. In fact, the two groups have very different perspectives. Whereas Black Shi'is have emphasized sameness based on the egalitarian principles of Islam, immigrants have accentuated otherness based on ethnicity. This binary opposition of sameness against otherness, universality versus particularity means that there is little impetus for creating a pan-ethnic American Shi'ism that could unite the diverse factions within the community.

While it could be argued that Black Sunnis face a similar challenge, the degree and intensity of ethnicity is definitely greater in American Shi'ism. Since they cannot be accommodated in the ethnic centers, Black Shi'is struggle to negotiate their identity and find a voice in an Islam that is dominated by Black Sunni and the immigrant communities. Due to the pervasive effect of the ethnic factor in American Shi'ism, it can be argued that for the African Americans, integration into the Sunni community is easier than it is to the Shi'i community.

Furthermore, Black Shi'is are largely absent in American Shi'i discourse, an arena dominated by immigrant Shi'is. At no time, whether in the *majalis* recited or in discussion groups, are issues of race, discrimination, and the integration of blacks within the Shi'i community discussed. Even UMAA, which purports to discuss issues that impact the American Shi'i community, has not devoted a single session in its conferences to address the issue of Black Shi'ism. The matter seems unimportant to the Shi'i community. Even the Shi'i religious leaders, the *maraji'*, have yet to address or acknowledge the particular needs of the African American community. I have yet to see directives or guidelines from the *maraji'* that address the specific needs of Black Shi'is, especially those who are incarcerated. In fact, the religious guides need to explore the possibility of establishing institutes that could effectively promote Shi'ism in America.

Black Shi'is are excluded not only from Shi'i mosques but also from Shi'i *da'wa* organizations, which, ironically, are trying to reach out to the black community. To be sure, there is little black representation in the institutions that purport to reach out to and embrace the African American community. They are also excluded from the very organizations that claim to speak on behalf of all Shi'is in America. Furthermore, most dialogue sessions that immigrant Shi'is arrange or participate in exclude members of the African American community. If they are hardly visible in immigrant mosques, Black Shi'is are largely absent in interfaith dialogue sessions. It is the immigrants who tend to control the agenda and list of invitees. The agendas ignore issues that are most germane to the African American community: relations between immigrant and black communities, race, poverty, welfare, and unemployment.

For the Black Shi'is, conversion to Shi'ism has meant a transition from being a minority in America to becoming a minority within the American, Muslim, and Shi'i communities. Black Shi'is have had to endure American racism, marginalization from the Shi'i community, alienation from the ethnic Shi'i centers, American prejudices against all Muslims, and prejudices from other Black Muslims because of their acceptance of Shi'ism. To offset these disadvantages, some Black Shi'is in cities like New York and Los Angeles have established their own mosques. For example, when Shi'i inmates in New York State are released, they often congregate at the Islamic Guidance Center on Atlantic Avenue in Brooklyn. This mosque offers Arabic and religion classes, but has yet to implement a program to assist its new arrivals from prisons.[31]

The Iranian Influence on the Black Shi'i Community

By the mid-1990s, Black Shi'is realized that they could not depend on the immigrant community to cater to their spiritual or financial needs. They decided to take matters into their own hands. As I explained earlier, many Blacks were attracted to Shi'i Islam by the anti-American rhetoric and defiance by the Iranian government. In the 1980s and 1990s, many Black Shi'is were invited to visit Iran; some of them decided to study in Qum. Along with several others Black Shi'is, Hashim 'Ali 'Ala al-Din studied under scholars in Qum who, he insists, were not affiliated to nor propagated on behalf of the Iranian government. While studying in Iran in the 1990s, he saw the need to help others understand Shi'ism. Hashim 'Ala al-Din helped establish the Islamic Foundation Cooperation (IFC), an institution that helps Black Shi'is visit the tomb of the eighth Imam, 'Ali al-Rida, in Mashad and encourages them to take short-term courses in Iran.[32] Besides teaching some of the traditional courses offered in the traditional seminaries, these courses deal with those issues confronting African

Americans, such as poverty, racism, and discrimination. The courses also focus on spiritual dimensions of Shiʻism like the purification of the self and how to deploy jihad as a weapon of spiritual resistance.

After returning to the States, these students tried to spread Shiʻism here by engaging in community services. In California, Hashim started an organization called "Slam-n-Jam," a youth basketball league. According to Hashim, many young African Americans embraced Shiʻism through this organization. Gradually, the league was able to produce a community of Black Shiʻis, a movement that has spread throughout the Bay Area

Black Shiʻism has splintered into small groups in different parts of America. Hashim states that there are three major Black Shiʻi groups in Los Angeles. These include the Masjid al-Rasool and a group that consists of Shiʻis of Moorish-American descent. These groups work in the inner city among gang members and have been successful in spreading Islam in Southern California. Hashim, who now lives in Houston, also notes that there are other Black Shiʻi groups on the East Coast such as the Islamic Party and the Dar al-Islam. In addition, another group of Black Shiʻis were students at a Shiʻi seminary in Madina, New York, in the 1990s. After graduating, they went to Qum for further studies. Some of them have returned to America as scholars; others have settled in Atlanta and Florida.[33]

The discussion on the interaction between immigrant and Black Shiʻis should not conceal the fact that there are a considerable number Black Shiʻis in correctional centers. Their education and spiritual nourishment is contingent, to a large degree, on the activities of the Shiʻi institutes mentioned in this section.

Shiʻism in the Correctional Facilities

Immigration of Shiʻis to America, the Iranian revolution, the advent of Hizbollah in Lebanon, the Internet, and greater access to Shiʻi literature have made Shiʻism an American rather than a purely foreign phenomenon. These factors, plus the Wahhabi denouement of Shiʻism have encouraged many African Americans, including those in correctional facilities, to look at Shiʻism as an alternative articulation of normative Islam. Since the 1980s there has been a gradual but steady increase in the number of African Americans converting to Shiʻism both inside and outside the correctional facilities.

Like Black Shi'is outside the prison facilities, the majority of Shi'i inmates seek empowerment through education. They seek a *da'wa* team that could educate and guide them. These inmates are concerned that the religious education offered in the prison system teaches Sunni Islam exclusively. Shi'i inmates do not have access to normative Shi'i texts or facilities to educate them about Shi'i history, theology, or jurisprudence. Most of their knowledge on Shi'ism is derived from their fellow Shi'i inmates who are better versed but certainly not experts in Shi'i Islam.

As we have seen, there are very few Shi'i institutes that have engaged in any *da'wa* activity and most have done this at their own initiative, with little financial or human resources. This has meant that Shi'i inmates are largely alienated from Shi'i institutes and community. In my correspondence with them, most inmates complained that Shi'i organizations do not respond or send them the books they request. They also reported that they lack communication with people in the Shi'i community who might be able to help them.

Significantly, many Shi'i inmates indicate that some of them accepted Shi'ism due to the proliferation of Sunni literature that vilified and denigrated the Shi'is. Derogatory remarks against Shi'i beliefs made them more curious and led them to investigate Shi'i beliefs and practices. Ironically, by their pernicious attacks against and denigration of Shi'ism, the Wahhabis aroused the curiosity of many converts who had not previously heard of this branch of Islam. After further exploration, some of these converts embraced Shi'ism.

Black Shi'ism has yet to evolve into a full-fledged movement. So far, it has been occupied with defending itself from attacks by the Wahhabis and Black Sunnis. Black Shi'is need to forge a distinct identity within and integrate into Shi'ism without compromising their distinctive African American consciousness. They also need to foster an ideology that will distinguish them from other African American movements. In addition, Black Shi'is need to nurture charismatic leadership and establish institutions in their fight against racism and socioeconomic injustice within the framework of American Shi'i Islam.

As I have stated, most Shi'i institutions have been introverted and focused largely on providing essential religious services to its members. However, the events of September 11, 2001, forced them to become more extroverted and open to the American public. Faced with alienation, prejudices, an abundance of hate literature, and a hostile media, Shi'is realized that they could no longer afford to remain the invisible other in America. To be sure, the events of 9/11 changed the shape of both the Sunni and Shi'i communities in America.

The Events of 9/11 and
Its Impact on the American Muslim Community

The terrorist attacks of September 11, 2001, revived prejudices of Islam as a religion that promotes the killing of innocent people and of Muslims as an inherently militant and irrational people. Indeed, the media has represented the "absent Muslim other"; it has sought to create a stereotypical representation of Islam and Muslims that has been impossible to ignore. In addition, the American global war on terror and the invasion of Iraq have invigorated stereotypes and suspicions against Muslims, especially those of Middle Eastern origins.

After 9/11, the U.S. government implemented a wide range of domestic legislative, administrative, and judicial measures in the name of national security and the war on terrorism. Most of them were designed and carried out by the executive branch of government, with little a priori public discussion or debate. These measures included mass arrests, secret and indefinite detentions, prolonged detention of "material witnesses," closed hearings and use of secret evidence, FBI home and work visits, wiretapping, seizures of property, removals of aliens with technical visa violations, and mandatory special registration.

Legal and political measures are augmented by continued public backlash of hate crimes, hate speech, and job discrimination, all of which sensationalized media portrayals of Muslims and strong anti-Muslim/anti-Islamic rhetoric from the political right. Not only do Muslims feel vulnerable in America, they also feel as if they are being continuously watched and under the constant threat of arrest.[34]

Since 9/11, Islamophobia and hatred toward Muslims have become legitimized and acceptable by-products of national media and American culture. This has left many migrants and second generation Muslims with a sense of alienation and marginalization. Furthermore, the vitriolic attacks on Islam and the Qur'an by some Christian fundamentalist groups have exacerbated the current conflict in America. Franklin Graham, the son of Billy Graham, labeled Islam as a "very evil and wicked religion"; Jerry Vines, a former president of the Southern Baptist Convention, said the Prophet Muhammad was a "demon-obsessed pedophile."[35]

On public television, Jerry Falwell called the Prophet a pedophile and a terrorist.[36] Such comments further amplified the prejudices against Islam and Muslims.

Incidents of discrimination and attacks against Muslims were accompanied by bias and hatred against Muslims. A study of more than 1,000 Muslim Americans by the Pew Research Center showed that about half of those surveyed indicated that their life has become more difficult after September 11.[37] Furthermore, one-fourth of respondants state that they have been victims of discrimination, and 54 percent feel Muslims are singled out for extra government surveillance.[38] In the summer of 2006, a Gallup poll of more than one thousand Americans showed that 39 percent were in favor of requiring Muslims in the United States, including those who are American citizens, to carry special identification.

In her book *Mecca and Main Street*, Geneive Abdo sums up the prevailing mood in America: "during the years I spent researching on this book, I had countless experiences with Americans who held negative views about Muslims, but who knew virtually nothing about Islam and had never met a Muslim. Some people talked about Muslims as if they were an alien species."[39]

Muslim Reaction to the Events of September 11, 2001

Since the events of 9/11, Muslims have sought to go beyond the history of hostility, caricature, and power struggles that have characterized relations between Christians and Muslims in the past. It is correct to state that the Muslims' struggle in America has been not only to coexist with the other but also to make themselves comprehensible in the American milieu, to de-mythify and de-code Islam, and to challenge the negative characterization of Islam.

Muslims have also realized that due to the activities of terrorists, both their Islamic identity and American citizenship are at stake. The Muslim community has acknowledged that the silent majority syndrome must come to an end simply because Muslim acquiescence has encouraged an extremist expression of Islam. It is the extremists who have spoken on behalf of Islam as their acts of violence have drowned out the silent voices of the Muslim majority. Thus, many Muslims have felt the need to integrate themselves into mainstream American society in order to make their voices heard. This integration of American Islam represents a silent revolution that many Muslims have been engaged in since September 11,

2001.[40] The creation of an American Muslim identity can be discerned from an advertisement placed by the Council on American-Islamic Relations (CAIR) in some newspapers. It shows a Muslim girl, wearing a head scarf, stating proudly, "I am an American, I am a Muslim." Interestingly, the American identity precedes the Islamic.

Muslims have expressed their patriotism in tangible ways. Denunciations of the 9/11 attacks appeared on the websites of every major Arab and Muslim organization. The display of American flags by Arabs in Detroit—on clothes, skin, cars, homes, storefront windows, and places of worship—was part of a heightened desire to "belong" or to obviate accusations of being un-American. In many American cities, Muslims have also engaged in civic responsibilities. There have been numerous food drives to help homeless Americans all over the country. In Denver, a group called Muslims Intent on Learning and Activism (MILA) has opened a weekly "Ansar Pantry" where anyone can collect food and house supplies. In September 2005, with the U.S. Capitol as a backdrop, several Muslim groups made a $1 million donation to Hurricane Katrina relief efforts and further stated that a portion of the money would be used to provide hot meals to all the survivors housed at the Houston Convention Center on September 11, 2005.[41] Even the tone of sermons delivered in many American mosques has changed. Instead of denouncing American society and values, Friday sermons have focused on devotional, ethical, and historical topics.

The Events of 9/11 and the American Shi'i Community

The prejudices, stereotyping of and attacks against Muslims and Islam ignore the multiplicity of voices and nuances prevalent within Islam. They also ignore that fact that Muslims are multivocal and hold different views. Since 9/11, in the media and the eyes of many Americans, all distinctions between Muslims have been obliterated. Distinctions between Shi'is and Sunnis, moderate or conservative, Christian or Muslim Arabs have been effaced. Instead, all Muslims and Arabs have been grouped together as the enemy other.

Like other Muslims, American Shi'is have been held equally responsible for the terrorist attacks even though none of the terrorists were Shi'is. They have had to apologize for acts they did not commit and condemn acts that they never condoned. Shi'is feel that they have been found guilty by religious association, drawn into a discourse on terrorism, and associated with a group (al-Qa'ida) that would, ironically, exterminate them if it could. Indeed, there is no record of any Shi'i group committing an act of terror in America, nor have Shi'i mosques or institutions been funded by foreign movements.

Shi'i scholars would not endorse Bin Laden's *fatwa* of jihad against America. It is important to understand that for the Shi'is, offensive jihad is held to be in abeyance until the appearance of the Mahdi, the promised messiah. He is expected to establish the kingdom of justice and equality and to eliminate injustice and tyranny. This belief is predicated on numerous apocalyptic traditions on the events that will unfold when he reappears. Whereas for the Sunnis, the caliph was empowered to declare and lead jihad, the Shi'is declared that the functions of calling people to respond to God's guidance and fighting those who undermine the creation of a just order was restricted to the figure of an infallible Imam or his deputy. In the absence of the Imam, offensive jihad was suspended until he reappears. This juridical ruling was based on the premise that infallibility protects the Imam from destroying or commanding to destroy any life without proper justification. Most Shi'i jurists even declared that to fight for an illegitimate ruler was a sin.[42]

Since 9/11 and especially since 2006, Shi'i organizations have been targeted by the government. The war between Israel and Hizbollah in 2006 was particularly damaging for American Shi'is. The U.S. government declared Hizbollah a terrorist organization, a move that led to several Shi'i nonprofit organizations being raided by the FBI. Such raids have been carried out in Detroit, where there is some sympathy for Hizbollah. Since the Bush administration declared Hizbollah a terrorist organization, Iran, Lebanon, and al-Qa'ida have now been grouped together, and American Shi'is have come under closer scrutiny.

Like other Muslims, Shi'is have been targeted and profiled and have had to endure much discrimination. A survey conducted by Qunoot Foundation, a Washington-based nonprofit group, shows that Shi'is in the United States are unlikely to report anti-Muslim hate crimes or other forms of discrimination. Nearly 80 percent of American Shi'is who were victims of "post 9-11 discrimination" reported the incidents either to family members or to no one, according to the nationwide survey. The survey found that few American Shi'i victims reported such incidents to the Council on American-Islamic Relations, which claims to represent American Muslims.[43]

For the Shi'i community, the ramifications of 9/11 have been varied. Many Shi'is whom I talked to stated that the events of 9/11 have exposed the true terrorists. Before the attacks, many Americans associated Shi'ism with acts of terror and militancy, especially after the Iranian hostage crisis and the taking of American hostages in Beirut in the 1980s. However, 9/11 showed that the true perpetrators of terror were extremist groups like al-Qa'ida, who base their ideology on Wahhabism.

Shi'is in different parts of the world were among the first to condemn the terrorist acts of 9/11 and show sympathy with the victims. Shi'is in Iran gathered on the night of 9/11 to hold a candlelight vigil and protest the attacks.[44] The *maraji'*, Ayatullah Seestani, and other Shi'i religious leaders throughout the world have repeatedly condemned acts of terror and the killing of innocent civilians. Ayatullah Fadlallah states,

> As for those suicide bombers who kill innocent people as well those who accuse others of unbelief, just because they differ with them in some sectarian views even within the same religion . . . or those who explode car bombs, killing women children, elderly and youth who have nothing to do with any war of aggression, to those we say that their inhuman brutal actions have nothing to do with Islam whatsoever, and that what they are doing will lead to God's wrath and not His satisfaction. It also undermines the image of Islam and Muslims and gives others a wrong idea about Islam and Muslims.[45]

Ayatullah Khamene'i, the supreme ruler of Iran states, "Killing of people, in any place and with any kind of weapons, including atomic bombs, long range missiles, biological or chemical weapons, passenger or war planes, carried out by any organization, country or individuals is condemned. . . . It makes no difference whether such massacres happen in Hiroshima, Nagasaki, Qana, Sabra, Shatila, Deir Yassin, Bosnia, Kosovo, Iraq or in New York and Washington."[46] Similarly, Ayatullah Seestani urged Muslims to obey the laws of the country of their residence. In June 2006, after the arrests of seventeen people connected to a bomb plot investigation in southern Ontario, he condemned all acts of violence.[47]

Ironically, the image of Shi'ism in America has improved somewhat since 9/11 and the American invasion of Iraq in 2003. Most of the resistance in Iraq and acts of terrorism have been perpetrated by Sunni and al-Qa'ida–inspired insurgents. Shi'i resistance has been restricted to Muqtada al-Sadr's al-Mahdi army. However, many other Shi'is, including Ayatullah Seestani, have not supported his movement nor have they called for armed resistance to the American invasion. According to Hisham Husainy, the imam of the Kerbala center in Dearborn, the late Ayatullah Baqir al-Hakim explicitly prohibited his followers from attacking American soldiers when they first invaded Iraq.[48] All this has improved the image of Shi'ism in America especially as the Bush administration had to rely on Shi'i support in its attempt at introducing democracy in Iraq.

Many Shi'is feel that the favorable image of Shi'ism has not been fully exploited by the Shi'i community. There have been few Shi'i voices in the public arena or in the media condemning terrorism; Shi'i institutions have also not engaged in political lobbying to represent their concerns. At a Shi'i imams' conference held in 2004 in New Jersey, imams from various Shi'i centers in North America stated that in the aftermath of the events of 9/11, more could have been done to promote a better image of Islam in general and Shi'ism in particular. Various imams stated that the events of 9/11 certainly changed a number of things. The American media has focused on the threat posed by the Wahhabis, Taliban, and on Saudi Arabia, and this has shifted the spotlight from the Shi'is.

For Shaykh Fyzee of Bait al-ilm in Chicago, the events of 9/11 provided Shi'is an opportunity to promote a better understanding of Islam in general and of Shi'ism in particular. However, their failure to capitalize on the situation allowed the media and non-Muslims to speak on behalf of Islam. For Shaykh Fyzee, it is only now that the community has realized what it has failed to do for the last twenty or thirty years, and that is to have an effective outreach program.[49]

Americans in general have also become more aware of the Sunni–Shi'i distinctions and that Shi'is have been a minority within the Muslim world. In the eyes of many Americans, Shi'is represent a more moderate school. In addition, Ayatullah Seestani's role in brokering peace between Muqtada al-Sadr and the American forces in Iraq in 2004 and his nonviolent position have all nurtured the view of Shi'ism as representing a more temperate stance.

The events of 9/11 have also impacted the vision of Shi'i scholars in America. Instead of focusing on community-related issues, they are now repositioning in order to reach out to non-Muslims. In November 2007, the Council of Shia Muslim Scholars in North America dedicated the theme of its annual conference to religious propagation. The *'ulama'* discussed topics such as strategies in *da'wa*, the challenges of reaching out to "the other" in America, the characteristics of a successful preacher, and modern tools and methodologies of *da'wa*.

Shi'i Interaction with Non-Muslim Communities

Even though the Shi'i community has been present in America since the late nineteenth century, there was limited integration with non-Muslims before the events of September 11, 2001. However, since then, Shi'is have recognized that they cannot afford to live in impregnable fortresses and that living in a pluralistic milieu requires an active engagement with the other. The events of 9/11 also proved to the American Shi'i community, if any proof were needed, that pluralism in America is a social reality from which it cannot escape. In fact, many Shi'is have become more visible, vocal, and extroverted while others have stressed their American rather than homeland identity.

In addition, Shi'is have become more aware of the need to give back something to American society. They realized that it is better to speak with, rather than about, the other. Shi'i leaders in America have exchanged visits with numerous Christian and Jewish groups, and many U.S. federal agencies and political figures have visited Shi'is in their places of worship. For example, Michael Chertoff, head of the Department of Homeland Security, visited local Muslim leaders in July 2007 at the Kerbala Center in Dearborn. He encouraged religious leaders in attendance to "not stand on the sidelines and watch people misrepresent our religions." He also encouraged Muslim youth in the direction of government service.[50]

American Shi'is have increasingly expressed themselves in various genres of discourses so that they can be both physically and intellectually visible. Exchange visits have occurred at different levels, not only from interfaith groups but with community leaders as well. In 2007 Cardinal Adam Maida, the Roman Catholic archbishop of Detroit, visited the Islamic Center of America in Dearborn to meet with imam Hassan Qazwini, the spiritual leader of the Islamic Center, along with Muslim leaders and representatives of various Muslim organizations in Michigan, such as CAIR, Islamic House of Wisdom, and Unity Center. In their meeting Cardinal Maida and the Muslim leaders discussed Catholic-Muslim relations.[51]

Various Shi'i groups in America have engaged in outreach programs. They have spoken at local events, conferences, and places of worship. Imam Hasan Qazwini, for example, was invited by the Michigan state senate to deliver a prayer and open a senate session in Lansing. He also visited the White House and led a prayer opening the session of Congress in Washington in 2003. In May 2008, he met with Senator Barack Obama, the Democratic presidential candidate.

Shi'i Contribution to Interfaith Dialogue

Increasingly, Americans have become aware that Islam in America is not a monolithic entity and that there are many dividing lines within the Muslim community. They know that Muslims hold a variety of opinions on a great number of issues, and they want to hear a wider range of Muslim voices. Consequently, many institutions want to hear both Sunni and Shi'i voices.

In several cities, it is the Christians and Sunnis who set the agenda for dialogue in which Shi'is are sometimes invited to participate. Shi'i representation at dialogue sessions tend to be minimal, often with only one participant alongside a number of Sunnis. In most cases, Sunnis and Shi'is share the same beliefs and practices. However, instances have arisen where Shi'is feel that the topics chosen for discussion do not reflect their distinctive beliefs or practices. A Christian friend once asked me why Muslims believe in predestination. I had to explain to him that this is an Ash'ari theological stance that not all Muslims share. Infact, Shi'is reject the belief in predestination and insist, instead, in free will, a view that only a few Sunnis accept. Similarly, when Sunnis and Shi'is dialogue together with Christians, they soon realize that their conception of post-Muhammadan authority differs quite radically. Sunnis believe that after his death, the charismatic authority of the Prophet was routinized among his companions. Shi'is, however, believe that the comprehensive Prophetic authority was transmitted to his family.[52]

Another instance where Shi'i and Sunni practices differ markedly is that of mourning over the dead. Sunni mourning ceremonies tend to be quite brief, but Shi'is, especially those from Iran, will hold ceremonies three and seven days after the death of a family member or friend. Most Shi'is will also hold special ceremonies forty days after the death of a person and even mark the death anniversary. Thus, when Shi'is join Sunnis to dialogue with Christians and questions such as post-Muhammadan authority or mourning ceremonies arise, disagreements between them surface near their non-Muslim friends.

Due to these differences and the Shi'i concern that Sunnis set the agenda for and dominate dialogue sessions, Shi'is in cities such as Washington, Los Angeles, and Dearborn have formed their own dialogue groups with Christians. In areas where there are smaller Shi'i groups, like Denver and Seattle, Shi'is and Sunnis often combine their dialogue sessions.

Shi'is have increasingly felt the need for self-representation rather than being represented by the Sunni majority. Especially after the American invasion and occupation of Iraq and the concomitant awareness of Shi'ism, Shi'is hope to counter the negative images most Christians may have about Islam by engaging in dialogue with their non-Muslim counterparts. The Islamic Education Council of Maryland organizes annual interfaith events that discuss topics affecting other faith groups in America. Issues like marriage and the importance of inculcating proper values in modern youth have been discussed with local Christian and Jewish communities. Al-Khoei Foundation of New York also participates in a number of national, international, interfaith, and intrafaith initiatives.

Another Shi'i institution, the Ithna'asheri Muslim Association of the Northwest (IMAN) was a founding member of an interfaith coalition of Muslims, Christians, and Jews that has, for six years, focused on seeking common-ground learning and working together to build homes for low income families.[53] IMAN has actively participated in various interfaith and intrafaith activities in the Greater Seattle area to help promote a better understanding of Islam, the teachings of the family of the Prophet, and to build intercommunity bridges in the process.

The Shi'i-based Institute of Islamic Learning in Metroplex (IILM) in Dallas has embarked on a series of initiatives focused on establishing religious understanding, community harmony, and interfaith communications through celebration of religious and cultural commonalities. Along with other faith groups, they convene an annual interfaith celebration of Mother's Day, which has been celebrated for seven years and has gradually attracted a diverse community.[54]

The substance of dialogue has changed since 9/11 according to a Shi'i activist, Najjah Bazzy. In conversations with non-Muslims, she realized that Islam 101 is no longer in demand. Especially after the American invasion of Iraq, Americans have gone beyond asking questions such as "why do they hate us, and why are Muslim women oppressed?" The themes covered now are as diverse as they are fascinating. Topics include issues like authority and scripture, mysticism, the law, challenges in the American milieu, holy days, and fundamentalism in the three monotheistic religions. Other topics may include the sources of authority, terrorism in the scriptures, the Sunni–Shi'i divide, justice, faith, and the treatment of Muslims in the media. Americans also want to know more about the relationship between Black and immigrant Muslims, Muslim perspectives on issues like abortion, gay marriages, aging, and euthanasia, which have now become part of the conversations that Muslims and non-Muslims engage in. In fact, it is possible to detect an evolution in dialogue from basic issues (terrorism, women's rights) to more sensitive and controversial topics.[55]

Najjah Bazzy adds that Shi'is who dialogue have introduced distinctly Shi'i themes and figures in their conversation. They have introduced their sheroes and heroes. Figures like Imam 'Ali, Fatima, and their daughter Zaynab have featured more in conversations. Shi'is have also accentuated their chiliastic vision of a just social order upon the appearance of the twelfth Imam, the Mahdi. They have also made others aware of what it means to be a Shi'i Muslim in America, and that the demonization of Islam, increasing surveillance of Muslims, and restriction of civil liberties have been extremely painful for all Muslims. They also make it clear that Shi'is have been drawn into a battle (the war against terror) that they are not a part of. As they relate their experiences in the past two years, the partners in dialogue have both communicated and internalized their pain.

Resistance to Dialogue

Not all Shi'is view interfaith dialogue as important to their lives. Shi'i immigrants who have arrived recently from overseas, especially those who may have come to America to escape political or economic oppression, do not see dialogue as their priority. The cultural shock and sense of displacement they experience means that they are drawn more into ethnic mosques than churches. They are more concerned with safeguarding their beliefs and obviating the threat of assimilation to American culture than talking with non-Muslims. This reasoning applies not only to recently arrived immigrants but even to conservative Shi'is who have lived in America for years.

This observation is corroborated by a question posed in my survey. Table 5 indicates that when asked if they engaged in interfaith dialogue, only 59 percent of the centers responded to the question. Of these, 68 percent reported that there was some form of interfaith dialogue whereas 32 percent said there was no dialogue at all. Many Shi'is are not accustomed to sitting around a table with a group of Sunnis and Christians to discuss their faith, which is often seen as a very personal matter. Many recently arrived and conservative Shi'is may construe dialogue as a subtle form of Christian evangelism, a comment that I have heard many times. As Jane Smith observed, "The truth is that the majority of Muslims in America are really not interested in interfaith dialogue, either by inclination or by ideology. Those who identify with what is perceived as a growing Wahhabi or Salafi influence in this country are among the Muslims who would probably decline the dialogue."[56]

Since Shi'is do not engage in interfaith dialogue or outreach activities in their home countries, they have not been able to construct an effective medium of conversation with non-Muslims in America. Rather than reaching out to non-Muslims, many Shi'is have been trained to vindicate the preponderance of Shi'i faith and liturgical practices over corresponding Sunni praxis.

The Shi'i Community and Civic Engagement

As I have stated, many Shi'is have a double consciousness as they navigate between a homeland and an American mentality. One important way of doing this is to engage in civic responsibility. Civic engagement is an important way of escaping marginalization, of feeling at home in America and, at the same time, stressing the "Americanness" of an American Islam.

According to Peter Berger, civil society consists of two parts, structural and cultural. Structurally, the term refers to the ensemble of institutions that stand between the private sphere on the one hand and the macro-institutions of the state and the economy on the other. Culturally, the term refers to those institutions that mitigate conflict and foster peace.[57] The term "civil society" can thus be seen as signifying types of social processes that relate to an intermediary participatory realm between the private and public spheres. This realm is determined by structures, processes, and institutions that stem from the voluntary, private actions of individual citizens.

Civil society itself is defined by three elements: civic life, citizenship, and civility in interaction. It is the first element that has been stressed as Shi'is in different parts of the country have increasingly identified themselves with American culture and values, and have tried to distance themselves from the back-home mentality. They have sought to articulate an Islamic response to the secularized civic conscience. Stated differently, they have tapped into Islam to activate ethical and moral universal imperatives and have highlighted Muslim role models to show how Islam can contribute to American civil society. Many Shi'i imams have educated their followers that they must see the American diaspora as their new home, and that they need to enter the civic and political realms of their adopted homeland.

This process has expressed itself in various forms. Shi'is have been involved in social programs like food drives and have sought to help homeless Americans. Centers have facilitated "open-mosques" hours and have tried to become more "people friendly" by encouraging their non-Muslim neighbors to visit mosques.

Bayt al-Zahra, which was opened in 2004 in Dearborn, helps with the transportation of and translation for the less fortunate in the area. The founders of another Shi'i institution, the United Muslim Foundation (UMF), were inspired by the paradigmatic model of Imam Husayn. Established in Orlando in 2003, Masuma Virjee, one of its founders, states that the UMF has engaged in various interfaith and networking opportunities to help clarify misconceptions about Islam. By 2007 UMF had extended its local Orlando and Pennsylvania chapters to include volunteers nationwide, with international interest in its work. UMF now assists Muslims and non-Muslims against hunger and reaches out to the homeless, hungry, and working poor in the area. UMF has participated in many events helping people in need. These have ranged from serving at soup kitchens to providing food pantries for the homeless. The UMF has also donated food and clothes to schools and encouraged its members to run in marathons and collect funds for the American Cancer Society. UMF also aims to promote greater Islamic awareness and cultural understanding while reaching out to those in need. Its "Project Downtown Orlando" is a group dedicated to helping the less fortunate in the city.[58]

Civil engagement within the Shi'i community has taken different forms. The community in Orlando, under the auspices of the Husseini Islamic Center (HIC), has organized projects that brought various Shi'i groups together. In 2005, fifteen volunteers took a delicious hot meal of Biryani to the Coalition of the Homeless in downtown Orlando and fed more than three hundred people in one hour. Student volunteers helped organize a wide variety of miniprojects including cleaning donated medical equipment, packing Christmas presents for mentally challenged children, sorting food at a food bank, talking to seniors at a seniors' home, and playing games with handicapped children. The intent, according to organizer Zuhair Ebrahim, was "to make our presence felt in the community with the benefit reaching a cross-section of members of different ages, different cultures, and religious backgrounds. At a time when Islam takes a continuous bashing in the media, it was heartening to see that so many members, young and old, male and female, came out to show the other communities that we are truly peaceful and law-abiding citizens."[59]

In Miami, Shi'is have cooperated with Sunnis in contributing to a wide variety of humanitarian projects. For example, the two communities have come together to organize free medical clinics for the indigent. Muslim students at the University of Miami started a feed-the-homeless program on Fridays. On the day of *'Ashura'*, the Shi'i community of Miami organizes a blood-donation drive in the name of Imam Husayn, and more than one hundred people participate in the annual drive.[60]

Based in Detroit, Zaman International seeks to inspire individuals to recognize and care for the needs of the indigent. In the words of Zaman's executive director, Najjah Bazzy, "Through our work and collaborative partnerships with other organizations, we strive to be "Hope for Humanity." Zaman International's vision is of a world in which all individuals realize their potential as servant leaders and join together—despite creed, ethnic background, race, or class—to impact, improve, and enhance the lives of others. In order to achieve this vision, Zaman International conducts social services and educational projects throughout the Detroit area and supports international humanitarian relief efforts worldwide.[61]

The Bait-ul-Ilm in Chicago raised about $25,000 after Hurricane Katrina and donated it to the Village of Streamwood (the suburb where the center is located) for relief work.[62] During the forest fires in California in 2006, local Shi'is donated money and brought food to displaced families. They also raised funds to help those affected by Hurricane Katrina. In Toronto, Canada, Shi'is have collaborated with Jewish and Christian groups to help the homeless in winter. The "Out of the Cold" program brings the homeless to the three places of worship and provides them with dinner, accommodation, and breakfast in winter. In cities like Denver, Shi'is and Sunnis work together to feed the hungry and to promote food drives for the Ansar pantry. Instead of focusing on Muslim refugees or earthquakes abroad, Shi'is have increasingly turned their attention to the streets of America.

Projects such as these show that Shi'is are increasingly committed to instilling a sense of civic awareness in their communities. They have promoted civic rather than just communal programs since the latter can foster exclusion and marginalization, elements that are not conducive to promoting a better image of Islam. As Shi'is explore the civilizing potential of Islam, their tone of discourse is also changing. Shi'i role models like 'Ali and Husayn are invoked to contribute to American civil society. Shi'i women are drawing upon female role models like Fatima and Zaynab to accentuate their own contribution in the American public sphere. This civil engagement with the non-Muslim other is predicated on principles like shared humanity, universal values of justice, and a concern for the less fortunate.

As American Shi'is become more closely identified with American civil society, their self-imposed marginalization is ending. Interaction with political, religious, and civic leaders have prompted Shi'is to accentuate humanitarian values that transcend the boundaries of religion, culture, and race. Gradually, the Shi'is will have to go beyond civic boundaries and enter into matters important in American political discourse, issues such as housing, unemployment, racism, and the environment.

Shi'i Political Discourse

Increased government surveillance and other measures have forced Shi'is to abandon their traditional ambivalent stance toward political engagement. They have realized that it is only by participation in the American political order that Shi'is can enjoy protection against government agencies that disregard the constitution and violate civil liberties. Integration into American society and the need to voice sociopolitical concerns necessitated a more politically active voice, which might also persuade policymakers to counteract American resentment against Muslims.

The question of political participation by the American Shi'i community is premised on two important considerations. Traditionally, Shi'is have eschewed political involvement since Shi'i political theory is based on a hermeneutic structure, which views that all governments in the prolonged absence of the twelfth Imam to be illegitimate.[63] Because of this approach, most Shi'is have remained politically inactive even in their own countries. Lack of Shi'i involvement in the American political process can also be explained by the relatively young age of the centers. This observation is corroborated by my survey. Table 2 indicates that only 29 percent of the centers thought it important to be involved in the political process.

Traditional Shi'i aversion to American politics can be discerned from the following anecdote. In 1996 there was a major discussion on the Shi'i-based Internet discussion group (the Ahl al-Bayt Discussion Group or ABDG) as to whether Shi'is should support candidates running for federal elections. The majority felt that since they are living in a non-Muslim country, Shi'is should eschew all political involvement. Others even argued that, given American penchant toward Israel, voting for a candidate would be tantamount to supporting the Israeli cause. Therefore, they maintained that it was *haram* (religiously prohibited) to support or vote for a candidate. A small minority disagreed, arguing that voting for a candidate of their choice might help the Shi'i cause in America and perhaps influence American foreign policy.

Shi'i political inactivity can also be explained by the fact that the Shi'is have yet to form politically active institutions or coalitions like CAIR, AMC, or AMA. The Shi'is are not represented in these Muslim organizations that participate in American civil discourse. Shi'i political exertions have yet to concretize into independent political bodies or lobby groups that would represent their political aspirations in America. In the absence of such political institutions, political activism has so far manifested itself in public discourse on moral and social issues that impact the community. And once again, 9/11 changed things dramatically.

Since the attacks, there has been greater Shi'i political engagement. According to imam Muhammad Ilahi, before 9/11 many Shi'is considered it *haram* (forbidden) to vote; now it is considered a religious obligation (*wajib*) to vote. Shi'is have felt the need to voice their concerns against American foreign policies, especially those which pertain to Iraq and Iran. Such instances have forced Shi'is to abandon their traditional ambivalent stance toward political activity. Shi'is have also come to the realization that civic engagement may be the most powerful way to fulfill their political aspirations in America. Vital issues such as civil rights, immigration, foreign policy, education, and social and economic justice can be positively affected by political lobbying.

The election of 2004 proved to the Shi'i community that political participation with Sunnis would benefit both groups. Sunnis and Shi'is cooperated as Muslims registered and voted in record numbers. During the election, several Muslim Political Alliance Committees (PACs) were established and a national Muslim voter database created by Muslim American Society (MAS) Freedom Foundation. Muslims gained valuable practical political experience by working in campaigns, performing such tasks as working the polls, canvassing, forming logistical teams, voter rights monitoring, and manning phone banks. In August 2008, there were fifty Muslim delegates at the Democratic National convention in Denver. Thirty of them attended the American Muslim caucus and both Shi'is and Sunnis participated in the event.[64] Shi'is participated with Sunnis to build a Muslim voting bloc, which they hoped would help unseat Republicans.

Increased politicization of the Muslim community during the November 2008 election can be discerned from a poll undertaken soon after Barack Obama's victory.[65] The American Muslim Taskforce on Civil Rights and Elections (AMT) released the results of a poll indicating that almost 90 percent of American Muslim voters backed Barack Obama in the election. The survey of more than six hundred American Muslim voters indicated that just 2 percent of respondents cast their ballots for Sen. John McCain. According to this poll:

- Of those who voted, 89 percent cast their ballot for Barack Obama.
- Just 2 percent of respondents said they voted for John McCain.
- Most of the respondents (78 percent) reside in ten states: Illinois, New York, Virginia, Michigan, California, Texas, New Jersey, Maryland, Florida, and Pennsylvania.
- Ninety-five percent of respondents said they voted in the presidential election, whether at the polls or by absentee ballot. This is the highest American Muslim voter turnout ever reported.
- Of those who voted, nearly 14 percent said they did so for the first time.
- One-fourth of respondents said they volunteered for or donated money to a political campaign in this election.
- American Muslim voters are increasingly identifying themselves with the Democratic Party. More than two-thirds said they consider themselves Democrats. Most of the rest, or 29 percent, still consider themselves independent. Only 4 percent said they are Republicans.
- More than two-thirds (63 percent) of respondents said the economy was the most important issue that affected their voting decision. This was followed by 16 percent who said the wars in Iraq and Afghanistan were the most important. (In January 2008, a sample of one thousand Muslim voters rated education and civil rights as the top issues.)[66]

Worried by what they saw as attacks on their civil liberties under the Bush administration, Muslims were eager to build and enhance political consciousness. In a 2006 survey of one thousand Muslim registered voters, about 12 percent identified themselves as Shiʻis, 36 percent said they were Sunnis, and 40 percent called themselves "just . . . Muslim," according to the Council on American-Islamic Relations (CAIR).

In some areas, Shiʻi political activity has taken the form of establishing eclectic bodies that transcend sectarian boundaries, cooperating with

Sunnis to create a unified and effective challenge for local posts. In cities like Detroit, Shi'is cooperate with Sunnis to provide Muslim candidates for school boards, municipal posts, and working for the election of Muslim mayors and state legislators. The intent is to get Shi'is to vote for fellow Muslim candidates, planning for an eventual Muslim presence in Congress or the Senate. In 2000, when the local school board planned an expansion project that was perceived to be against the interests of the Muslim community, local Sunni and Shi'i communities rallied together to defeat the plan. Gradually, Muslims are playing more active roles in the policies adopted by local school boards and other regional agencies.

In Chicago, Shi'is have organized fund-raisers for congressmen, senators, and presidential candidates.[67] Other Shi'is like Masom 'Ali in Chicago organize breakfast meetings with the mayor, state representatives, and candidates running for Congress in order to introduce community members to these figures. Candidates were invited to Shi'i religious centers to make them aware of Shi'i contribution to American civil society and to urge Shi'is to exercise their right to vote.[68]

In other cases, Shi'is have joined Sunnis so that Muslim voters could make a difference in the political process. In 2006 the Muslim American Society (MAS) set up booths in 150 mosques across the country. The booths have a computer monitor with a link to a website (http://www.masvip.org/) to enable Muslims to register online during Friday prayers.

Shi'i political activism is also demonstrated within the Iranian community. For a long time, Iranian Americans have remained political outsiders. They blame their lack of political activism to their own politically shy sensibilities, which were formed as they were immigrants from a country where they had no say in the political process. Now, some Iranian Americans in the Bay Area are running for office. Susan Irene Etezadi campaigned to be a San Mateo County Superior Court judge. Others have set up a political action committee; a national group has tried to urge Iranian Americans to be more involved by instructing them on ways to write letters to editors and helping them register to vote.

Some Shi'is have allied themselves with the Sunni-based American Muslim Council (AMC). Dr. Hashim, a Shi'i proselyte living in Maryland, recalls how he used the offices of AMC to write to senators who made. statements deemed offensive by Muslims. Like Dr. Hashim, many Shi'is have subscribed to CAIR's mailing list and have taken positive steps to defend Muslim interests. They have also taken CAIR's advice to seek out "Muslim friendly" candidates in the election year.[69]

Political activism is visible in different segments of the American Shi'i community. The Islamic Information Center (IIC) is based in Maryland and run by Mawlana Rafiq Naqavi, a religious scholar of South Asian origins. In February 2008 the IIC issued a communiqué stating:

> The IIC strongly encourages all Muslims to take part in the primary elections taking place in Maryland, DC and Virginia tomorrow February 12th, 2008. For those who have already registered it is imperative that they take part in this election process, especially considering how close the candidates are to each other at this point. The outcome of this year's elections will have a great impact on issues related to the affairs of Muslims domestically as well as internationally, and thus it is our duty to take part in this process.

Since it is one of the largest and the oldest Shi'i group, the Detroit Shi'i community has always played a more active civic and political role. As the second-generation Shi'is in America identify with and assimilate into American culture, they develop a sense of patriotism leading to a greater politicization of the community and a sense of American national consciousness. Increasing political activism in the Detroit community is apparent from the fact that many community members are politically engaged with Arab organizations. The Arab American Political Committee (APAC) in Detroit has lobbied for certain specific political issues. Although many APAC members are Shi'is, they prefer to identify themselves with an Arab rather than an Islamic political entity. In all probability, this is to avoid stereotypical images associated with Islamic organizations.

The rise of political consciousness within the Detroit Shi'i community has precipitated a concomitant desire for participation within the political system. In the voter registration drive prior to the elections in 2000, imam Hasan Qazwini of ICA urged its members to register to vote. According to imam Qazwini, the majority of the Muslims in Michigan (at least 70 percent) voted for George Bush. Participation by local mosques and centers in the American political process is not restricted to lobbying. Some mosques are fostering closer ties with local political figures so that their particular concerns are addressed. The October 1999 edition of the Islamic House of Wisdom's (IHW) newsletter '*Salaam*' contains a letter from the former U.S. Senator from Michigan, Spencer Abraham. He states that he is "sponsoring the first congressional resolution regarding tolerance towards Islam that is aimed at expressing Congress' view of religious tolerance in America today." The resolution further calls upon the Congress to take the lead in condemning anti-Muslim intolerance and discrimination and recognizes the contributions of Islam.

Increasingly, American politicians are acknowledging the need to rely on Muslim support in their constituencies. They are developing closer relations with local Muslim communities and seek support from the Michigan Muslim community in running for various posts. The fact that Senator Abraham informed the Muslim community in Detroit of his pro-Muslim political stance is indicative of the close ties being fostered by some centers with local politicians.

Even the Shi'i youth in Dearborn have become politically active since 9/11. Every year, during the Arab International festival, a group of young Shi'i volunteers register as many people as possible for local elections. They seek to educate people regarding the benefits of voter registration and why it is critical to vote. Increasingly, young Shi'is are participating in changing the American political landscape. These young Muslims, who seek both political and cultural citizenship, join political campaign groups and have urged Shi'is to become active political figures. In a local election in 2007, 70 percent of the Shi'is in Dearborn voted.[70] This was a great example of political involvement and representation. By 2007, Dearborn and the surrounding areas had Shi'i councilors, Shi'i members of various school boards, and even a Shi'i mayor in the city of Wayne, Michigan. David Turfe, a Shi'i, became a judge in a district court in 2006. He was elected by the people and serves in the people's court. Shirley Elder is another Shi'i judge in Wayne County, Michigan.

Political awakening of American Shi'ism is premised on the necessity to contribute Islamic values and norms to a wider notion of American civilization as well as improve the Shi'i position in the United States. The activities of Shi'i youth have inspired the elders to make Shi'ism a more prominent and vocal feature of the American political landscape, and these engagements by Muslim youth are catalyzing a transfer of political identification from the national level to the local level.

As the second generation of Shi'is has come to see the United States as their permanent home, it has appropriated distinctly American values and outlook. Shi'is all over this country have opted for voluntary social activism; they identify with American culture and develop a sense of patriotism leading to a greater politicization of the community and a sense of American national consciousness. This is their way to counter marginality, Islamophobia, and social exclusion.

The events of 9/11 forced them to become both politically active and socially extroverted. The concern by the imams and Shi'is of Dearborn to be involved in American civil and political lives is not matched by a similar concern by the *'ulama'* from the Iranian, South Asian, or Khoja communities who have chosen to remain largely apolitical. As the Shi'is settle here, based on the Dearborn experience, we can indeed expect that the next generation of Shi'is will exert their political rights as they integrate into American culture and identify with America as their homeland.

Religious communities often show the preponderance of their faith rather than seek accommodation when confronted with an alien faith. However, existence in an American pluralistic milieu has forced Shi'is to seek an appropriate response to religious and interfaith diversity. Shi'is have realized that they cannot afford to isolate themselves. Especially since the events of 9/11, American Shi'is, along with peoples of other faiths, have searched for a global ethic that can provide a basis for interreligious relations among people of diverse spiritual commitment.

For many years, American Shi'is were politically dormant, content to remain within their ethnic enclaves and practice their faith within the confines of the mosques. American Shi'is have engaged in a major paradigm shift, from preservation of religious boundaries to social and political activism. Increasingly, domestic rather than foreign issues have become important for them. Before the events of 9/11, like other Muslims, Shi'is in America focused primarily on changing U.S. policy toward Palestine, Kashmir, Iran, and Iraq. Since 9/11, though, the attempt to reconstitute their identity as American Shi'is is making domestic relations—and civil rights and interfaith relations—more important. Shi'is have become more vocal and visible in their adopted homeland.

Conclusion

American Shiʻism is interwoven with different cultures, for, like other religious communities, its structures and rituals are impacted by the cultural markings of its members. The community is constituted in an environment in which its members form a conglomerate of disparate ethnic groups. This confluence of Shiʻis sharing common space has proved to be problematic. Shiʻis face the challenge of reconstituting themselves into more Islamic and less ethnically stylized institutions. They also face the challenge of cultural homogenization, meaning coming to terms with a common culture that is evolving among the second- and third-generation Shiʻis. The youth seek to foster interethnic social interaction and pluralistic centers anchored on bonds of faith that would transcend other differences.

The freedom that America offers has also precipitated different strands of Shiʻism in America. This book has focused primarily on the ethnic and cultural distinctions. However, this emphasis betrays the differences that undergird the community. Circles are drawn based on interpretation of Islamic law, openness to American society, and nationalistic fervor. Other dividing lines include tensions between conservatism and change, the dichotomy between preservation and reformation, and the discourse on gender segregation in the community. These distinctive markers underscore the persistence of disparities, despite creedal and juridical uniformity, between indigenous African American and immigrant communities. They also relate to differences between and within the immigrant community. It is the internal pluralism that has led to the fragmentation of the Shiʻi community, mainly because elements of American culture and values are interfacing with the culture of immigrant and American-born Shiʻis.

As Shiʻis search for ways to chart out their existence in America, they also need to reevaluate their normative texts. This exercise is contingent on recognizing that they are not bound to erstwhile juridical or exegetical hermeneutics. Communities often construct a paradigmatic interpretation of a text and force it on their readers. Once it is defined, the authoritative legacy of the text is transmitted to the next group of scholars and becomes entrenched as the normative and "authentic" position. Gradually, the texts construct an increasingly restrictive and specific well-defined position on an issue. The contents of the sacred texts are frequently less important than the social and historical settings in which they are interpreted.

The reading of a text is interwoven with the closing of the interpretive process, restricting, thereby, the text to a specific determination. This determination is then submitted as the final and only possible interpretation of the text.[1] In this sense, juridical hermeneutics are no different from the interpretive activities evident in other fields. There is a need to differentiate between the Qur'anic vision and the sociopolitical context in which that vision was interpreted and articulated by classical and medieval exegetes. This reinterpretive task demands that Shi'is undertake the task of reevaluating the classical and medieval juridical corpus.

American Shi'is are making their presence felt in different spheres. Since the 1980s, they have realized that they cannot depend on Sunni institutions to represent their interests. In many cities, they have formed their own institutions. However, so far there is no systematic crystallization of Shi'i thought or vision within the institutions. Even though they live in a multiethnic and a largely pluralistic milieu, Shi'is in America often encounter isolation and resistance from elements of the larger Muslim community and the host society. Since they are a minor component of American Islam, they have to negotiate their boundaries against both groups. They must resist the homogenizing affects of American culture and confront the perpetual charge of heresy from the Wahhabis and Salafis.

Like other Muslims, since the horrific events of September 11, 2001, the Shi'is have affirmed their sense of loyalty to America and sought to demarginalize themselves. They have engaged in more civic duties and tried to become more visible in the American public square. In many ways, Shi'is are involved in a paradigm shift, from being Shi'is in America to becoming American Shi'is. This silent revolution indicates that they are transitioning from being "the other" within the "Muslim other" to becoming a more visible and vocal minority group in America.

We need to understand the role of Shi'i Muslims in weaving the religious as well as social tapestry of America and to see several gaps—between religion and culture, between religion and politics, between religious loyalty and ethnic identity, and the lacuna between normative religious texts and the reality of American life. With time, these gaps will be filled. It is here that the challenge for the next generation of Shi'is lies.

Appendix

TABLE 1

Year of Establishment of Shi'i Institutions in America: Base (32)

Decade	Number of Organizations
1970s	3
1980s	9
1990s	14
2000s	5
No Response	1
Total	32

Conclusion

31 (96.88%) of the 32 organizations surveyed responded to this question. Of these organizations, 9.68% were established in the 1970s, 29.03% were established in the 1980s, 45.16% were established in the 1990s, and 16.13% were established in the 2000s.

TABLE 2

Challenges Facing Shi'i Institutions: Base (32)

Challenge	Number of Organizations
Facility	21
Finances	17
Achieving regular attendance	12
Division in the community	11
Obtaining a resident Alim	10
Using English in programs	8
Transmitting religion to youth	21
Developing literature for non-Muslims	8
Cooperation with non-Shi'a Muslims	8
Having women involved in the programs	5
Getting involved in the political process	6
Maintaining Shi'a values/identity	10
Increasing membership	10
Responding to the needs of new converts	2
Speakers	1
No Response	2

*Note: Nearly all of the organizations listed more than one challenge and thus are represented more than once in the above table.

Conclusion

93.75% of the organizations surveyed responded to this question. The top challenges given by the responding organizations are facility (70%), transmitting religion to youth (70%), finances (56.67%), and attendance (40%).

TABLE 3
Thursday Majalis at Shi'i Institutions: Base (32)

Response	Number of Organizations
Yes	14
No	9
No Response	9
Total	32

Conclusion

71.88% of the organizations surveyed responded to this question. Of those that responded, 68.87% have Thursday *majalis*, while 39.13% do not.

TABLE 4
Celebration of Birthdays/Wafats of Imams at Shi'i Institutions: Base (32)

Response	Number of Organizations
Have celebration	16
No celebration	1
No Response	15
Total	32

Conclusion

53.13% of the organizations surveyed responded to this question. Out of the organizations that responded, 94% celebrate birthdays/wafats of Imams at their center.

TABLE 5
Interfaith Dialogue held by Shi'i Institutions: Base (32)

Response	Number of Organizations
Yes	13
No	6
No Response	13
Total	32

Conclusion

Of the nineteen (59.38%) organizations that responded to this question, 68.42% reported to having interfaith dialogue while 31.58% reported no interfaith dialogue at their center.

TABLE 6
Ethnic Diversity of Shi'i Institutions: Base (32)

Ethnicity	Number of Organizations
Iran	18
Pakistan	15
India	14
Iraq	10
Afghanistan	10
Lebanon	5
"Arab"	4
United States	3
Khojas	3
East Africa	2
Gulf Countries	2
South America	2
Syria	2
Bosnia	1
Tunis	1
Egypt	1
Jordan	1
Palestine	1
Turkey	1
Sudan	1
"Africa"	1
No Response	0

*Note: Twenty-two organizations are represented more than once in the above data as they listed more than one country from which their constituents originate. Also, four organizations responded with unclear data, such as "everywhere" or "mixed," thus the responses of only twenty-eight organizations are represented above.

Conclusion
100% of the organizations surveyed responded to this question. 64.29% of organizations reported some constituents from Iran, 53.57% reported some from Pakistan, 50% reported some from India, 35.71% reported some from Iraq, and 35.71% reported constituents from Afghanistan.

TABLE 7
Languages used in Shi'i Institutions: Base (32)

Language	Number of Organizations
English	24
Arabic	7
Farsi	7
Urdu	6
No Response	5

*Note: Twenty-four (88.89%) of the twenty-seven organizations that responded reported using at least two primary languages at their center and thus are represented more than once in the above table.

Conclusion
84.38% of the organizations surveyed responded to this question. Of these organizations, 88.89% (24 organizations) use English as one of their primary languages. 25.93% use Arabic, 25.93% use Farsi, and 22.22% use Urdu.

TABLE 8
Da'wa/Tabligh by Shi'i Institutions: Base (32)

Presence of Da'wa/Tabligh Work	Number of Organizations
Yes	18
No	2
No Response	12
Total	32

Conclusion
It is noteworthy that twelve (37.5%) of the organizations surveyed did not answer the question about Da'wa/Tabligh work. However, 90% of the organizations that did respond reported positively to Da'wa/Tabligh work.

Notes

NOTES TO INTRODUCTION

1. An exception to this is Yvonne Haddad and Jane Smith, *Mission to America: Five Islamic Sectarian Communities in North America* (Gainesville: University Press of Florida, 1993).

2. In this study, the term *Shi'is* is used to refer to Twelver Shi'is only. Therefore it excludes other Shi'i groups like the Zaydis and the Bohra and Agha Khani Isma'ilis.

3. For a more detailed study of the origins and doctrines of Twelver Shi'ism see the following: Lynda Clarke, ed., *The Shi'ite Heritage: Essays on Classical and Modern Traditions* (Binghamton: Global, 2001); Hamid Dabashi, *Authority in Islam: From the Rise of Muhammad to the Establishment of the Umayyads* (New Brunswick: Transaction, 1989); Jassim Hussain, *The Occultation of the Twelfth Imam* (Cambridge: Muhammadi Trust, 1982); Syed Husain Jafri, *The Origins and Early Development of Shi'ite Islam* (London: Longman, 1978); Etan Kohlberg, ed., *The Formation of the Classical Islamic World: Shi'ism* (Burlington: Ashgate, 2003); Hossein Modarresi, *Crisis and Consolidation in the Formative Period of Shi'ite Islam* (Princeton: Darwin, 1993); Mojan Momen, *An Introduction to Shi'i Islam: The History and Doctrines of Twelver Shi'ism* (New Haven: Yale, 1985); Liyakat Takim, *The Heirs of the Prophet: Charisma and Religious Authority in Shi'ite Islam* (Albany: SUNY Press, 2006).

4. For details of these, see Syed Hussein Jafri, *Origins*, chaps. 2 and 3.

5. Muhammad b. 'Isma'il al-Bukhari, *Sahih al-Bukhari*, trans. Muhammad Khan, 9 vols. (Beirut: Dar al-Arabia, 1985), 4:183; 4:260.

6. Examples are the revolts of Muhammad b. 'Abd Allah (Nafs al-Zakiyya) (d. 762), Husayn b. 'Ali (d. 786), and Abu Saraya (d. 815). For a discussion on various 'Alid revolts against the 'Abbasids, see Hugh Kennedy, *The Early 'Abbasid Caliphate: A Political History* (London: Croom Helm, 1981); C. Huart, "'Alids," *Shorter Encyclopedia of Islam*, eds. H. A. Gibb and J. H. Kramers (Leiden: E. J. Brill, 1974), 32–33.

7. See Liyakat Takim, *Heirs of the Prophet*, 27.

8. Muhammad b. 'Umar Kashshi, *Ikhtiyar Ma'rifa al-Rijal*, ed. al-Mustafawi (Mashad: Danishgahi Mashad, 1969), 209. In another tradition, the Imam is

quoted as saying, "Anything that does not come from this house is invalid." Muhammad b. al-Hasan al-Saffar, *Basa'ir al-Darajat fi Fada'il Al Muhammad* (Qum: Maktabat Ayat Allah al-Mar'ashi, 1983), 511.

9. Wilferd Madelung, "Authority in Twelver Shi'ism in the Absence of the Imam," in George Makdisi et al., *La Nation D'autorite au Moyen Age* (Byzance: Occidental Paris, 1982), 164.

10. See Abdulaziz Sachedina, *Islamic Messianism: The Idea of the Mahdi in Twelver Shi'ism* (Albany: SUNY Press, 1981).

11. For a detailed and nuanced discussion on the development of the authority of the jurists see Ahmad Kazemi Moussavi, *Religious Authority in Shi'ite Islam: From the Office of the Mufti to the Institution of Marja'* (Kuala Lumpur: Institute of Islamic Thought and Civilization, 1996); Abdulaziz Sachedina, *The Just Ruler in Shi'ite Islam: The Comprehensive Authority of the Jurist in Imamite Jurisprudence* (New York: Oxford University Press, 1988); Norman Calder, "The Structure of Authority in Imami Shi'i Jurisprudence" (Ph.D. diss., School of Oriental and African Studies, 1979).

12. See Vernon Schubel, "Karbala as Sacred Space Among North American Shi'a," in Barbara Metcalf, ed., *Making Muslim Space in North America and Europe* (Berkeley: University of California Press, 1996). Schubel has also examined the significance of Muharram rituals in North America in his "The Muharram Majlis: The Role of a Ritual in the Preservation of Shi'a Identity," in E. Waugh, S. M. Abu-Laban, and R. Qureshi, eds., *Muslim Families in North America* (Edmonton: University of Alberta Press, 1991).

13. Ron Kelley, "Muslims in Los Angeles," in Yvonne Haddad and Jane Smith, eds., *Muslim Communities in North America* (Albany: SUNY Press, 1994).

14. See Abdulaziz Sachedina, "A Minority Within a Minority: The Case of the Shi'a in North America," in Haddad and Smith, *Muslim Communities.*

15. Liyakat Takim, "Foreign Influences on American Shi'ism," in *Muslim World* 90 (Fall 2000): 459–77; "Multiple Identities in a Pluralistic World: Shi'ism in America," in Yvonne Haddad, ed., *Muslims in the West: From Sojourners to Citizens* (Oxford University Press: New York, 2002), 218–32.

NOTES TO CHAPTER 1

1. See Abdullah Hakim Quick, *Deeper Roots: Muslims in the Americas and the Caribbean from before Columbus to the Present* (London: Ta-Ha Publishers, 1998).

2. Mandiko was a prominent West African tribe. See Mohammad Abderrazzaq, "Native Americans," in Joselyn Cesari, ed., *Encyclopedia of Islam in the United States*, 2 vols. (Westport: Greenwood, 2007), 463.

3. Jane Smith, *Islam in America* (New York: Columbia University Press, 1999), 50.

4. Richard B. Turner, *Islam in the African-American Experience* (Indianapolis: Indiana University Press, 1997), 11.

5. The term refers to those Muslims who remained in Spain after the reconquest. Most of these Muslims were forced to convert to Christianity.

6. See Darcy Zabel, "The Arab Diaspora in the Americas: Latin America, the United States, and Canada," in Darcy Zabel, ed., *Arabs in the Americas: Interdisciplinary Essays on the Arab Diaspora* (New York: Peter Lang, 2006), 4.

7. In the late nineteenth century, Lebanese migrants migrated to Latin and South America too. See Zabel, ed., *Arabs in the Americas*, chap. 2.

8. Yvonne Haddad and Adair Lummis, *Islamic Values in the United States: A Comparative Study* (New York: Oxford, 1987), 13–14.

9. On the different reasons why Arab immigrants came to America during the first wave, see Zabel, "The Arab Diaspora in the Americas: Latin America, the United States and Canada," in Zabel, ed., *Arabs in the Americas*, 6.

10. This was confirmed by a friend who saw grave inscriptions that indicate the presence of Shi'i figures among the early migrants.

11. Geneive Abdo, *Mecca and Main Street: Muslim Life in America After 9/11* (New York: Oxford University Press, 2006), 71.

12. I am grateful to Ron Amen, the facility manager at the Arab American National Museum in Detroit, for sharing with me a transcribed copy of an interview that Hussein Ayad gave to John P. Brennan, a representative of the Public Library of Michigan City, n.d.

13. I am grateful to Julia Harajali for sharing this information with me in May 2008.

14. These accounts were confirmed to me in July 2007.

15. Linda Walbridge, *Without Forgetting the Imam: Lebanese Shi'ism in an American Community* (Detroit: Wayne State University Press, 1997), 16–17.

16. Ibid., 17.

17. Ibid.

18. Sulayman Nyang, *Islam in the United States of America* (Chicago: Kazi Publications, 1999), 51.

19. Linda Walbridge, "The Shi'a Mosques and Their Congregations in Dearborn," in Haddad and Smith, *Muslim Communities*, 340.

20. Interview with Khalil Alwan. July 2007.

21. Interview with Marium 'Uthman, 1996.

22. Richard B. Turner, *Islam in the African-American Experience*, 121.

23. Haddad and Smith, *Mission to America*, 60–61.

24. Walbridge, *Without Forgetting the Imam*, 45.

25. Interview with Eid Alwan. The term *jahiliyya* refers to the period of moral deprivation before the coming of Islam.

26. Muharram is the month when Husayn was killed in Kerbala. Shi'is mark the event by holding commemorative gatherings combined with a series of elaborate rituals (see chap. 2 of the present study).

27. See Islamic Center of America, Grand Opening, Commemorative Journal (May 2005), 31.

28. Ibid., 32.

29. Abdo, *Mecca and Main Street*, 46.

30. Mary Lahaj, "The Islamic Center of New England: The Immigrant Generation," in Haddad and Smith, *Muslim Communities*, 293.

31. Interview with Haj Muhammad Omar (Awad) by Mary Lahaj, October 4, 1983, Weymouth, MA.

32. Diana Eck, *A New Religious America: How a "Christian Country" Has Become the World's Most Religiously Diverse Nation* (New York: HarperCollins, 2001), 246.

33. Interview with Nayfee Krugler, March 2008.

34. Eck, *New Religious America*, 245.

35. Abdo Elkholy, *The Arab Moslems in the United States: Religion and Assimilation* (New Haven: College and University Press, 1966), 143.

36. Garbi Schmidt, *Sunni Muslims in Chicago: Islam in Urban America* (Philadelphia: Temple, 2004), 19.

37. Ibid., 26.

38. Marcia Hermansen, "Chicago," in Cesari, ed., *Encyclopedia of Islam in the United States*, 135.

39. Theresa Alfaro Velcamp, "Mexican Muslims in the Twentieth Century: Challenging Stereotypes and Negotiating Space," in Haddad, ed., *Muslims in the West*, 284.

40. Ibid.

41. See *al-Ilmu Noorun*, Edmonton, Alberta (June 1995), 4.

42. Abdulaziz Sachedina, "A Minority Within a Minority: The Case of the Shi'a in North America," in Haddad and Smith, *Muslim Communities*, 6.

43. Ibid.

44. John Voll, "Muslims in the Caribbean: Ethnic Sojourners and Citizens," in Yvonne Haddad and Jane Smith, eds., *Muslim Minorities in the West: Visible and Invisible* (Walnut Creek, CA: AltaMira Press, 2002), 268.

45. Youssef M'roueh, "Shi'a Population in North America," in Sayyed M. Hejazi and A. Hashim, eds., *Ahlul Bayt Assembly of North America: Abstract of Proceedings of 1996* (Beltsville: International Graphics, 1997), 44.

46. Ibid.

47. Yvonne Haddad, *Not Quite American? The Shaping of Arab and Muslim Identity in the United States* (Waco, TX: Baylor University Press, 2004), 5.

48. Carol Stone, "Estimate of Muslims Living in America," in Yvonne Haddad, ed., *The Muslims of America* (New York: Oxford University Press, 1991), 31.

49. Sharon McIrvin Abu-Laban, "Family and Religion among Muslim Immigrants and Their Descendants," in Waugh, S. Abu-Laban, and Qureshi, *Muslim Families in North America*, 21–22.

50. Haddad, *Not Quite American?*, 5–6.

51. A temporary marriage is contracted for a limited period. Some Shi'i jurists do allow Muslims to marry Christian and Jewish women on a permanent basis.

52. Ayatullah al-Uzama Syed 'Ali al-Husaini Seestani, *Islamic Laws: English Version of Taudhihul Masae'l* (London, 1994), 443.

53. Karen Leonard, *Muslims in the United States: The State of Research* (New York: Russell Sage, 2003), 4.

54. Ibid., 52.

55. J. Smith, *Islam in America*, 30. See also Yvonne Haddad, Jane I. Smith, and Kathleen M. Moore, eds., *Muslim Women in America: The Challenge of Islamic Identity Today* (Oxford: Oxford University Press, 2006), 7.

56. Ghulam Abbas Sajan, "The Status of the Ahlul Bayt's Devotees in Canada," in Hejazi et al., *Ahlul Bayt Assembly*, 95.

57. Ibid.

58. Larry Poston, *Islamic Da'wah in the West: Muslim Missionary Activity and the Dynamics of Conversion to Islam* (New York: Oxford University Press, 1992), 30.

59. Ilyas Ba-Yunus and Kassim Kone, "Muslim Americans: A Demographic Report," in Zahid H. Bukhari, Sulayman S. Nyang, Mumtaz Ahmad, and John L. Esposito, eds., *Muslims' Place in the American Public Square: Hope, Fears, and Aspirations* (Walnut Creek, CA: AltaMira Press, 2004), 320.

60. Youssef M'roueh, "Shi'a Population," 57. The author does not cite the source of his figures.

61. Al-Jibouri, "A Glance at Shi'a Communities in the U.S.," in *Islamic Affairs*, Virginia (1993), 1. See also Smith, *Islam in America*, 61.

62. Larry Poston, *Islamic Da'wah*, 30.

63. See details in Ron Kelley, "Muslims in Los Angeles," in Haddad and Smith, *Muslim Communities*, 160–61.

64. According to some estimates, there are approximately a million Iranians in America, most of whom are Shi'is although a considerable number follow the Baha'i faith. See Smith, *Islam in America*, 53.

65. Discussion with Hisham Husainy, July 2007.

66. Some statistics indicate that over 3 million Iraqis have been displaced since the American invasion in 2003.

67. A *marji'* is the most learned juridical authority in the Shi'i community whose rulings on the *shari'a* (Islamic moral-legal law) are followed by his adherents. In the absence of the twelfth Shi'i Imam, the *marji'* assumes the responsibility of reinterpreting the relevance of Islamic norms to the modern era. He is thus able to impinge on the religious and social lives of his followers.

68. Walbridge, *Without Forgetting the Imam*, 211–13.

69. Confirmed by an imam of a Shi'i center.

70. See for example, Ron Kelley, "Muslims in Los Angeles," in Haddad and Smith, *Muslim Communities*, 156.

71. Smith, *Islam in America,* 53.

72. Carol Stone, "Estimate of Muslims Living in America," in Haddad, *Muslims of America,* 33.

73. Frederick Denny, "Church/Sect Theory and Emerging North American Muslim Communities: Issues and Trends," in Earle Waugh and Frederick Denny, eds., *The Shaping of an American Islamic Discourse: A Memorial to Fazlur Rahman* (Atlanta: Scholars Press, 1998), 235.

74. M. K. Hermansen, "The Muslims of San Diego," in Haddad and Smith, *Muslim Communities,* 187. It should be noted that not all Iranians are Muslims. The figures quoted include members from the Bahai, Jewish, and Christian Armenian communities.

75. George Sabagh and Mehdi Bozorgmehr, "Secular Immigrants: Religiosity and Ethnicity Among Iranian Muslims in Los Angeles," in Haddad and Smith, *Muslim Communities,* 456–57.

76. Bruce Lawrence, *New Faiths, Old Fears: Muslims and Other Asian Immigrants in American Religious Life* (New York: Columbia University Press, 2002), 95.

77. Sabagh and Bozorgmehr, "Secular Immigrants," in Haddad and Smith, *Muslim Communities,* 451.

78. Ron Kelley, "Muslims in Los Angeles," in Haddad and Smith, *Muslim Communities,* 148.

79. Sabagh and Bozorgmehr, "Secular Immigrants," in Haddad and Smith, *Muslim Communities,* 451.

80. Ibid., 453.

81. Lawrence, *New Faiths, Old Fears,* 98.

82. Sabagh and Bozorgmehr, "Secular Immigrants," in Haddad and Smith, *Muslim Communities,* 452.

83. Ibid., 457.

84. The first Iranian mosque in Los Angeles was built in 1986.

85. Eck, *New Religious America,* 47.

86. For a sample list of Iranian-American Organizations see Charles Dilley, "The Iranian Diaspora in Los Angeles: From Islamic Revolution to an Iranian-American Community" (honors thesis, University of Denver, May 2006), app. C.

87. Kambiz GhaneaBassiri, *Competing Visions of Islam in the United States: A Study of Los Angeles* (Westport: Greenwood Press, 1997), 33.

88. See details in Kelley, "Muslims in Los Angeles," in Haddad and Smith, *Muslim Communities,* 149.

89. Ron Kelly, Jonathan Friedlander, and Anita Colby, eds., *Irangeles: Iranians in Los Angeles* (Los Angeles: University of California Press, 1993), 84.

90. M. K. Hermansen, "The Muslims of San Diego," in Haddad and Smith, *Muslim Communities,* 173.

91. Kelly, *Irangeles,* fig. 3. 6.

92. Haddad and Lummis, *Islamic Values*, 15.

93. Sally Howell and Andrew Shryock, "Cracking Down on Diaspora: Arab Detroit and America's War on Terror," *Anthropological Quarterly* (March 2003): 446.

94. C. Eric Lincoln, "The American Muslim Mission in the Context of American Social History," in Earle Waugh, Baha Abu-Laban, and Regula Qureshi, eds., *The Muslim Community in North America* (Edmonton: University of Alberta Press, 1991), 219.

95. Haddad and Lummis, *Islamic Values*, 171.

96. Ibid., 134.

97. Walbridge, *Without Forgetting the Imam*, 59.

98. Leonard, *Muslims in the United States*, 12.

99. M. K. Hermansen, "The Muslims of San Diego," in Haddad and Smith, *Muslim Communities*, 171.

100. Ilyas Ba-Yunus and Kassim Kone, "Muslim Americans," in Bukhari, *Muslims' Place in the American Public Square*, 312.

101. Hermansen, "The Muslims of San Diego," in Haddad and Smith, *Muslim Communities*, 171.

102. Carol Stone, "Estimate of Muslims Living in America," in Haddad, ed., *Muslims of America*, 32.

103. Leonard, *Muslims in the United States*, 13.

104. Carol Stone, "Estimate of Muslims Living in America," in Haddad, *Muslims of America*, 32.

105. Schmidt, *Sunni Muslims in Chicago*, 3.

106. Wilferd Madelung, "Khodjas," in *Encyclopedia of Islam (EI)*, 2nd ed.

107. http://www.world-federation.org/Misc/KSI+History/.

108. This refers to the Shi'i practice of giving one-fifth of their net savings to a *marji'* or his representative. See chap. 4 of the present study for more details.

109. See chap. 3 of the present study for a discussion on the Wahhabis and Salafis.

110. For a brief history of some Sufi movements in America, see Amina Beverly McCloud, *African American Islam* (New York: Routledge, 1995), 91–94.

111. For a summary of the main Sufi groups in America, see also Marcia Hermansen, "Hybrid Identity Formation in Muslim America: The Case of American Sufi Movements," *Muslim World* 1/2 (2000): 90.

112. For a discussion on spiritual exercises in esoteric Shi'ism, see Allamah Mutahhari, Allamah Tabataba'i, and Imam Khumayni, *Light Within Me* (Qum: Ansariyan Publications, n.d.).

113. Muhammad b. Ibrahim al-Nu'mani, *Kitab al-Ghayba* (Tehran: Maktaba al-Saduq, n.d.), 38. See also Ahmad b. Muhammad b. Khalid al-Barqi, *Kitab al-Mahasin* (Najaf: Matba'a al-Haydariyya, 1964), 201.

114. Muhammad b. al-Hasan al-Saffar, *Basa'ir al-Darajat fi Fada'il Al Muhammad* (Qum: Maktabat Ayat Allah al-Mar'ashi, 1983), 21, 23.

115. Seyyed Hossein Nasr, *Sufi Essays* (Albany: SUNY Press, 1991), 107–8.

116. Annemarie Schimmel, *Mystical Dimensions of Islam* (Chapel Hill: University of North Carolina Press, 1975), 223.

117. Arthur Buehler, *Sufi Heirs of the Prophet: The Indian Naqshbandiyya and the Rise of the Mediating Sufi Shaykh* (Columbia: University of South Carolina Press, 1998), 90. The term "golden chain" was coined because a Samanid ruler had a tradition on the unity of God, reported from 'Ali al-Rida, written and inserted in his shroud. See Muhammad al-Baqir al-Majlisi, *Bihar al-Anwar: al-Jami'a Lidurari Akhbar al-A'imma al-Athar*, 110 vols. (Beirut: Dar al-Ihya al-Turath al-'Arabi, 1983), 49:127.

118. Michael David Cooperson, "The Heirs of the Prophet in Classical Arabic Biography," (Ph.D. diss., Harvard University, 1994), 306.

119. Ibid., 306–7.

120. Colin Turner, *Islam Without Allah? The Rise of Religious Externalism in Safavid Iran* (Richmond: Curzon Press, 2002), 56.

121. Buehler, *Sufi Heirs of the Prophet*, 90.

122. Kelley, "Muslims in Los Angeles," in Haddad and Smith, *Muslim Communities*, 160.

123. See http://www.nimatullahi.org. See also http://www.nimatullahi.org/nurbakhsh.

124. Hermansen, "Hybrid Identity Formation," 174.

125. On this movement see William Chittick, "Sufism," in John Esposito, ed., *Encyclopedia of the Modern Islamic World* (New York: Oxford University Press, 1995), 4, 108. For a brief history of the Ni'matullahiya, including this branch, see Alan A. Godlas, "Ni'matullahiyah" in *Encyclopedia of the Modern Islamic World*, 3:252; Shaykh Muhammad Hasan Salih Ali Shah, *The Illustrious Treatise of Salih's Advice* (Pand-i Salih) (Tehran: n. p., 1986), 10.

126. Marcia Hermansen, "In the Garden of American Sufi Movements: Hybrids and Perennials," in Peter B. Clarke, ed., *New Trends and Developments in the World of Islam* (London: Luzac Oriental, 1997), 165.

127. For a history of the Nimatullahis, including a brief section on the biography of Javad Nurbakhsh and the history of the order in America, see Javad Nurbakhsh, "The Nimatullahi" in Seyyed Hossein Nasr, ed., *Islamic Spirituality II: Manifestations* (New York: Crossroad, 1991), 144–59. A further historical source is Nasrollah Pourjavady and Peter Lamborn Wilson, *Kings of Love: The Poetry and History of the Ni'matullahi Sufi Order* (Tehran: Imperial Iranian Academy of Philosophy, 1978). For basic practices of the order the best sources are Javad Nurbakhsh, *In the Tavern of Ruin* (New York: Khaniqahi Nimatullahi, 1978) and *In the Paradise of the Sufis* (New York: Khaniqahi Nimatullahi, 1979).

128. Kelley, "Muslims in Los Angeles," in Haddad and Smith, *Muslim Communities*, 161.

129. See www.icchome.org.

130. Haeri has published extensively on Islamic topics including "Songs of Iman on the Roads of Pakistan" (a series of talks given during a tour of Pakistan) (Blanco, TX: Zahra Publications, ca. 1983); Beams of Illumination from the Divine Revelation. Juz' 'Amma (the last section of the Qur'an) (Blanco, TX: Zahra Publications, ca. 1985); *Beginning's End* (London and New York: KPI in association with Zahra Publications, 1987); *The Journey of the Self: a Sufi Guide to Personality* (San Francisco: Harper, 1991); *Keys to the Qur'an, Shaykh Fadlalla Haeri,* new ed. (Reading, UK: Garnet, ca. 1993); *Living Islam* (Dorset: Element, 1989). For a time Zahra Press issued a magazine available as *Nuradeen, An Islamic Sufi Journal: Selections* (Blanco, TX: Zahra Publications, 1983).

131. "Uwaysi" or "Oveyssi" in Persian pronunciation refers to a line of Sufis who received their original initiate transmission spiritually rather than through direct contact with the Prophet Muhammad. The order is named after Uways al-Qarani, a contemporary of the Prophet and reported to have received such a transmission from him.

132. http://mto.shahmaghsoudi.org/.

133. A biographical note states that he is the "present master of the School of Islamic Sufism" with 300,000 students worldwide. *Shah Maghsoud Angha, al-Rasa'el* (Lanham, MD: University Press, 1986), 121.

134. Hermansen, "Hybrid Identity Formation," 175.

135. Kelley, "Muslims in Los Angeles," in Haddad and Smith, *Muslim Communities,* 160–61.

136. http://www.ias.org/.

137. See also http://www.ias.org/resources.html.

NOTES TO CHAPTER 2

1. "City's Mohammedans Open New Mosque, First in U.S.," *Detroit News,* June 9, 1921.

2. I am grateful to Sally Howell, a doctoral student at the University of Michigan, for sharing her research with me.

3. "Moslems Celebrate Feast of Id-Ul-Filtr." *Detroit Free Press,* June 8, 1921.

4. *Highland Parker,* October 21, 1926.

5. I am grateful to Ron Amen of the Arab American Museum in Detroit for making a copy of the booklet available to me.

6. The booklet states that the new name was incorporated on May 15, 1924. According to the certificate of incorporation, it was actually incorporated on May 10, 1924.

7. Larry Poston, *Islamic Da'wah,* 108. Yasin al-Jibouri later relocated to Virginia where he founded the Islamic Society of Virginia Inc. See also Yasin al-Jibouri, *Memoirs of a Shi'a Missionary in America: Two Decades of Da'wa,* vol. 1 (Virginia, n.p., 1993), 32.

8. This number is based on a list that I compiled. It includes centers of worship, daily Islamic schools, and other educational institutions.

9. Shi'is believe that Imam 'Ali taught a special supplication to a companion of his, Kumayl b. Ziyad. Most Shi'i centers congregate on Thursday nights to recite the supplication.

10. See Council on American-Islamic Relations, *The Mosque in America: A National Portrait*, www.cair-net.org (April 2001) 3, 24.

11. I do not mean to suggest that cultural or religious pluralism do not exist in the homeland countries; however, they are not as pronounced as they are in America.

12. Walbridge reports a more intense and dramatic atmosphere during the 'Ashura' commemorations after the arrival of Iraqis. See Walbridge, *Without Forgetting the Imam*, 211–13. In my conversation with members of the Dearborn community, I was surprised to find that Muharram rituals were not observed by members of the community until after 1963, when the Islamic Center of America was established. This coincided with the arrival of newer immigrants. Similarly, Julia Harajali does not remember the commemoration of 'Ashura' when she was living in Michigan City.

13. Other factors, such as the spread of Wahhabi and Salafi ideologies, have rekindled traditional Sunni–Shi'i disputes (see chap. 3 of the present study).

14. Discussion with Najjah Bazzy, July 2007.

15. See Ateqah Khaki, "Identity Negotiation among Second-generation South Asian Muslim Americans" (senior thesis, Whitman College, 2005), 19.

16. Ibid., 19–20.

17. As quoted in Christine Soriea Sheikh, "Religious and Ethnic Variation among Second-generation Muslim Americans" (Ph.D. Dissertation, University of Arizona, 2007), 55.

18. See Gary David and Kenneth Ayouby, "Being Arab and becoming Americanized: Forms of Mediated Assimilation in Metropolitan Detroit," in Haddad and Smith, *Muslim Minorities in the West*, 128.

19. Ron Kelley, "Muslims in Los Angeles," in Haddad and Smith, *Muslim Communities*, 156.

20. Discussion with Hisham Husainy, July 2007.

21. Garbi Schmidt, *Sunni Muslims in Chicago*, 26.

22. See also Vernon Schubel, *Religious Performance in Contemporary Islam: Shi'i Devotional Rituals in South Asia* (Columbia: University of South Carolina Press, 1993), 71.

23. *Husayniyya* refers to a place where Shi'is congregate to commemorate the death and birthdays of the Imams and other festivals. It is distinguished from a mosque in that rules governing ritual purity of mosques are not applied there.

24. See Council on American-Islamic Relations, *Mosque in America*, 3. See also Geneive Abdo, *Mecca and Main Street*, 64.

25. Leonard, *Muslims in the United States*, 76.

26. Ibid.

27. Lawrence, *New Faiths, Old Fears*, 135.

28. I am grateful to Mariam Meghjee of Boulder for an elucidation of Khoja weddings.

29. I am grateful to Maryam Derbehesht of Denver for sharing this information with me.

30. I am grateful to Shazia Razvi of Denver for a colorful description of Pakistani weddings.

31. This refers to the Shiʻi visitation to the shrines of the Imams. See Takim, "Charismatic Appeal or Communitas? Visitation to the Shrines of the Imams," *Journal of Ritual Studies* 18, no. 2 (2004): 106–20.

32. ʻAbbas was the half brother of Husayn. A very courageous and skilled horseman, he was also killed in Kerbala.

33. A *mujtahid* is an expert in Islamic law who is able to independently extrapolate legal rulings from the Islamic revelatory sources.

34. Ayatullah Sayyid Fadhel Milani, *Frequently asked Questions on Islam: Islamic Answers for Modern Problems* (London: Islam in English Press, 2001), vol. 1, 164.

35. Roy Mottahedeh, *The Mantle of the Prophet: Religion and Politics in Iran* (New York: Pantheon, 1985), 176.

36. David Pinault, "Self-Mortification Rituals in the Shiʻi and Christian Traditions," in L. Clarke, *Shiʻite Heritage*, 384.

37. David Pinault, *The Shiites* (New York: St. Martin's Press, 1992), 103.

38. During the Umayyad dynasty (681–750), poets composed elegies for Husayn in the *majalis*. An important poet, Ismaʻil b. Muhammad al-Himyari (d. 886/891?), is reported to have composed numerous odes (*qasaʼid*) arousing sadness and passion for Husayn. See Mahmoud Ayoub, *Redemptive Suffering in Islam* (New York: Mouton, 1978), 165–66. The Imams encouraged the recitation of poetry in memory of Husayn. Jaʻfar al-Sadiq is reported to have told the poet Abu Harun al-Makfuf: "Heaven is decreed for one who recites poetry about Husayn, weeps, and makes others weep," Ayoub, *Redemptive Suffering*, 18.

39. Jean Calmard, "Shiʻa Rituals and Power II. The Consolidation of Safavid Shiʻism: Folklore and Popular Religion," in *Safavid Persia*, Charles Melville, ed. (New York: I. B. Tauris and Co Ltd, 1996), 143.

40. David Pinault, *Horse of Kerbala: Muslim Devotional Life in India* (New York: Palgrave, 2001), 144–45.

41. Pnina Werbner, "Stamping the Earth with the Name of Allah: Zikr and the Sacralizing of Space among British Muslims," in Metcalf, *Making Muslim Space*, 182.

42. Toby Howarth: *The Twelver Shiʻa as a Muslim Minority in India: Pulpit of Tears* (New York: Routledge, 2005), 16.

43. Vernon Schubel, "Karbala as Sacred Space among North American Shi'a," in Metcalf, *Making Muslim Space*, 187.

44. For a further discussion on how Karbala is re-created in both time and space, see ibid., 188.

45. In the classical period, Shi'is were often labeled as *Rafidis* (rejecters) by their opponents. They are reported to have dissociated themselves from the first three caliphs and maintained that the community had apostatized by rejecting 'Ali's Imamate after the Prophet's death. According to the Mu'tazili al-Hakim b. al-Jushami (d. 1101), Hisham b. al-Hakam, a companion of the fifth and sixth Imams, had introduced into Islam the idea of *takfir al-sahaba* (considering the companions to be infidels). For details, see Liyakat Takim, *Heirs of the Prophet*, chap. 4.

46. On the concept of signification and resistance to it, see Turner, *Islam in the African-American Experience*, 45. I must emphasize that signification of the Shi'is in America occurs within a small segment of the Sunni community.

47. On how rituals are enacted in Dearborn, see Walbridge, *Without Forgetting the Imam*, 92.

48. Yasin al-Jibouri, *Memoirs of a Shi'a Missionary*, 23.

49. In the Shi'i context, the term *hadith* refers to the reports and statements of the Prophet and the Imams.

50. Vernon Schubel, "The Muharram Majlis: The Role of a Ritual in the Preservation of Shi'a Identity," in Waugh, Abu-Laban, and Qureshi, *Muslim Families*, 128.

51. See Lori Peek, "Becoming Muslim: The Development of a Religious Identity," *Sociology of Religion* 66:3 (2005): 217.

52. On why immigrants may stress their religious as opposed to other identities see ibid., 218–19.

53. Looking at why people adopt a particular identity in a given situation is not my thesis here. To do this, it would be necessary to conceive of identity through multiple frames of reference, including such factors as race, ethnicity, class, age, gender, etc. My main concern here is to show how, rather than why, Shi'is express their religious identity, particularly in their centers of worship.

54. For a discussion on this see Sharaf al-Din al-Musawi, *Questions of Jurisprudence: A Comparative Study of Muslim Ritual Practices*, trans. Liyakat Takim (Toronto: Hydery Press, 1996), chap. 1.

55. See Takim "From *Bid'a* to *Sunna*: The *Wilaya* of 'Ali in the Shi'i *Adhan*," *Journal of the American Oriental Society* 120, no. 2 (2000): 66–77.

56. This refers to a famous *hadith* narrated from the Prophet. He is reported to have stated "I leave behind me two weighty things, [they are] the book of God and my family; as long as you cling on to them you will not go astray."

57. The horse of Husayn is also called *Dhu'l-jinah*. However, this appellation was given to the horse much later. The actual name of the horse was Lahiq.

See Muhammad b. Jarir al-Tabari, *Ta'rikh al-Umam Wa'l-Muluk*, 8 vols. (Beirut: Mu'assasa al-A'lami, 1983), 4:322.

58. The Shi'i school of law is called the Ja'fari school after its founder, the sixth Shi'i Imam, Ja'far al-Sadiq.

59. Fatima Haji-Taki, "My Journey to Identity" (honors thesis, University of Minneapolis, 2004), 20.

60. See Luis Leon, *La Llorona's Children: Religion, Life, and Death in the U.S.-Mexican Borderlands* (Berkeley: University of California Press, 2004), 116.

61. Lawrence, *New Faiths, Old Fears*, xv.

62. Steven Barboza, *American Jihad: Islam after Malcolm X* (New York: Doubleday, 1994), 58–59.

63. Hamid Naficy, "Identity Politics and Iranian Exile Music Videos," *Iranian Studies* vol. 31, No. 1. (1998): 64.

64. Charles Dilley, "The Iranian Diaspora in Los Angeles: From Islamic Revolution to an Iranian-American Community" (honors thesis, University of Denver, May 2006), 38.

65. Leonard, *Muslims in the United States*, 125.

66. See chap. 5 for details of these institutions.

67. http://www.muslimcongress.org/contentmc/conferences/conference-2008.aspx.

68. I am grateful to Madina Humkar for sharing this information with me.

69. Jocelyn Cesari, "Islam in France: The Shaping of a Religious Minority," in Haddad, *Muslims in the West*, 42.

70. The survey of the Shi'i youth in Toronto is incorporated in a book that marks an important milestone in understanding the youth predicament in North America. See Sadik Alloo, ed., *Muslim Youth at the Crossroads: Advancing into the Twenty First Century* (Toronto: Hyderi, 1995), 61.

71. Ibid., 62.

72. Ibid., 63.

73. Ibid., 71–72.

74. Ibid., 83.

75. Interview with 'Ali Dabaja in Dearborn, July 2007.

76. On Shi'i internet sites see Abdul Hamid Lotfi, "Spreading the Word: Communicating Islam in America," in Haddad and Smith, *Muslim Minorities in the West*, 22, n. 42. Other Shi'i sites include:

http://al-shia.com/html/eng/lib/lib/index.html
http://al-islam.org/organizations/dilp/index.htm#texts
http://www.shiasearch.net/ENGLISH/library/index.html
http://www.rafed.net/english/general/book.html
http://www.rafed.net/books/other-lang.html
http://rafed.net/ftp/lokat-e.html

http://www.geocities.com/ahlulbayt14/lib1.html
http://www.geocities.com/ahlulbayt14/lib2.html
http://www.geocities.com/ahlulbayt14/lib3.html
http://www.imamali-s.com/en/k/ind-lib.HTM
http://www.shiaa.8m.com/frame_files/s_book1.html
http://islam.web1000.com/books/contents.htm
http://home.swipnet.se/islam/books/contents.htm
http://www.almujtaba.com/english.html
http://shia.mine.nu/media/Books/
http://www.shiaofali.com/soa/
http://www.ahlebait.s5.com/islam.htm
http://www.khamenei.de/books/books.htm
http://www.yamahdi.com/books/books.htm
http://www.ic-el.org/english/html/menu/imam/portrait.htm
http://www.irib.com/Ouriran/imam/writing/html/en/a.htm
http://www.najafi.org/book/
http://www.najaf.org/
http://www.dartabligh.org/books/ebooks/
http://islamica.addr.com/literature/literature.htm
http://islamica.addr.com/scholast/scholast.htm
http://www.angelfire.com/al/gardez/
http://www.wabil.com/digbooks.htm
http://www.almuntazar.com/book.htm
http://members.tripod.com/~mdhasan/Ali/
http://www25.brinkster.com/imamah/library.html
http://www.sicm.org.uk/index.php?page=suduk/index.html
http://www.shia.net/islamicbooks.asp.

77. See chap. 4 of the present study for a discussion of the *marji'iyya* in America.

78. In private circles, many jurists do not recognize Fadlallah as a competent *marji'*. Thus, they do not accord him the status of one who can issue religious edicts.

79. Ayatullah al-'Uzma al-Sayyid Muhammad Husayn Fadlullah, *World of Our Youth*, trans. Khaleel Mohammed (Montreal: Organization for the Advancement of Islamic Learning and Humanitarian Services, 1998), 216.

80. Ibid., 225. Most jurists prohibit playing chess as it was used as an instrument for gambling.

81. Ibid., 102.

82. Abdul Hadi al-Hakim, *A Code of Practice for Muslims in the West (in accordance with the edicts of Ayatullah al-Udhma as-Sayyid Ali al-Husaini as-Seestani)*, trans. Sayyid Muhammad Rizvi (London: Imam Ali Foundation, 1999), 236.

NOTES TO CHAPTER 3

1. Walbridge, *Without Forgetting the Imam*, 44.
2. Walbridge, "The Shi'a Mosques," in Haddad and Smith, *Muslim Communities*, 340.
3. Abdo Elkholy, *Arabs in the United States*, 75–78; 125–26.
4. Mary Lahaj, "The Islamic Center of New England," in Haddad and Smith, *Muslim Communities*, 295.
5. Ibid., 296.
6. Emily Kalled Lovell, "Islam in the United States: Past and Present," in Earle Waugh, Baha Abu-Laban, and Regula Qureshi, eds., *The Muslim Community in North America* (Edmonton: University of Alberta, 1987), 105.
7. Personal interview with Yasin al-Jibouri.
8. Yasin al-Jibouri, *Memoirs of a Shi'a Missionary*, 22.
9. Ibid., 25–26.
10. Haddad, "The Impact of the Islamic Revolution in Iran on the Syrian Muslims of Montreal," in Waugh, Abu-Laban, and Qureshi, *Muslim Community in North America*, 174–77.
11. Ibid., 166.
12. Ibid., 166–68.
13. Haddad and Smith, *Mission to America*, 166.
14. Fatima Haji-Taki, "My Journey to Identity," 7.
15. Islamic Center of America, Grand Opening, Commemorative Journal, 32.
16. Yitzhak Nakash, *Reaching for Power: The Shi'a in the Modern Arab World* (Princeton: Princeton University Press, 2006), 51–52.
17. Vali Nasr, *The Shia Revival: How Conflicts Within Islam Will Shape the Future* (New York: W. W. Norton, 2006), 95.
18. I am aware of the problem of using the term *fundamentalism* in the Islamic context. However, the difficulty of finding a precise equivalent in the Islamic languages should not deter us from applying the term to Muslims, because attitudes similar to those found among other fundamentalist religious groups are characteristic of many activist Muslims as well. For a discussion of the term in an Islamic context, see Abdulaziz Sachedina, *The Islamic Roots of Democratic Pluralism* (Oxford: Oxford University Press, 2001), 52.
19. Nasr, *Shia Revival*, 94.
20. Yitzhak Nakash, *Reaching for Power*, 50.
21. See chap. 2 for a definition of the *Rafidis*.
22. See *International Herald Tribune*: "Africa and the Middle East," December 29, 2006.

23. Muhammad Qasim Zaman, *The Ulama in Contemporary Islam: Custodians of Change* (Princeton: Princeton University Press, 2002), 123.

24. Jocelyne Cesari, *When Islam and Democracy Meet: Muslims in Europe and in the United States (New York: Palgrave, 2004)*, 93.

25. Nasr, *Shia Revival*, 164.

26. Mohammad Manzoor Nomani, Khomeini, *Iranian Revolution and the Shi'ite Faith* (London: Furqan Publications, 1988), 4.

27. Ibid., 11–12.

28. Ibid., 17.

29. Nasr, *Shia Revival*, 165.

30. Muhammad b. Muhammad al-Mufid, *Awa'il al-Maqalat fi al-Madhahib wa'l-Mukhtarat* (Tabriz, 1950), 94–95.

31. Muhammad Qasim Zaman, *Ulama in Contemporary Islam*, 121–22.

32. Ibid., 119–22.

33. Ibid., 118.

34. Ibid., 142, 234, n 41.

35. Nasr, *Shia Revival*, 166. On past incidents of violence against Shi'is see Zaman, *Ulama in Contemporary Islam*, 53.

36. Ibid., 246. For a discussion on Sunni–Shi'i tensions and violence in Pakistan see Andreas Rieck, "The Struggle for Equal Rights as a Minority: Shia Communal Organizations in Pakistan 1948–1968," in Rainer Brunner and Werner Ende, eds., *The Twelver Shia in Modern Times: Religious Culture and Political History* (Leiden: Brill, 2001), 268ff.

37. Nasr, *Shia Revival*, 156.

38. See the example cited by Mohammed Muqtedar Khan, "Muslims and Identity Politics in America," in Yvonne Haddad and John Esposito, eds., *Muslims on the Americanization Path?* (Atlanta: Scholars Press, 1998), 114.

39. Schmidt, *Sunni Muslims in Chicago*, 146.

40. Khaled Abou El Fadl, "The Ugly Modern and the Modern Ugly," in Omid Safi, ed., *Progressive Muslims: On Justice, Gender, and Pluralism* (Oxford: Oneworld Publications, 2003), 57.

41. For more details on the Salafis see Quintan Wiktorowicz, *Radical Islam Rising: Muslim Extremism in the West* (New York: Rowman and Littlefield, 2005), 186–87.

42. Steve Johnson, "Political Activity of Muslims in America," in Haddad, *Muslims of America*, 113.

43. Ibid., 119.

44. Nasr, *Shia Revival*, 155.

45. Khaled Abou el-Fadl, *The Great Theft: Wrestling Islam from the Extremists* (San Francisco: HarperCollins, 2005), 70.

46. Olivier Roy, *Globalized Islam: The Search for a New Ummah* (New York: Columbia University Press, 2004), 236.

47. Poston, *Islamic Da'wah*, 30.

48. Robert Dannin, "Understanding the Multi-Ethnic Dilemma of African-American Muslims," in Haddad and Esposito, *Muslims on the Americanization Path?*, 331–32.

49. Haddad and Lummis, *Islamic Values in the United States*, 5.

50. Poston, *Islamic Da'wah*, 127.

51. Ibid., 128.

52. Haddad and Lummis, *Islamic Values in the United States*, 62–63.

53. See the example of an imported imam in Lac La Biche, Canada, cited by Harold Barclay in Poston, *Islamic Da'wah*, 40.

54. Laurent Murawiec, *Princes of Darkness: The Saudi Assault on the West* (Lanham: Rowman and Littlefield, 2003), 34.

55. Cesari, *When Islam and Democracy Meet*, 94.

56. See Barbara Metcalf, "New Medinas: The Tablighi Jama'at in America and Europe," in Metcalf, *Making Muslim Space*, 113.

57. Cesari, *When Islam and Democracy Meet*, 94.

58. Abdulaziz Sachedina, *Islamic Roots*, 54.

59. Quintan Wiktorowicz, *Radical Islam Rising*, 7.

60. Ihsan Bagby, "The Mosque and the American Public Square," in Z. Bukhari et al. eds., *Muslims' Place in the American Public Square*, 329.

61. On the presence of Hizb al-Tahrir on campuses see Schmidt, *Sunni Muslims in Chicago*, 121.

62. Saeed Khan, "Muslim Brotherhood," in Cesari, ed., *Encyclopedia of Islam in the United States*, 447–48.

63. See Roy, *Globalized Islam*, 241, n 19.

64. Cesari, *When Islam and Democracy Meet*, 95.

65. Steve Johnson, "Political Activity of Muslims in America," in Haddad, *Muslims of America*, 119.

66. Roy, *Globalized Islam*, 244–45, n. 26.; www.allaahuakbar.net.

67. Ibid., 238.

68. http://www.washingtonpost.com/wpdyn/content/article/2005/11/18/AR2005111802427_2.html?sub=AR.

69. Steve Johnson, "Political Activity of Muslims in America," in Haddad, *Muslims of America*, 119.

70. Muhammad al-Tijani al-Samawi, *Ask Those who Know* (Toronto: Hyderi, 1993), chap. 7.

71. UMAA press release, February 2006. See chap, 5 for details of UMAA.

72. Christa Kuberry, "Globalization and Identity: Deterritorialization and Reterritorialization Examined" (masters thesis, University of Denver, May 2006), 50–51.

73. Roy, *Globalized Islam*, 239.

74. For further examples of Shiʻi–Sunni Internet polemics, see the following sites:

> http://www.geocities.com/antishia/
> http://www.khayma.com/fnoor/
> http://pub22.ezboard.com/ffnoorfrm1
> http://www.humanists.net/alisina/facts.htm
> http://www.kafir.8m.net/
> http://www.geocities.com/WestHollywood/Park/6443/Shia/shiaCreed.html
> http://www.murabitun.org/documents/amal/defence/protec2p1.html
> http://www.homa.org/khomeneiSayings.html
> http://hometown.aol.com/ahreemanx/page35.html
> http://www.murabitun.org/documents/amal/defence/protec2p1.html
> http://www.jamiat.co.za/library/pamphlets/shia_beliefs.htm.

Shiʻi Sites that reply to Wahhabi/Sunni attacks include the following in English:

> http://www.answering-ansar.org/
> http://www.islamoriginal.co.uk/Shia_defence.htm
> http://www.al-shia.com/html/eng/books/beliefs/are-shia-muslims/are-shia-muslims.htm
> http://rafed.net/books/other-lang/spurious-arguments/index.html
> http://al-islam.org/underattack/
> http://al-islam.org/shiism/
> http://al-islam.org/encyclopedia/
> http://www.wahhabism-info.com/books.htm
> http://www.wahhabism-info.com/books.htm.

Others include:

> http://members.ozemail.com.au/%7Eazma/misconeptions.htm
> http://www.al-islam.org/links.asp?CatId=117
> http://al-islam.org/nutshell/
> Ahlul Bayt Digital Library:
>   http://al-islam.org/organizations/dilp/index.htm#texts.

Below are some Shiʻi sites in Arabic that respond to Wahhabi accusations:

> http://www.geocities.com/Tokyo/Spa/7220/wahabia.html
> http://www.alhagega.net/
> http://www.alhagega.net/sb1.htm

http://www.geocities.com/antiwahabies/abrar1.html
http://www.alfakih.org/akazib/akazib/alhag11-22.htm
http://www.alfakih.org/wahabia/garaeb.htm
http://www.alfakih.org/wahabia/garaeb2.htm
http://www.aqaed.com/shialib/04.html
http://www.najaf.org/Arabic/shobohat/index.htm
http://alwelaya.8m.net/shobhat.htm
http://www.al-shia.com/html/ara/books/khotut/fehrest.html
http://www.al-shia.com/html/ara/books/al-rad/indexs.html
http://www.al-shia.com/html/ara/books/wahabie5/indexs.html
http://www.al-shia.com/html/ara/books/magazine/vahabyat/fehrest.htm
http://rafed.net/books/turathona/17/008.html
http://7adath.tripod.com/.

75. Abdo, *Mecca and Main Street,* 189.
76. Ibid., 188–89.
77. Poston, *Islamic Da'wah,* 130. For an example of Mawdudi's impact among Americans, see Robert Dannin, *Black Pilgrimage to Islam* (New York: Oxford University Press, 2002), 69. On Qutb's influence on the Islamic Party of North America, see McCloud, *African American Islam,* 68.
78. Roy, *Globalized Islam,* 240–41.
79. Abdo, *Mecca and Main Street,* 188–89.
80. Abbas Barzegar, "Dominant Themes in Muslim Communities of the United States: A Survey of Five Organizations in Denver, Colorado" (masters thesis, University of Colorado, 2004), 105.
81. Ibid., 104.
82. Personal email discussion with 'Abbas Kanji, June 2007.
83. See http://www.msapsg.org/disp37SummaryReport.htm.
84. Neil MacFarquhar, "Iraq's shadow widens Sunni-Shiite split in United States" in *International Herald Tribune:* "America," February 4, 2007.
85. http://www.umd.thaqalayn.org/.
86. Email message from Zeinab Chami, July 2007.
87. MacFarquhar, "Iraq's Shadow Widens."
88. This refers to the Shi'i practice of placing their foreheads on a clay tablet or on any element that is made from earth when they prostrate on the ground.
89. MacFarquhar, "Iraq's Shadow."
90. Ibid.
91. See chap. 5 of the present study for a more extensive discussion of UMAA and its activities.
92. UMAA Flyer, 6–7.
93. Ibid., 4–5.

94. http://web.jrn.columbia.edu/newmedia/2008/masters/islam/conviction_slideshow.html.

95. This observation is based on comments made in letters received from inmates.

96. http://islamicinsights.com/index.php?option=com_content&task=view&id=322&Itemid=1.

97. See *Islamic Insights,* September 2007.

98. Frankie Cancel letter, 2000.

99. Steve Johnson, "Political Activity of Muslims in America," in Haddad, ed., *Muslims of America,* 119.

100. *Wall Street Journal,* February 5, 2003.

101. Ibid.

102. Joseph Goldstein, "Muslim Rivalry Hits New York Prisons," *New York Sun,* November 2007), http://www.nysun.com/article/65974.

103. See the examples cited by Kathleen Moore, "Muslims in Prison: Claims to Constitutional Protection of Religious Liberty," in Haddad, ed., *Muslims of America,* 141.

104. Ibid., 142.

105. Robert Dannin, *Black Pilgrimage to Islam,* 171–73.

106. This refers to the invocation, "In the name of God, the Most Merciful and the Most Compassionate."

107. Frankie Cancel letter, 2000.

108. http://www.scoc.state.ny.us/pdfdocs/clr01-1.pdf; see also http://caselaw.lp.findlaw.com/data2/circs/2nd/020030pv2.pdf.

109. http://www.al-khoei.org/al-huda/download/alh_rm1422.pdf.

110. Based on an email exchange with an official from al-Khoei Foundation.

111. I am grateful to imam al-Qazwini for sharing his personal observations with me.

112. I am grateful to imam Muhammad Ilahi for this information.

113. http://news.bbc.co.uk/2/hi/middle_east/7436212.stm.

114. http://bayynat.org.

115. *Takfir* refers to the act of pronouncing someone to be a non-Muslim.

116. A link to the text of the code of honor is at the website of the Muslim Public Affairs Council at http://www.mpac.org.

117. *Muslim Observer,* vol. 8, no. 13 (March 24–30, 2006).

118. Ibid., vol. 8, no. 17 (April 21–27, 2006).

119. Lawrence, *New Faiths,* 13.

120. Mohammed Nimer, "Muslims in the American Body Politic," in Z. Bukhari et al. eds., *Muslims' Place in the American Public Square,* 149.

121. Schubel, *Religious Performance in Contemporary Islam,* ix.

122. Omid Safi, "Introduction," in Omid Safi, ed., *Progressive Muslims,* 2.

123. Ibid., 2.

124. See their essays in L. Clarke, *Shi'ite Heritage.*

NOTES TO CHAPTER 4

1. The need to follow the most learned jurist was first stated by al-Sharif al-Murtada (d. 1044). See 'Ali b. al-Husayn al-Murtada, *al-Dhari'a ila Usul al-Shari'a* (Tehran: Daneshghah Tehran, 1983), 2nd ed., 2 vols., 2:317.

2. The view that a stratified and hierarchical leadership is a recent phenomenon in Shi'ism is refuted by Devin Stewart who finds abundant evidence of strong hierarchical religious leadership in both Shi'i and Sunni legal establishments in premodern times. See Devin Stewart, "Islamic Juridical Hierarchies and the Office of Marji' al-Taqlid," in L. Clarke, *Shi'ite Heritage*, 149. However, according to Ayatullah Taskhiri, a number of Shi'i scholars who lived after Shahid al-Thani (d. 1558) did not hold *a'lamiyya* to be a necessary requirement in following a religious leader. See Ayatullah Muhammad Ali Taskhiri, "Supreme Authority (Marji'yah) in Shi'ism," in L. Clarke, *Shi'ite Heritage*, 169. After reviewing arguments for and against following the most learned, Taskhiri concludes, "while *taqlid* is certainly necessary, following the most learned is not." Clarke, 176.

3. Ayatullah al-Uzama Syed 'Ali al-Husaini Seestani, *Islamic Laws: English Version of Taudhihul Masae'l*, 1.

4. Ibid., 4.

5. Muhammad Kazim Yazdi, *al-'Urwa wa'l Wuthqa* (Tehran: Dar al-Kutub al-Islamiyya, n.d.), 3.

6. Yusuf Talal DeLorenzo, "The Fiqh Councilor in North America," in Haddad and Esposito, *Muslims on the Americanization Path?* 83.

7. See for example,

http://www.Seestani.org. http://english.bayynat.org.lb/
http://www.jannaati.com/eng/index.php?page=6
http://www.lankarani.org/eng/index.html
http://www.saanei.org/
http://amontazeri.com/farsi/default.asp
http://www.leader.ir/
http://www.makaremshirazi.org/
http://www.mesbahyazdi.org/english/index.htm.

8. Walbridge, *Without Forgetting the Imam*, 64.

9. According to Hossein Modaressi, al-Baqir and al-Sadiq did not collect the *khumus* from their followers because the Mahdi, the messianic Imam, was expected to collect it when he reappeared. It was the ninth Imam, Muhammad al-Taqi al-Jawad (d. 835), who instituted the collection of *khumus* on certain kinds of income. See Hossein Modarressi, *Crisis and Consolidation in the Formative Period of Shi'ite Islam* (Princeton: Darwin, 1993), 12.

10. Telephone discussion with imam Mustafa al-Qazwini, July 2008.

11. William Wininger, "*Dar al-Harb* and *Dar al-*Islam," in Cesari, ed., *Encyclopedia of Islam in the United States*, 170.

12. Ibid., 171. There are at least six different definitions of *dar al-Islam* in Islamic law. See Cesari, *When Islam and Democracy Meet*, 160.

13. See Liyakat Takim, "Holy Peace or Holy War: Tolerance and Co-existence in the Islamic Juridical Tradition," *Islam and Muslim Societies* 4, no. 2 (2007); "Peace and Conflict Resolution in the Islamic Tradition," in K. Kuriakose, ed., *Religion, Terrorism and Globalization, Nonviolence: A New Agenda* (New York: Nova Science Publishers, 2006).

14. Muhammad b. Muhammad al-Mufid, *Awa'il al-Maqalat*, 109–10.

15. Khaled Abou El-Fadl, "Islamic Law and Muslim Minorities: The Juristic Discourse on Muslim Minorities from the Second/Eighth to the Eleventh/Seventeenth Centuries," *Islamic Law and Society* 1, no. 2 (1994): 152.

16. Najm al-Din Ja'far b. al-Hasan (Muhaqqiq) al-Hilli, *Shara'i al-Islam* (Qum: Ansariyan, 2002), 1/270.

17. Omar Khalidi, "Living as a Muslim in a Pluralistic Society," in Zahid Bukhari et al., *Muslims' Place in the American Public Square*, 44.

18. Khalid Abou El-Fadl, "Striking a Balance: Islamic Legal Discourse on Muslim Minorities," in Haddad and Esposito, *Muslims on the Americanization Path?*, 61. 'Ali b. Abi Talib is reported to have stated that the best country is the one that treats you well. See imam Hasan Qazwini, *American Crescent: A Muslim Cleric on the Power of his Faith, the Struggle against Prejudice and the Future of Islam in America* (New York: Random House, 2007), xii.

19. Ayatullah Muhammad Mujtahid Shabistari, "Religion, Reason and the New Theology," in L. Clarke, *Shi'ite Heritage*, 256.

20. See, for example, al-Sayyid Husayn al-Husayni, *Ahkam al-Mughtaribin* (Tehran: Markaz al-Taba'a wa'l-Nashr Lil-Majma' al-'Alami li ahl al-Bayt, 1999), 126–27, which explains how to pray with Sunnis.

21. Taha Jabir al-Alwani, "Towards a Fiqh for Minorities: Some Reflections," in Bukhari et al., *Muslims' Place in the American Public Square*, 4.

22. Ibid., 11.

23. Tariq Ramadan, *Western Muslims and the Future of Islam* (Oxford: Oxford University Press, 2004), 42.

24. Ayatullah Fadlullah, *World of Our Youth*, 217. Ayatullahs al-Khu'i and Seestani rule along the same lines. See al-Sayyid Husayn al-Husayni, *Ahkam al-Mughtaribin*, 187–88.

25. Husayn al-Husayni, *Ahkam al-Mughtaribin*, 188.

26. Muhammad Qasim Zaman, *Ulama in Contemporary Islam*, 186.

27. Ayatullah Muhaghegh-Damad, "The Role of Time and Social Welfare in the Modification of Legal Rulings," in L. Clarke, *Shi'ite Heritage*, 218.

28. Mohsen Kadivar, "Freedom of Religion and Belief in Islam," in Mehran Kamrava, *The New Voices of Islam: Rethinking Politics and Modernity* (Berkeley: University of California Press: 2006), 132–33.

29. The views of Ayatullah Bojnourdi appeared in an Iranian newspaper, *Morning Daily*, in August 2001.

30. Abdul Hadi al-Hakim, *Jurisprudence Made Easy: According to the Edicts of His Eminence Grand Ayatullah as-Sayyid Ali al-Hussaini as-Seestani*, trans. Najim al-Khafaji (London: Imam Ali Foundation, 1998), 10.

31. 'Abdul Hadi al-Hakim, *A Code of Practice for Muslims in the West in Accordance with the Edicts of Ayatullah al-Udhma as-Sayyid Ali al-Husaini as-Seestani*, transl. Sayyid Muhammad Rizvi (London: Imam 'Ali Foundation, 1999), 8.

32. *Current Legal Issues According to the Edicts of Ayatullah al-Sayyid 'Ali al-Seestani* (London: Imam Ali Foundation, 1997), 40. Al-Khu'i also rules that it is forbidden (*haram*) to disobey the laws of the land even if one is living in a non-Muslim country. See al-Sayyid Husayn al-Husayni, 407.

33. 'Abdul Hadi al-Hakim, *A Code of Practice*, 138.

34. *Contemporary Legal Rulings in Shi'i Law in Accordance with the Rulings (fatawa) of Ayatullah al-'Uzma al-Sayyid 'Ali al-Husayni al-Seestani*, trans. Hamid Mavani (Montreal: Organization for the Advancement of Islamic Knowledge and Humanitarian Services, 1996), 74–75.

35. 'Abdul Hadi al-Hakim, *Code of Practice*, 47.

36. Ibid., 136.

37. Al-Sayyid Husayn al-Husayni, *Ahkam al-Mughtaribin*, 408.

38. *Contemporary Legal Rulings in Shi'i Law*, 8.

39. Ibid., 36. He states that gelatin taken from all animals apart from pigs is permissible to consume since it is extracted from the bones of animals. Since bones do not have life they are ritually pure (*tahir*).

40. Ibid., 29. He rules it is not mandatory to abide by such laws, although it is better to seek the permission of the author.

41. Sayyid Ali Khamene'i, *Replies to Inquiries about the Practical Laws of Islam* (Tehran: Islamic Culture and Relations Organization, 1997), 97.

42. Hasan Qazwini, *American Crescent*, 192–93.

43. Olivier Roy, *Globalized Islam*, 199, 279.

44. Ibid., 216.

45. *Current Legal Issues*, 48.

46. 'Abdul Hadi al-Hakim, *Code of Practice*, 70, 84.

47. Stephan Rosiny, "The Tragedy of Fatima al-Zahra in the Debate of Two Shi'ite Theologians in Lebanon," in Rainer Brunner and Werner Ende eds., *The Twelver Shia in Modern Times* (Leiden: Brill, 2001), 210.

48. Ayatullah Fadlullah, *World of Our Youth*, 218.

49. Email from Ayatullah Fadlullah, December 8, 2002.

50. Ziba Mir-Hosseini, *Islam and Gender: The Religious Debate in Modern Iran* (Princeton: Princeton University Press, 199), 160.

51. http://aawsat.com/english/news.asp?section=3&id=8554.

52. http://imam us.org/DesktopModules/Fiqh/FiqhBooks. aspx?book=code_of_practice_for_muslims_in_west&no=0.

53. See al-Sayyid Husayn al-Husayni, *Ahkam al-Mughtaribin*, 444.

54. Fadlullah, *World of Our Youth*, 220.

55. Ibid., 222.

56. For the views of other *maraji'* on what genres of music are permissible see al-Sayyid Husayn al-Husayni, *Ahkam al-Mughtaribin*, 443–44.

57. http://www.saanei.org/page.php?pg=showistifta&id=5&lang=en.

58. http://imam us.org/DesktopModules/Fiqh/FiqhBooks. aspx?book=code_of_practice_for_muslims_in_west&no=0.

59. *Current Legal Issues*, 102.

60. Khamene'i, *Ajwibat al-Istifta'at* (Beirut: al-Dar al-Islamiyya, 2003), 69. I base this segment of my discussion on an excellent article written by Morgan Clarke, "Children of the Revolution: 'Ali Khamene'i's 'liberal' views on *in vitro* fertilization," *British Journal of Middle Eastern Studies* Dec. 2007, 34 (3): 287–303.

61. M. Clarke, "Children of the Revolution," 298.

62. Khamene'i, *Ajwibat*, 70. Like most jurists, Ayatullah Khumayni prohibits fertilizing a woman with the sperm of a stranger. See Ayatullah Ruhullah al-Musawi Khumayni, *Tahrir al-Wasila*, 2 vols. (Qum: 1982), 2:621.

63. M. Clarke, "Children of the Revolution," 299. Email from istifta@saanei. org, Monday, October 23, 2006.

64. M. Clarke, "Children of the Revolution," 300.

65. Ibid., 301. Khamene'i, *Ajwibat*, 72.

66. Husayn al-Husayni, *Ahkam al-Mughtaribin*, 439–440.

67. Abdulaziz Sachedina, Brain Death and Organ Retrieval, http://www.is-lamiclearning.org/Article6.htm.

68. Sachedina, "Islamic Bioethics," in John F. Peppin Mark Cherry and Ana Iltis, eds., *The Annals of Bioethics: Religious Perspectives in Bioethics* (London and New York: Taylor and Francis, 2004), 168.

69. *Current Legal Issues*, 49.

70. Ibid.

71. See also http://english.bayynat.org.lb/Issues/Mercykilling%20.htm.

72. 'Abdul Hadi al-Hakim, *Code of Practice*, 191.

73. *Contemporary Legal Rulings*, 50; See also 'Abdul Hadi al-Hakim, *Code of Practice*, 194–95; *Current Legal Issues*, 100.

74. Khaled Abou El Fadl, "Between Functionality and Morality: The Juristic Debates on the Conduct of War," in *Islamic Ethics of Life: Abortion, War and Euthanasia*, ed. Jonathan Brockopp (Columbia: University of South Carolina Press, 2003), 114.

75. *Current Legal Issues*, 25–26.

76. Ayatullah Sanei and other jurists agree with al-Khu'i on this ruling. See http://www.saanei.org/page.php?pg=showistifta&id=10&lang=en.

77. 'Abdul Hadi al-Hakim, *Code of Practice*, 89–90; http://media.whatcounts. com/wired_jamaat/Information-on-Eid-Moon_1428.pdf.

78. Talib Aziz, "Fadlallah and the Remaking of the Marja'iyya," in Linda Walbridge, ed., *The Most Learned of the Shi'a: The Institution of the Marja' Taqlid* (New York: Oxford University Press, 2001), 211.

79. Email from YMA Dearborn, December 18, 2007.

80. Husayn al-Husayni, *Ahkam al-Mughtaribin*, 214.

81. Moussavi, *Religious Authority in Shi'ite Islam*, 245.

82. See also Ann Lambton, "A Reconsideration of the Position of the Marja al-Taqlid and the Religious Institution," *Studia Islamica* 20 (1964): 117.

83. See Juan Cole, *Sacred and Holy Space: The Politics, Culture and History of Shi'ite Islam* (New York: Tauris, 2002), 174–75.

84. Taha Jabir al-Alwani, "Towards a Fiqh for Minorities: Some Reflections," in Bukhari et al., *Muslims' Place in the American Public Square*, 4.

85. Tariq Ramadan, *Western Muslims and the Future of Islam*, 53.

86. Based on a discussion with Mustafa al-Qazwini, July 2008.

87. Talib Aziz, "Baqir al-Sadr's Quest for the Marja'iyya," in Walbridge, ed., *Most Learned of the Shi'a*, 144.

88. Ibid., 146.

89. Ibid.

90. See Mortaza Motahhari, "The Fundamental Problem in the Clerical Establishment," in Walbridge, *Most Learned of the Shi'a*, 161.

91. Talib Aziz, "Fadlallah and the Remaking of the Marja'iyya," in Walbridge, *Most Learned of the Shi'a*, 213.

92. See Muhammad Baqir al-Sadr, *Durus fi 'Ilm al-Usul* (Beirut: Dar al-Kitab al-Lubnani, 1978), 1:175.

93. http://www.leader.ir/tree/index.php?catid=39. Traditionally, Shi'is do not adorn themselves in the months of Muharram and Safar when they mourn for Husayn's death and for his family members who were imprisoned in Damascus.

94. Walbridge, *Without Forgetting the Imam*, 69.

95. Ibid., 71.

96. Based on a discussion with Ilahi, July 2007.

97. Based on a discussion with Sahlani, May 2005.

98. See http://www.imam-us.org/.

99. I am grateful to Shaykh Fadhil Sahlani, who was the chairman of the Council of Shi'a Muslim Scholars of North America, for sharing the council's constitution with me.

100. http://www.imam-us.org/.

NOTES TO CHAPTER 5

1. Abdul Hadi al-Hakim, *Code of Practice*, 41.

2. Ibid., 47.

3. Poston, *Islamic Da'wah*, 128–29.

4. See Robert Dannin, "Understanding the Multi-Ethnic Dilemma," in Haddad and Esposito, *Muslims on the Americanization Path?*, 356, n. 9.

5. On the early history of the FIA, see Gutbi Mahdi Ahmed, "Muslim Organizations in the United States," in Haddad, *Muslims of America*, 12–14.

6. For a list of American Muslim organizations see Cesari, *When Islam and Democracy Meet*, 185ff. For a brief account of some of their activities see Liyakat Takim, "To Vote or not to Vote: The Politicization of American Islam," in Alec Hargreaves, John Kelsay, and Sumner B. Twiss, eds., *Politics and Religion in France and the United States* (Lanham, MD: Lexington Books / Rowman and Littlefield, 2007).

7. Many of the mosques are affiliated to these organizations. For a list of the organizations and when they were established, see Leonard, *Muslims in the United States*, 102.

8. Based on a telephone conversation with Aunali Khalfan, August 2003.

9. Based on a discussion with Dr. Hakim in 2002.

10. http://www.al-khoei.org/.

11. See the UMAA constitution (distributed brochure).

12. See MuslimCongress.org.

13. See http://www.islamiclearning.org/.

14. See chap. 1 of the present study for NASIMCO'S activities in North America.

15. Hujjatul Islam al-Sayyid Mohammad Reza Hejazi, preface to the proceedings of the *Ahlul Bayt Assembly of America*, 3.

16. Ibid., 74.

17. I am grateful to Zahir Janmohammed, a founding member of Qunoot, for this information.

18. Robert Dannin, "Island in a Sea of Ignorance: Dimensions of the Prison Mosque," in Metcalf, *Making Muslim Space*, 132; Robert Dannin, *Black Pilgrimage to Islam*, 169.

19. Robert Dannin, "Island in a Sea of Ignorance," in Metcalf, *Making Muslim Space*, 132.

20. By stating this, I do not mean to suggest that there is no racism in the Muslim community.

21. Jane Smith, *Muslims, Christians and the Challenges of Interfaith Dialogue* (New York: Oxford University Press, 2007), 57.

22. On the close relationship between Warith al-Din and Saudi Arabia see Robert Dannin, "Understanding the Multi-Ethnic Dilemma," in Haddad and Esposito, *Muslims on the Americanization Path?* 333; also 356, n. 9.

23. Haddad and Smith, *Mission to America*, 133.

24. Ibid.

25. As quoted by Sherman Jackson, "Preliminary Reflections on Islam and Black Religion," in Bukhari et al., *Muslims' Place in the American Public Square*, 206.

26. Ignaz Goldziher, *Muslim Studies*, 2 vols. (Albany: SUNY Press, 1971), 2:94–95. See also Bryan Turner, *Weber and Islam: A Critical Study* (London: Routledge and Kegan Paul, 1974), 92.

27. Based on a telephone conversation with Jihad Saleh, August 2007.

28. Cesari, *When Islam and Democracy Meet*, 11.

29. Sherman Jackson, "Preliminary Reflections," in Bukhari et al., *Muslims' Place in the American Public Square*, 201.

30. See Sherman Jackson, *Islam and the Blackamerican: Looking Toward the Third Resurrection* (New York: Oxford University Press, 2005), 70.

31. There are only two African American Shi'i mosques that I am aware of, one in New York (Islamic Guidance Center) and the other in Los Angeles (Masjid al-Rasul).

32. See http://www.islamifc.org/test/index.php.

33. I am grateful to Hashim 'Ali 'Ala al-Din for sharing this information with me.

34. Cesari, *When Islam and Democracy Meet*, 41.

35. Amir Hussain, "Muslims, Pluralism, and Interfaith Dialogue," in Safi, *Progressive Muslims*, 261.

36. Abdo, *Mecca and Main Street*, 85.

37. *Muslim Americans: Middle Class and Mostly Mainstream* (PewSearch.org. retrieved July 25, 2007) http://pewresearch.org/pubs/483/muslim-americans.

38. Ibid.

39. Abdo, *Mecca and Main Street*, 6.

40. See Liyakat Takim, "From Conversion to Conversation: Interfaith Dialogue in Post-911 America," *Muslim World* 94, no. 3 (2004): 343–55.

41. http://www.masnet.org/masnews.asp?id=2739.

42. For details see Liyakat Takim, "Islam–Shi'a," in *Encyclopedia of Religion and War*, Gabriel Palmer-Fernandez, ed. (New York: Routledge, 2004).

43. http://www.washingtonpost.com/wpdyn/content/article/2005/11/18/AR2005111802427_2.html?sub=AR.

44. Vali Nasr, *Shia Revival*, 251.

45. Excerpts from an email received on 8/22/2007. Several American Muslim groups also condemned the 9/11 attacks. Those who condemned the attacks include the new Grand Mufti in Saudi Arabia and Yusuf al-Qaradawi. See also Olivier Roy, *Globalized Islam*, 255, n 48.

46. *Islamic Republic News Agency*, September 16, 2001. A BBC website quotes Khamene'i as strongly condemning the suicide terrorist attacks in New York and Washington. See http://news.bbc.co.uk/1/hi/world/middle_east/1549573.stm.

47. http://www.aimislam.com/forums/index.php?showtopic=313.

48. Personal discussion with Hisham Husainy, July 2007.

49. Based on a telephone conversation with Shaykh Fyzee, 2006.

50. See *Muslim Observer*, vol. 9, no. 29, July 12–18, 2007.

51. Imam Hasan Qazwini, *American Crescent*, 139.

52. See Takim, *Heirs of the Prophet*, for a fuller discussion on this.

53. www.togetherwebuild.org. I am indebted to Jawad Khaki for this information.

54. I am grateful to Dr. Hasnain Walji for sharing the information with me.

55. On the different genres of dialogue possible, see Smith, *Muslims, Christians and the Challenges*, chap. 4.

56. Ibid., *Muslims, Christians and the Challenges*, 87.

57. See Peter Berger, "Religion and Global Civil Society," in Mark Juergensmeyer, ed., *Religion in Global Civil Society* (Oxford: Oxford University Press), 12.

58. See www.UnitedMuslimFoundation.org.

59. Based on an email received from Zuhair Ebrahim, August 2007.

60. I am grateful to Dr. Mohsin Jaffer for this information.

61. See www.zamaninternational.org.

62. I am grateful to Abbas Kanji for providing this information.

63. Said Arjomand, *The Shadow of God and the Hidden Imam: Religion, Political Order and Societal change in Iran from the Beginning to 1890* (Chicago: University of Chicago Press, 1986), 36–38. See also Ann Lambton, "A Reconsideration of the Position," 115.

64. http://www.muslimsforamerica.us/?emaillink.

65. http:///www.newsweek.com/id/168062.

66. CAIR website, Nov. 7, 2008-11-15.

67. I am grateful to Dr. Ali Syed for the information.

68. Based on an email received from Masom Ali, March 2008.

69. I am grateful to Dr. Hashim for sharing his political experiences with me in an interview conducted in 2004.

70. This was relayed to me by many Shi'is when I visited Dearborn in July 2007.

NOTE TO CONCLUSION

1. Khaled Abou El Fadl, *Speaking in God's Name: Islamic Law, Authority and Women* (Oxford: Oneworld, 2001), 92.

Bibliography

Abd-Allah, 'Umar. *A Muslim in Victorian America: The Life of Alexander Russell Webb*. New York: Oxford, 2006.

Abdul Ghafur, Saleema, ed. *Living Islam Out Loud: American Muslim Women Speak*. Boston: Beacon Press, 2005.

Abdo, Geneive. *Mecca and Main Street: Muslim Life in America After 9/11*. New York: Oxford University Press, 2006.

Abou El Fadl, Khaled. "Between Functionality and Morality: The Juristic Debates on the Conduct of War." In Jonathan Brockopp, ed. *Islamic Ethics of Life: Abortion, War and Euthanasia*. Columbia: University of South Carolina Press, 2003.

———. *The Great Theft: Wrestling Islam from the Extremists*. San Francisco: HarperCollins, 2005.

———. "Islamic Law and Muslim Minorities: The Juristic Discourse on Muslim Minorities from the Second/Eight to the Eleventh/Seventeenth Centuries." *Islamic Law and Society* 1, no. 2 (1994): 140–87.

———. "9/11 and the Muslim Transformation." In Mary L. Dudziak, ed., *September 11 in History—A Watershed Moment?* Durham, NC: Duke University Press, 2003.

———. *The Place of Tolerance in Islam*. Boston: Beacon Press, 2002.

———."Striking a Balance: Islamic Legal Discourse on Muslim Minorities." In Haddad and Esposito, *Muslims on the Americanization Path?*

———. "The Ugly Modern and the Modern Ugly." In Omid Safi, ed., *Progressive Muslims: On Justice, Gender, and Pluralism* (Oxford: Oneworld Publications, 2003).

Abu-Laban Sharon, McIrvin. "Family and Religion Among Muslim Immigrants and Their Descendants." In Waugh et al., *Muslim Families in North America*. Edmonton: University of Alberta Press, 1991.

Abu-Rabi', Ibrahim M. *Intellectual Origins of Islamic Resurgence in the Modern Arab World*. Albany: SUNY Press, 1996.

——— and Ian Markham, eds. *September 11: Religious Perspectives on the Causes and Consequences*. Oxford: Oneworld, 2003.

Ahmed, Gutbi Mahdi. "Muslim Organizations in the United States." In Haddad, ed. *Muslims of America*.

Akhtar, Shabbir. *A Faith for all Seasons: Islam and Western Modernity*. London: Bellew Publishing, 1990.

Alloo, Sadik, ed. *Muslim Youth at the Crossroads: Advancing into the Twenty First Century*. Toronto: Hyderi, 1995.

Al-Alwani, Taha Jabir. "Towards a Fiqh for Minorities: Some Reflections." In Bukhari et al., *Muslims' Place in the American Public Square*.

Amanat, Abbas, and Frank Griffel, eds. *Shari'a: Islamic Law in the Contemporary Context*. Stanford: Stanford University Press, 2007.

Anway, Carol. *Daughters of Another Path: Experiences of American Women Choosing Islam*. Lee's Summit, MO: Yawna Publications, 1995.

Aswad, Barbara C., ed. *Arabic Speaking Communities in American Cities*. Staten Island, NY: Center for Migration Studies of New York, 1974.

Austin, Allan. *African Muslims in Antebellum America: Transatlantic Stories and Spiritual Struggles*. New York: Routledge, 1997.

Aziz, Talib. "Baqir al-Sadr's Quest for the Marja'iyya." In Walbridge, *Most Learned of the Shi'a*.

———. "Fadlallah and the Remaking of the Marja'iyya." In Walbridge, *Most Learned of the Shi'a*.

Bagby, Ihsan, Paul M. Perl, and Bryan T. Froehle, eds. "The Mosque and the American Public Square." In Bukhari et al., *Muslims' Place in the American Public Square*.

———. *The Mosque in America: A National Portrait*. Washington: Council on American–Islamic Relations, 2001.

Bannerman, Patrick. *Islam in Perspective: A Guide to Islamic Society, Politics and Law*. London: Routledge, 1988.

Barboza, Steven, ed. *American Jihad: Islam After Malcolm X*. New York: Doubleday, 1993.

Barret, Paul. *American Islam: The Struggle for the Soul of a Religion*. New York: Farrar, Straus and Giroux, 2007.

Ba-Yunus, Ilyas, and Kassim Kone. "Muslim Americans: A Demographic Report." In Bukhari et al., *Muslims' Place in the American Public Square*.

Barzegar, Abbas. "Dominant Themes in Muslim Communities of the United States: A Survey of Five Organizations in Denver, Colorado." Masters thesis, University of Colorado, 2004.

Berger, Peter. "Religion and Global Civil Society." In Juergensmeyer, *Religion in Global Civil Society*.

Bloul, Rachel. "Engendering Muslim Identities: De-territorialization and the Ethnicization Process in France." In Metcalfe, *Making Muslim Space*.

Brunner, Rainer, and Werner Ende, eds. *The Twelver Shia in Modern Times: Religious Culture and Political History*. Leiden: Brill, 2001.

Bukhari, Zahid. *Muslims' Place in the American Public Square: Hope, Fears, and Aspirations*. Zahid H. Bukhari, Sulayman S. Nyang, Mumtaz Ahmad, and John L. Esposito, eds. Walnut Creek: AltaMira Press, 2004.

Calmard, Jean. "Shi'a Rituals and Power II. The Consolidation of Safavid Shi'ism: Folklore and Popular Religion." In Charles Melville, ed. *Safavid Persia*. New York: I. B. Tauris and Co Ltd., 1996.

Cesari, Jocelyne. *Encyclopedia of Islam in the United States*. 2 vols., Westport, CT: Greenwood, 2007.

———, ed. "Islam in France: The Shaping of a Religious Minority." In Haddad, *Muslims in the West*.

———. *When Islam and Democracy Meet: Muslims in Europe and in the United States*. New York: Palgrave, 2004.

Clarke, Lynda, ed. *Shi'ite Heritage: Essays on Classical and Modern Traditions*. Binghamton: Global, 2001.

Clarke, Morgan. "Children of the Revolution: 'Ali Khamene'i's 'Liberal' Views on In Vitro Fertilization." *British Journal of Middle Eastern Studies* 34, no. 3 (Dec 2007).

Coward, Harold, and Leslie Kawamura, eds. *Religion and Ethnicity*. Waterloo: Wilfrid Laurier University Press, 1978.

Current Legal Issues According to the Edicts of Ayatullah al-Sayyid 'Ali al-Seestani. London: Imam 'Ali Foundation, 1997.

Curtis, Edward, IV. *Black Muslim Religion in the Nation of Islam 1960-1975*. Chapel Hill: University of North Carolina, 2006.

———, ed. *The Columbia Sourcebook of Muslims in the United States*. New York: Columbia University Press, 2007.

———. *Islam in Black America: Identity, Liberation, and Difference in African-American Islamic Thought*. Albany: SUNY Press, 2002.

Dannin, Robert. *Black Pilgrimage to Islam*. New York: Oxford University Press, 2002.

———. "Island in a Sea of Ignorance: Dimensions of the Prison Mosque." In Metcalf, *Making Muslim Space*.

———. "Understanding the Multi-Ethnic Dilemma of African-American Muslims." In Haddad and Esposito, *Muslims on the Americanization Path?*

DeCaro, Louis A. Jr, *Malcolm and the Cross: The Nation of Islam, Malcolm X, and Christianity*. New York: New York University Press, 1998.

———. *On the Side of My People: A Religious Life of Malcolm X*. New York: New York University Press, 1996.

DeLorenzo, Yusuf Talal. "The Fiqh Councilor in North America." In Haddad and Esposito, *Muslims on the Americanization Path?*

Denny, Frederick Mathewson. "Church/Sect Theory and Emerging North American Muslim Communities: Issues and Trends." In Waugh and Denny, *Shaping of an American Islamic Discourse*.

———. "Islamic Theology in the New World: Some Issues and Prospects." *Journal of the American Academy of Religion* 62, no. 4 (1994): 1069–84.

Dilley, Charles. "The Iranian Diaspora in Los Angeles: From Islamic Revolution to an Iranian-American Community." Honors thesis, University of Denver, May 2006.

Diouf, Sylviane. *Servants of Allah: African Muslims Enslaved in the Americas.* New York: New York University Press, 1998.

Eck, Diana L. *A New Religious America: How a "Christian Country" Has Become the World's Most Religiously Diverse Nation.* New York: HarperCollins, 2001.

Elkholy, Abdo A. *The Arab Moslems in the United States: Religion and Assimilation.* New Haven: College and University Press, 1966.

Fadlallah, Ayatullah al-ʿUzma al-Sayyid Muhammad Husayn. *World of Our Youth.* Translated by Khaleel Mohammed. Montreal: Organization for the Advancement of Islamic Learning and Humanitarian Services, 1998.

Fischer, Michael, M. J. Abedi, and Mehdi Abedi. *Debating Muslims: Cultural Dialogues in Post Modernity and Tradition.* Madison: University of Wisconsin Press, 1990.

Gardell, Mattias. *In the Name of Elijah Muhammad: Louis Farrakhan and the Nation of Islam.* Durham, NC: Duke University Press, 1996.

Gerges, Fawaz. *America and Political Islam: Clash of Cultures or Clash of Interests?* Cambridge: Cambridge University Press, 1999.

GhaneaBassiri, Kambiz. *Competing Visions of Islam in the United States: A Study of Los Angeles.* Westport, CT: Greenwood Press, 1997.

Gottschalk, Peter, and Gabriel Greenberg, eds. *Islamophobia: Making Muslims the Enemy.* Lanham: Rowman and Littlefield, 2008.

Geaves, Ron, Theodore Gabriel, Yvonne Haddad, and Jane I. Smith, eds. *Islam and the West Post 9/11.* Burlington: Ashgate, 2004.

Greeley, Andrew. *The Denominational Society: A Sociological Approach to Religion in America.* Glenview, IL: Scott, Foresman and Company, 1972.

Gutbi, Ahmed. "Muslim Organizations in the United States." In Haddad, *Muslims of America.*

Haddad, Yvonne. *Contemporary Islam and the Challenge of History.* Albany: SUNY Press, 1982.

——. "The Impact of the Islamic Revolution in Iran on the Syrian Muslims of Montreal." In Waugh et al., *Muslim Community in North America.*

——, ed. *Muslims in the West: From Sojourners to Citizens.* New York: Oxford University Press, 2002.

——. *Muslim Women in America: The Challenge of Islamic Identity Today.* Oxford: Oxford University Press, 2006.

——. *The Muslims of America: The Challenge of Islamic Identity Today.* New York; Oxford University Press, 1991.

——. *Not Quite American? The Shaping of Arab and Muslim Identity in the United States.* Waco: Baylor University Press, 2004.

Haddad, Yvonne, and John L. Esposito, eds. *Muslims on the Americanization Path?* Atlanta: Scholars Press, 1998.

Haddad, Yvonne, John L. Esposito, Elizabeth Hiel, and Hibba Abugideiri, eds. *The Islamic Revival since 1998: A Critical Survey and Bibliography.* Westport: Greenwood Press, 1997.

Haddad, Yvonne, and Wadi Zaydan Haddad, eds. *Christian-Muslim Encounters.* Gainesville: University Press of Florida, 1995.

Haddad, Yvonne, and Adair Lummis. *Islamic Values in the United States.* New York: Oxford University Press, 1987.

Haddad, Yvonne, and Jane Smith, eds. *Mission to America: Five Islamic Sectarian Communities in North America.* Gainesville: University Press of Florida, 1993.

———. *Muslim Communities in North America.* Albany: SUNY Press, 1994.

———. *Muslim Minorities in the West: Visible and Invisible.* Walnut Creek: Alta-Mira Press, 2002.

Haddad, Yvonne, Jane I. Smith, and Kathleen M. Moore, eds. "American Foreign Policy in the Middle East and Its Impact on the Identity of Arab Muslims in the United States." In Haddad, *Muslims of America.*

Haddad, Yvonne, and Barbara Freyer Stowasser, eds. *Islamic Law and the Challenges of Modernity.* Walnut Creek: AltaMira Press, 2004.

Haji-Taki, Fatima. "My Journey to Identity." Honors thesis, University of Minneapolis, 2004.

Al-Hakim, 'Abdul Hadi. *A Code of Practice for Muslims in the West in Accordance with the Edicts of Ayatullah al-Udhma as-Sayyid Ali al-Husaini as-Seestani.* Translated by Sayyid Muhammad Rizvi. London: Imam 'Ali Foundation, 1999.

———. *Jurisprudence Made Easy: According to the Edicts of His Eminence Grand Ayatullah as-Sayyid Ali al-Hussaini as-Seestani.* Translated by Najim al-Khafaji. London: Imam Ali Foundation, 1998.

Hamdani, Daood Hassan. "Canadian Muslims on the Eve of the Twenty-First Century." *Journal of Muslim Minority Affairs* 19, no. 2 (1999): 197–209.

———. *Muslims in Canada: A Century of Settlement, 1871–1976.* Ottawa: Council of Muslim Communities of Canada, 1978.

———. "Muslims in the Canadian Mosaic." *Journal of Muslim Minority Affairs* 5, no. 1 (1983): 7–16.

Haney, Marsha Snulligan. *Islam and Protestant African American Churches: Responses and Challenges to Religious Pluralism.* Lanham, MD: University Press of America, 1998.

Hasan, Asma Gull. *American Muslims: The New Generation.* New York: Continuum, 2000.

Hejazi, Sayyed Mohammed, and A. Hashim, eds. *Ahlul Bayt Assembly of America: Abstract of Proceedings Convention of 1996.* Beltsville, MD: International Graphics, 1997.

Hermansen, Marcia. "Hybrid Identity Formations in Muslim America: The Case of American Sufi Movements." *Muslim World* 90, no. 1/2 (2000): 158–97.

————."In the Garden of American Sufi Movements: Hybrids and Perennials." In Peter B. Clarke, ed. *New Trends and Developments in the World of Islam*. London: Luzac Oriental, 1997.

————. "The Muslims of San Diego." In Haddad and Smith, *Muslim Communities in North America*.

————. "What's American about American Sufi Movements?" In David Westerlund, ed. *Sufism in Europe and North America*. New York: Routledge Curzon, 2004.

Howarth, Toby. *The Twelver Shi'a as a Muslim Minority in India: Pulpit of Tears*. New York: Routledge, 2005.

Howell, Sally, and Andrew Shryock. "Cracking Down on Diaspora: Arab Detroit and America's War on Terror." *Anthropological Quarterly* (March 2003).

Hughes, Aaron. "Mapping Constructions of Islamic Space in North America: A Framework for Further Inquiry." *Studies in Religion / Sciences Religieuses* 33, no. 3/4 (2004), 339–57.

Al-Husayni, al-Sayyid Husayn. *Ahkam al-Mughtaribin*. Tehran: Markaz al-Taba'a wa'l Nashr Lil-Majma' al-'Alami li ahl al-Bayt, 1999.

Hussain, Amir. "Muslims, Pluralism, and Interfaith Dialogue." In Safi, *Progressive Muslims*.

————. *Oil and Water: Two Faiths: One God*. Kelowna, BC: Copperhouse, 2006.

————. "Teaching Inside-Out: On Teaching Islam." *Method and Theory in the Study of Religion* 17, no. 3 (2005): 248–63.

Jackson, Sherman. *Islam and the Blackamerican: Looking toward the Third Resurrection*. New York: Oxford University Press, 2005.

————. "Preliminary Reflections on Islam and Black Religion." In Bukhari et al. *Muslims' Place in the American Public Square*.

Al-Jibouri, Yasin. "A Glance at Shi'a Communities in the US." In *Islamic Affairs, Virginia*, October, 1993.

Juergensmeyer, Mark, ed. *Religion in Global Civil Society*. Oxford: Oxford University Press, 2005.

Johnson, Steve. "Political Activity of Muslims in America." In Haddad, *Muslims of America*.

Kadivar, Mohsen. "Freedom of Religion and Belief in Islam." In Kamrava, *New Voices of Islam*.

Kamrava, Mehran, ed. *The New Voices of Islam: Rethinking Politics and Modernity*. Berkeley: University of California Press, 2006.

Kashshi, Muhammad b. 'Umar. *Ikhtiyar Ma'rifa al-Rijal*. al-Mustafawi, ed. Mashad: Danishgahe Mashad, 1969.

Kelley, Ron. "Muslim in Los Angeles." In Haddad and Smith, *Muslim Communities in North America*.

Kelley, Ron, Jonathan Friedlander, and Anita Colby, eds. *Irangeles: Iranians in Los Angeles*. Los Angeles: University of California Press, 1993.

Kepel, Gilles. *Allah in the West: Islamic Movements in America and Europe.* Translated by Susan Milner. Stanford: Stanford University Press, 1997.

Khalidi, Omar. "Living as a Muslim in a Pluralistic Society and State: Theory and Experience." In Bukhari et al., *Muslims' Place in the American Public Square.*

Khaki, Ateqah. "Identity Negotiation among Second Generation South Asian Muslim Americans." Seniors thesis, Whitman College, 2005.

Khamenei, Sayyid Ali. *Ajwibat al-Istifta'at.* Beirut: al-Dar al-Islamiyya, 2003.

———. *Replies to Inquiries about the Practical Laws of Islam.* Tehran: Islamic Culture and Relations Organization, 1997.

Khan, Mohammed Muqtedar. "Living on Borderlines: Islam Beyond the Clash and Dialogue of Civilizations." In Bukhari et al., *Muslims' Place in the American Public Square.*

———. "Muslims and Identity Politics in America." In Haddad and Esposito, *Muslims on the Americanization Path?*

Khan, Shahnaz. *Aversion and Desire: Negotiating Muslim Female Identity in the Diaspora.* Toronto: Women's Press, 2002.

———. *Muslim Women: Crafting a North American Identity.* Gainesville: University Press of Florida, 2000.

Klausen, Jytte. *The Islamic Challenge: Politics and Religion in Western Europe.* Oxford: Oxford University Press, 2007.

Lahaj, Mary. "The Islamic Center of New England: The Immigrant Generation." In Haddad and Smith, *Muslim Communities.*

Lambton, Ann. "A Reconsideration of the Position of the Marja al-Taqlid and the Religious Institution." *Studia Islamica* 20 (1964): 115–35.

Lang, Jeffrey. *Struggling to Surrender: Some Impressions of an American Convert to Islam.* Maryland: Amana Publications, 1994.

Lawrence, Bruce. *New Faiths, Old Fears: Muslims and Other Asian Immigrants in American Religious Life.* New York: Columbia University Press, 2002.

Lee, Martha F. *The Nation of Islam: An American Millenarian Movement.* Syracuse: Syracuse University Press, 1996.

Leon, Luis. *La Lorona's Children: Religion, Life, and Death in the U.S.- Mexican Borderlands.* Berkeley: University of California Press, 2004.

Leonard, Karen. *Muslims in the United States: The State of Research.* New York: Russell Sage Foundation, 2003.

———. "South Asian Leadership of American Muslims." In Haddad, *Muslims in the West.*

———. "State, Culture, and Religion: Political Action and Representation Among South Asians in North America." *Diaspora* 9, no. 2 (2000): 21–38.

LeVine, Mark. *Why They Don't Hate Us: Lifting the Veil on the Axis of Evil.* Oxford: Oneworld Publications, 2005.

Lincoln, Eric. "The American Muslim Mission in the Context of American Social History." In Waugh et al., *Muslim Community in North America.*

————. *The Black Muslims in America,* rev. ed. New York: Kayode Publications, 1991.

Lovell, Emily Kalled. "Islam in the United States: Past and Present." In Waugh et al., *Muslim Community in North America.*

MacFarquhar Neil. "Iraq's shadow widens Sunni-Shiite split in United States." *International Herald Tribune: America,* February 4, 2007.

Mahajan, Rahul. *The New Crusade: America's War on Terrorism.* New York: Monthly Review Press, 2002.

Mallon, Elias. *Neighbors: Muslims in North America.* New York: Friendship Press, 1989.

Mazrui, Ali. "Muslims Between the Jewish Example and the Black Experience: American Policy Implications." In Bukhari et al., *Muslims' Place in the American Public Square.*

McAlister, Melani. *Epic Encounters: Culture, Media, and U.S. Interests in the Middle East, 1945–2000.* Berkeley: University of California Press, 2001.

McCarthy, Kate. *Interfaith Encounters in America.* New Brunswick, NJ: Rutgers University Press, 2007.

McCloud, Aminah Beverly. *African American Islam.* New York: Routledge, 1995.

Metcalf, Barbara Daly, ed. *Making Muslim Space in North America and Europe.* Berkeley: University of California Press, 1996.

————. "New Medinas: The Tablighi Jama'at in America and Europe." In *Making Muslim Space in North America and Europe.*

Milani, Ayatollah Sayyid Fadhel. *Frequently Asked Questions on Islam: Islamic Answers for Modern Problems.* London: Islam in English Press, 2001.

Mir-Hosseini, Ziba. *Islam and Gender: The Religious Debate in Modern Iran.* Princeton: Princeton University Press, 1999.

Mohammad-Arif, Amina. *Salaam America: South Asian Muslims in New York.* London: Anthem Press, 2002.

Moore, Kathleen. *Al-Mughtaribun: American Law and the Transformation of Muslim Life in the United States.* Albany: SUNY Press, 1995.

————. "Muslims in Prison: Claims to Constitutional Protection of Religious Liberty." In Haddad, *Muslims of America.*

Mottahedeh, Roy. *The Mantle of the Prophet: Religion and Politics in Iran.* New York: Pantheon, 1985.

Motahhari, Mortaza. "The Fundamental Problem in the Clerical Establishment." In Walbridge, *Most Learned of the Shi'a.*

M'roueh, Youssef. "Shi'a Population in North America." In Hejazi and A Hashim. *Ahlul bayt Assembly of North America.*

Moussavi, Ahmad Kazemi. *Religious Authority in Shi'ite Islam: From the Office of the Mufti to the Institution of Marja'.* Kuala Lumpur: Institute of Islamic Thought and Civilization, 1996.

Al-Mufid, Muhammad b. Muhammad. *Awa'il al-Maqalat fi al-Madhahib wa'l-Mukhtarat.* Tabriz: n.p., 1950.

Muhaghegh-Damad, Ayatullah. "The Role of Time and Social Welfare in the Modification of Legal Rulings." In L. Clarke, *Shi'ite Heritage*.

Al-Murtada, 'Ali b. al-Husayn. *Al-Dhari'a ila Usul al-Shari'a*. 2nd ed. 2 vols. Tehran: Daneshghah Tehran, 1983.

Naficy Hamid, "Identity Politics and Iranian Exile Music Videos." *Iranian Studies* 31, no. 1 (1998).

An-Na'im, Abdullahi. "The Politics of Religion and the Morality of Globalization." In Juergensmeyer, *Religion in Global Civil Society*.

Nakash, Yitzhak, *Reaching for Power: The Shi'a in the Modern Arab World*. Princeton: Princeton University Press, 2006.

Nasr, Seyyed Hossein, ed. *Islamic Spirituality II: Manifestations*. New York: Crossroad, 1991.

Nasr, Vali. *The Shia Revival: How Conflicts Within Islam Will Shape the Future*. New York: W. W. Norton, 2006.

Nimer, Mohamed, ed. *Islamophobia and Anti-Americanism: Causes and Remedies*. Beltsville: Amana, 2007.

———. "Muslims in the American Body Politic." In Bukhari et al., *Muslims' Place in the American Public Square*.

———. *The North American Muslim Resource Guide: Muslim Community Life in the United States and Canada*. New York: Routledge, 2002.

Nomani, Mohammad Manzoor. *Khomeini, Iranian Revolution and the Shi'ite Faith*. London: Furqan Publications, 1988.

Nurbakhsh, Javad. "The Nimatullahi." In Seyyed Hossein Nasr, ed. *Islamic Spirituality II: Manifestations*. New York: Crossroad, 1991.

Nyang, Sulayman. *Islam in the United States of America*. Chicago: Kazi Publications, 1999.

———. "Challenges Facing Christian-Muslim Dialogue in the United States." In Haddad and Haddad, *Christian-Muslim Encounters*.

Omar, Irfan. *A Muslim View of Christianity: Essays on Dialogue by Mahmoud Ayoub*. New York: Orbis, 2007.

Patel, Eboo. *Acts of Faith: The Story of an American Muslim; the Struggle for the Soul of a Generation*. Boston: Beacon, 2007.

Peek, Lori. "Becoming Muslim: The Development of a Religious Identity." *Sociology of Religion* 66, no. 3 (2005).

Pinault, David. *Horse of Kerbala: Muslim Devotional Life in India*. New York: Palgrave, 2001.

———. "Self-Mortification Rituals in the Shi'i and Christian Traditions." In L. Clarke, *Shi'ite Heritage*.

Pinn, Anthony. *Varieties of African American Religious Experience*. Minneapolis: Fortress Press, 2000.

Poston, Larry. *Islamic Da'wah in the West: Muslim Missionary Activity and the Dynamics of Conversion to Islam*. New York: Oxford University Press, 1992.

Qazwini, Imam Hasan. *American Crescent: A Muslim Cleric on the Power of His Faith; The Struggle against Prejudice and the Future of Islam in America.* New York: Random House, 2007.

Quick, Abdullah Hakim. *Deeper Roots: Muslims in the Americas and the Caribbean From Before Columbus To the Present.* London: Ta-Ha Publishers, 1996.

Qureshi, Emran, and Michael A. Sells, eds. *The New Crusades: Constructing the Muslim Enemy.* New York: Columbia University Press, 2003.

Ramadan, Tariq. *Western Muslims and the Future of Islam.* Oxford: Oxford University Press, 2004.

Rieck, Andreas. "The Struggle for Equal Rights as a Minority: Shia Communal Organizations in Pakistan, 1948–1968." In Brunner and Ende, *Twelver Shia in Modern Times.*

Roald, Anne-Sofie. *Women in Islam: The Western Experience.* New York: Routledge, 2001.

Roy, Olivier. *Globalized Islam: The Search for a New Ummah.* New York: Columbia University Press, 2004.

Rouse, Carolyn. *Engaged Surrender: African American Women and Islam.* Berkeley: University of California Press, 2004.

Sabagh, George, and Mehdi Bozorgmehr. "Secular Immigrants: Religiosity and Ethnicity Among Iranian Muslims in Los Angeles." In Haddad and Smith, *Muslim Communities in North America.*

Al-Saffar, Muhammad b. al-Hasan. *Basa'ir al-Darajat fi Fada'il Al Muhammad.* Qum: Maktabat Ayat Allah al-Mar'ashi, 1983.

Sachedina, Abdulaziz. "Islamic Bioethics." In John F. Peppin, Mark Cherry, and Ana Iltis, eds. *The Annals of Bioethics: Religious Perspectives in Bioethics.* London and New York: Taylor and Francis, 2004.

———. *The Islamic Roots of Democratic Pluralism.* Oxford: Oxford University Press, 2001.

———. "A Minority Within a Minority: The Case of the Shi'a in North America." In Haddad and Smith, *Muslim Communities in North America.*

Safi, Omid, ed. *Progressive Muslims: On Justice, Gender, and Pluralism.* Oxford: Oneworld, 2003.

Said, Edward W. *Covering Islam: How the Media and the Experts Determine How We See the Rest of the World.* New York: Vintage Books, 1997.

Sajan, Ghulam Abbas. "The Status of the Ahlul Bayt's Devotees in Canada." In Hejazi and Hashim, *Ahlul Bayt Assembly of America.*

Sajoo, Amyn, ed. *Civil Society in the Muslim World: Contemporary Perspectives.* London: Tauris, 2002.

Salvatore, Armando. *Islam and the Political Discourse of Modernity.* Reading, NY: Ithaca Press, 1997.

al-Samawi, Muhammad al-Tijani. *Ask Those who Know*. Toronto: Hyderi, 1993.

Schmidt, Garbi. "The Complexity of Belonging: Sunni Muslim Immigrants in Chicago." In Haddad and Smith, *Muslim Minorities in the West*.

———. *Sunni Muslims in Chicago: Islam in Urban America*. Philadelphia: Temple University Press, 2004.

Schubel, Vernon. "Karbala as Sacred Space among North American Shiʿa." In Metcalf, *Making Muslim Space*.

———. "The Muharram Majlis: The Role of a Ritual in the Preservation of Shiʿa Identity." In Waugh et al., *Muslim Families in North America*.

———. *Religious Performance in Contemporary Islam: Shiʿi Devotional Rituals in South Asia*. Columbia: University of South Carolina Press, 1993.

Al-Seestani, Ayatullah al-Sayyid ʿAli al-Husayni. *Contemporary Legal Rulings in Shiʿi Law*. Translated by Hamid Mavani. Montreal: Organization for the Advancement of Islamic Knowledge and Humanitarian Services, 1996.

———. *Islamic Laws: English Version of Taudhihul Masaeʾl*. London: World Federation, 1994.

Shabistari, Muhammad Ayatullah. "Religion, Reason and the New Theology." In L. Clarke, *Shiʿite Heritage*.

Smith, Jane I. *Islam in America*. New York: Columbia University Press, 1999.

———. *Muslims, Christians, and the Challenge of Interfaith Dialogue*. New York: Oxford University Press, 2007.

Stewart, Devin. "Islamic Juridical Hierarchies and the Office of Marjiʿ al-Taqlid." In L. Clarke, *Shiʿite Heritage*.

Stone, Carol. "Estimate of Muslims Living in America." In Haddad, *Muslims of America*.

Takim, Liyakat. "Foreign Influences on American Shiʿism." *Muslim World* 90 (2000): 459–77.

———. "From Conversion to Conversation: Interfaith Dialogue in Post-911 America." *Muslim World* 94, no. 3 (2004): 343–55.

———. *The Heirs of the Prophet: Charisma and Religious Authority in Shiʿite Islam*. Albany: SUNY Press, 2006.

———. "Holy Peace or Holy War: Tolerance and Co-existence in the Islamic Juridical Tradition." *Islam and Muslim Societies* 4, no. 2 (2007).

———. "Khomeini Ayatollah." In Cesari, *Encyclopedia of Islam in America*.

———. "Seestani, Ayatollah." In Cesari, *Encyclopedia of Islam in America*.

———. "Shiʿi Institutes in North America." In Hejazi and Hashim, *Ahlul Bayt Assembly of America*.

———. "Shiʿite Movements." In Gary Laderman and Luis Léon, eds. *Religion and American Cultures: An Encyclopedia of Traditions, Diversity, and Popular Expression*. Santa Barbara, CA: ABC-CLIO, 2003. vol. 1

———."To Vote or not to Vote: The Politicization of American Islam." *In Alec Hargreaves, John Kelsay, and Sumner B. Twiss, eds.* Politics and Religion in France and the United States. *Lanham, MD: Lexington Books / Rowman and Littlefield, 2007.*

Taskhiri, Ayatullah Muhammad Ali. "Supreme Authority (*Marji'iyah*) in Shi'ism." In L. Clarke, *Shi'ite Heritage.*

Turner, Richard Brent. *Islam in the African-American Experience.* Bloomington: Indiana University Press, 1997.

Theresa, AlfaroVelcamp. "Mexican Muslims in the Twentieth Century: Challenging Stereotypes and Negotiating Space." In Haddad, *Muslims in the West.*

Voll, John. "Muslims in the Caribbean: Ethnic Sojourners and Citizens." In Haddad and Smith, *Muslim Minorities in the West.*

Walbridge, Linda. *The Most Learned of the Shi'a: The Institution of the Marja' Taqlid.* New York: Oxford University Press, 2001.

———. "The Shi'a Mosques and Their Congregations in Dearborn." In Haddad and Smith, *Muslim Communities in North America.*

———. *Without Forgetting the Imam: Lebanese Shi'ism in an American Community.* Detroit: Wayne State University Press, 1997.

Waldman, Marilyn. "Reflections on Islamic Tradition, Women and Family." In Waugh et al., *Muslim Families in North America.*

Waugh, Earle H., Baha Abu-Laban, and Regula Qureshi, eds. *The Muslim Community in North America.* Edmonton: University of Alberta Press, 1983.

Waugh, Earle H., Sharon Abu-Laban, and Regula Qureshi, eds. *Muslim Families in North America.* Edmonton: University of Alberta Press, 1991.

Waugh, Earle H., and Frederick M. Denny, eds. *The Shaping of an American Islamic Discourse: A Memorial to Fazlur Rahman.* Atlanta: Scholars Press, 1998.

Webb, Gisela, ed. *Windows of Faith: Muslim Women Scholar-Activists in North America.* Syracuse: Syracuse University Press, 2000.

Werbner, Pnina. "Stamping the Earth with the Name of Allah: Zikr and the Sacralizing of Space among British Muslims." In Metcalf, *Making Muslim Space.*

White, Jr., Vibert L. *Inside the Nation of Islam: A Historical and Personal Testimony of a Black Muslim.* Gainesville: University Press of Florida, 2001.

Wiktorowicz, Quintan. *Radical Islam Rising: Muslim Extremism in the West.* New York: Rowman and Littlefield, 2005.

Wininger, William. "*Dar al-Harb* and *Dar al-Islam.*" In Cesari, *Encyclopedia of Islam in the United States.*

Wormser, Richard. *American Islam: Growing up Muslim in America.* New York: Walker and Company, 1994.

Yazdi, Muhammad Kazim. *al-'Urwa wa'l-Wuthqa.* Tehran: Dar al-Kutub al-Islamiyya, n.d.

Yousif, Ahmad F. *Muslims in Canada: A Question of Identity.* Ottawa: Legas, 1993.

Zabel, Darcy. "The Arab Diaspora in the Americas: Latin America, the United States, and Canada." In Zabel, *Arabs in the Americas.*

Zabel, Darcy, ed. *Arabs in the Americas: Interdisciplinary Essays on the Arab Diaspora.* New York: Peter Lang, 2006.

Zaman, Muhammad Qasim. *The Ulama in Contemporary Islam: Custodians of Change.* Princeton: Princeton University Press, 2002.

Zogby, John. *Arab America Today: A Demographic Profile of Arab Americans.* Washington, D.C.: Arab American Institute, 1990.

Index

About the Author

LIYAKAT NATHANI TAKIM is Associate Professor of Islamic Studies at the University of Denver.